MILES PER GALLON

Mike Magrann

DiWulf
Publishing
EST. 2014

we make punk rock books

Miles Per Gallon
First published in September 2023
by DiWulf Publishing
Morrisville, PA
diwulf.com

Editing by Steven DiLodovico
Cover & interior design by Steven DiLodovico &
Amy Yates Wuelfing

ISBN: 9798854733663

For K-

This book, while based on actual events, is to be read as autobiographical fiction rather than a strict, linear chronicle of history. While much of the material contained herein is supported by photographic evidence and the journal entries, much is culled from a memory that may or may not have been dulled by… sensory overload. Some instances have been combined to fit a timeline, some details slightly altered so as not to incriminate anyone, and some names have been changed to protect both the innocent and the not-so-innocent.

-Michael Magrann

PART I

A **Highway Patrol car is coming up in the oncoming**, heading west on the 10. It appears to float above the highway, held aloft by the heat waves shimmering across the asphalt.
I'm in the passenger seat, Chris at the wheel.
He turns his head to the side but keeps his eyes on the road, shouts to the back of the van.
"Keep the got-damned cans out of sight, fellas. We got a copper coming."
He turns to me, grinning, and shakes his head. "We're a bust."

Behind us, in the van, they cannot hear.
Misfits playing on the Blaupunkt, "I Turned Into a Martian" cranked to distortion and everyone howling the *whoa-ohs* in lupine harmony.
The hangovers that chased us from Cerritos are fading now, I can tell.
The music is louder, everyone up from sweating van naps, the ice chest being opened again for another beer just as soon as it is shut.

Feet on the dash, a Coors between my legs.
The cop car is almost upon us, I can make out a single trooper inside.
And there it is.
That primal urge to reach across the van's console and push the steering wheel up by just a few degrees.
Just enough to swing us across the dotted lines and into a head on crash.

I wonder at our matched inertia, 70mph mirrored, and at the fantastic tableau of carnage strewn across the road after the impact at a combined speed of 140.

I can see the blood and skin on the asphalt, the Blue & White Chevy on its side with one wheel still spinning.

Eviscerated of passenger and cargo, like a beached whale finally exploded outward in the summer heat.

Guitars ripped from cases, only their shattered necks visible, reaching out from the baked desert sand: headstocks as headstones.

The terrible silence after, flawed only by the groans of a lone survivor: Me.

No, no survivors.
The fantasy works better that way.

Only the dead would be dignified by silence.

Finally respected in death (*How did I miss these guys*? Robert Hilburn at *The Times* would moan, *the genius was right there all along!*), we would become more popular in a split second of disaster than a lifetime of touring.

Forever remembered in the golden light of youth, having never to suffer the indignity of decay.

But the cop car passes us without incident, and I recognize a tinge of disappointment in my chest.
Chris and I both watch the side mirrors until the patrol car melts into the desert haze, then we each raise up our beers to take a sip.
Chris finishes his beer and tosses the empty can into the van's side door well.
He opens the ice chest wedged between our seats and takes out another beer.
He looks at me and shakes his head again, smiling now.
"We're a fuckin' bust man. Tell you what."
The sun finally drops low on the highway, one last display of orange hatred before mercifully sinking below the horizon.

The shadows dripping blue across the desert as we pass the 85, just an hour more until Phoenix, night one of tour.
And we're running late.
As always, late.

We'd played a last-minute farewell gig at the Cathay the night before, really just an excuse to break in the new bass player, Jay.

We played a late set, cocky and loose.
Drunk.
"_You won't have Channel 3 to kick around this summer, you fuckers!_" I screamed into the mic at one point, before falling back into Jack's drum set.
Jack jumped clear like a bird startled from its nest, and the song died with a clatter of hardware.
A belt loop of my 501s caught one of the kick drum tuning keys and I dragged it over as I tried to stand.
Jay looked across the stage and raised an eyebrow to Kimm.
Kimm shrugged. "Normal." he said. "You'll get used to it."
He then nudged my prone body away with his creeper to tune his guitar.
I wallowed about the sticky stage, swatting at the forest of cymbal stands closing in on me.

I woke next to the Seal Beach pier in the morning to the chime of a buoy marker, its mating call finally answered by the moan of a foghorn out by the breakwater.
It was one of those gloomy June mornings, the clouds hugging the coast, defying the season.
I watched a lone metal detectorist solemnly waving his wand above the sand as if in benediction.
He stooped to examine a treasure he conjured out of the filthy sand.
He picked it up, sniffed it, then dropped it into a netted sack and moved on.

I patted at my pockets for wallet and keys, and any clue to the night's end.

There were blurry memories of a slashed blonde haircut, a girl driving, riding in a dark blue VW rabbit.

Damned on the stereo: *Strawberries*.

Shouting along to "Stranger on the Town," her fishnet-stockinged legs working the pedals, a marching ballet of clutch, gas, and brake.

A hand slipping from stick shift to my knee.

Then: wrestling on the beach with the grit of sand between our fencing tongues.

I had no memory beyond that, just the disconnected cinematic flashes familiar to all blackout drunks.

But there, tucked into the odd coin pocket of my jeans, a slip of notepaper with a 562 number in red ink, the digits followed only by "–K" and beyond that, a wee heart.

Now, driving through the purple desert sunset, I tuck the cold can of beer back between my legs, the chill of the can teasing answers from my tingling balls.

My groin held tightness, of denial or exhaustion I didn't know.

A blackout drinker gifted with nightly mysteries:

Had I come twice or not at all?

Kimm puts a hand on each of our seat backs and pulls his head in line with ours. He still has to shout above the music.

"How much longer ya think? I need a piss here." Kimm says.

Chris says, "What? Again?"

Kimm looks back at Jay and Jack in the back row. "Anyone else?"

Doug is sitting right behind me, first bench starboard.

He pounds on my headrest. "Piss, piss, piss" he chants.

We pull over on the next frontage road, get out to pee.

Jay joins us, Jack stays in the van.

I look back and see his head barely visible among the pile of amplifiers and guitar cases piled against the van's passenger windows.

The Blue & White was a 1978 Chevrolet Beauville van that was

originally used to haul motocross bikes out to the track on weekends.
It was a long wheelbase, 3/4-ton, Heritage Blue with a fat white stripe
bisecting its hull.
And though the hard saddled motocross bikes have been replaced by a
pawnshop backline, in the back hold is still the stuff to make noise.
Black Tolex covered speaker cabinets, their ripped grills showing the
12″ speakers that will translate the 100-watt language from the tubed
amplifier heads.
A stack of drum hardware tangled and rusting, like the swords of a
defeated tribe piled on a smoking battlefield.
Guitar cases and drumshells, everything covered with peeling stickers
and dried beer.
The payload is different now, but the possibility of violent outcome
remains.

Back to the pavement, no more stops 'til the club.
We each finish another can and toss the empties in the wheel well.
I open the cooler and swirl my hand through the melted ice water, toss
back the last of the cans.
We toast the end of the day, the start of the night, start of the tour.
Soon the shapes of Phoenix come into view, and I feel that familiar
quickening of pulse.

It's already crowded outside the club, punkers smoking and trying hard
to look bored. Or scrounging for change to make the cover charge.
An old block building on the outskirts of town, the venue is an old
boxing and wrestling hall that still had a turnbuckled ring in the middle
where the bands would set up.
We can see the green Dodge Ram van driven by The Stretchmarks, a
band from Winnipeg we'd met only a couple weeks before while they
were camped out in LA.
They seemed like good-natured guys, with that Canadian workman-like
approach to getting steadily and completely beer drunk each day.
We got along immediately.
Bill, the wiry guitar player, waved us in like a parking attendant,

standing with his brother Kelly, their own bewildered young drummer to match our own.

Their manager Matt came up to my window grinning, shaking his head at our late arrival.

"Jeez, thanks for showing up." he said.

"Hey, let us know when you guys finish your set, will ya," I said, "then we'll come in and give these good people what they *really* want."

Mark the bassist and singer Dik, both barrel chested lumberjacks in shorts and boots, stood clutching beer bottles in one paw, flipping me off with the other.

I got out the passenger door then unlatched the sliding door.

As I pushed it back open, a couple dozen empty aluminum cans fell to the parking lot.

Metallic clatter, live as firecrackers in the desert air: this became our intro song that summer.

Kimm gathered his calendars and folders, got out to go meet the promoter who was pacing the front entry at our late arrival.

Chris met Doug at the back of the van to start hauling out gear, both already sighting the crowd outside for girls.

Doug came along at the last minute.

He'd decided to take the summer off from his backbreaking construction job to come along on this trip, though he and Chris despised being called *roadies.*

("I'm the fuckin' *driver* of this here buggy," I would hear Chris tell countless girls that summer. Doug would simply point to his muscled chest: "*Security*").

Doug opens the back doors, and the first thing he unloads is not a drum or cabinet, but the black Hefty bags filled with merch.

He opens one of the bags, pulls out one of the shirts.

Thin white T-shirts, silk screened in red or green.

CH3 above a solid circle, the Rising Sun.

On either side the *kanji* symbols for *kamikaze*, and below that, *Lights Out Tour 1983.*

"Who's in charge of selling merch? Me?" he asks.
Doug raises an eyebrow to some punk girls smoking by a phone booth
and waves the shirt toward them with a matadorian flair.
"I'm selling merch," he says.

Jay and Jack stay in the back bench of the van, as if unwilling to start
this story just yet.
Jay had been writing his girlfriend a long letter on the ride, as they had
promised correspondence *every day*.
He shakes the cramp out of his pen hand as he emerges from the Blue
& White, looks up at the cinderblock club. We stand in a gravel parking
lot, kids smoking, sipping at brownbagged cans.
A squeal of laughter goes up as a scandal is confessed.
The bark of electric guitar through distortion pedal leaks from the club
as the door is opened a moment.
"Hey, wow," Jay says in his relaxed drawl. "Punk rock."
Jack was the last out of the van.
He got out blinking in the twilight, shaking off the ride.

The desert sky was finally a proper dark, that rich darkness that we
never got to see in our light-flooded suburban tracts.
The stars brilliant against the night, stolen jewels spilled upon black
velvet.
The air clean and hot, infused with promise and dust.
I stretched and swiped my arms at the swirling galaxies above us, as if
to erase the last moment of stillness before a great rush of motion.

TWO

***B**efore I opened my eyes* I felt something drip on my face.
Viscous as a spent bodily fluid, sickly-sweet smelling.
I taste it.
It's fucking candy.

I looked up to see a pink wad of bubble gum, placed on the ceiling of
the van above me by some monster.
It had melted in the morning heat, became a stalactite of goo.
Perhaps Chris got a girl in here last night during the show, persuaded
her to wrestle in the dark recesses of the van while we were on stage.
He'd play on her sympathies, being so far from home, you know,
so *lonely.*
Like the doe-eyed pilot chatting up the USO gal on the eve of his final
flight into glory.
He'd promise to write as she lifted her Bad Brains shirt above her head.
She would then surrender to her passions for the good of the war effort.
Then, just before lowering her head to his lap, she'd take the huge wad
of bubble gum from her grinning mouth, the same piece of candy that
had been hockeyed between their tongues the last twenty minutes.
And then she'd place it above her head on the van's stickered rail.

Before the next drip could humiliate me again, I sat up.

The sudden shift in elevation started a headache all too familiar.

I tried to remember where I was, how the night before had ended.
Sure, we played a gig, but it took a moment of looking out at the cactus
and rock landscape (the Southwestern architecture applied even to the
low rent apartment complex where we'd parked), to remember we were
in New Mexico.
We were parked in front of the promoter's pad, I understood now, and
they had left me in the van to sleep it off.

It became our security system: whoever was the drunkest would spend the night in the van and play watchdog. I happened to get the job most often.

But I preferred it out there, alone with a paperback in the morning, while Kimm would have to sit and be sociable with the local promoters or punkers that let us crash.

Talk *punk*, man.

People always assume the singer is the communicator of the band, but when we got off the stage, when the booze wore off, I was quiet.

Shy and awkward around strangers.

Kimm had that gift for looking people in the eye and holding conversation.

Me, I mumbled, looked over people's heads.

I came across: *asshole.*

I took a notebook down from the dash, flipped to the first blank page and wrote *June24, 1983* at the top.

I underlined the date twice, wrote *ABQ* beneath that, and then stared out the window.

It was a vinyl covered, college ruled Mead that my mom had handed to me when we left.

"Here," she said, giving me the notebook along with a paper bag.

She stood on the curb in front of our Cerritos suburban tract home, the sidewalks baking on a summer solstice day.

"Write when you can. Maybe a postcard to your sisters?"

Beside her, my little Japanese grandma, *Bachan*, wiped her hands on her apron and looked up at me, squinting in the sun.

"Goodbye, *Michael-chan*'" she said in her clipped accent. "*Sayo-nara*, hmm?"

I leaned down and kissed the top of her grey head, her waist length silver hair wrapped in its usual hair net above a mysterious network of hairpins and origami-like braiding.

My mom gave me a hug then and raised a playful fist to my face.

"Hey," she said. "No funny business."

I looked into the bag now and found a stack of envelopes bound by rubber band, and half a roll of twenty cent stamps.
She'd also included five extra Japanese *kamikaze* headbands that she probably bought at a Little Tokyo gift shop, and a little handwritten note that just read *"Be safe."*

I took one of the headbands and smelled it, then tied it around my head. I had taken to wearing the headbands on stage that year, treating each night as a one-way suicide mission.
Only to be surprised once again, when I opened my eyes each morning. Still alive.

We got to Albuquerque early, even though we stopped off in Truth or Consequences, NM, for no reason other than its game show name.

It was comfort to see the ugly green Stretchmarks van in the side view mirror as we drove through the desert.
We stood around at rest stops trading beers while Kimm and their manager Matt shut themselves in phone booths to plot out gigs weeks away.
We had achieved a team rhythm to our piss stops now, our bladders achieving a menstrual-like synchronization, and were making decent time on the highway.

It was still daylight when we got to a cinderblocked VFW hall, parked on gravel.
We loaded in, untangled the sticky guitar cords that were tossed together in Tucson the night before, changed strings on the guitars.
One amp head was already blown, and Jack had a crack on a cymbal.
We would track that split in his Paiste crash through the next few months, the crack zigzagging toward the bell like the steady decline of a failing penny stock.

We'd finished setting up the amps and were tuning when a dreadlocked whiteboy soundman wandered in.
He nodded to us and brought a crate of microphones to the stage.
We were happy to see him miking the drums and cabinets, even setting direct line out for bass signal.
Most clubs guarded their precious stage gear from the punk bands, offering us only two or three battered microphones for the front vocals.
It was hard to blame them, as most good shows featured flying beer bottles and stage divers, guitars cords ripped from input jacks, amp cabinets knocked over in succession, like scale buildings toppled by a Godzilla-costumed dwarf.
We counted on the stage and gear to be destroyed on a good night, the chaotic blending of the crowd and the band onstage and in pit.
I still have a faint crosshatch scar on my lower lip, the calloused kiss of a Shure SM58 smashed yet again into my face.

We wandered onstage separately, in shorts and shirtless, to begin the preshow routine of a soundcheck.
First the bass drum pounding like a catching heartbeat, muffled.

Then, channel found on the board, the room filled with percussive booms.
The *snack snack* of the snare next, then the toms, the *snick* of the hi hat, then the soundman chimes in with go *ahead and play the whole kit.*
Now Jack has his drum solo for the night, and we all gather round and stare at him as he plays simple time.
We make funny faces, try to make him drop a stick.

The Stretchers are loading in from the back of hall, Chris and Doug are setting up a small merch booth. Naturally, it's right by the women's bathroom.
It is that rare time to be shy, our meager craft on display in the harsh light of an unlit stage, songs played recital style without booze or crowd to dampen the mistakes.

We play a song, "I Wanna Know Why," an easy one and not too rough a vocal warmup.

Song ends, a beat of silence, then the soundman picks up the board mic and tells us to turn down the guitars.

Mark from the Stretchmarks turns, bends at the waist and unveils his large ass to the stage.

During the intro to "Take My Chances," Jay makes the *cut it* sign, index finger slashing across throat.

"Hey, this one… you do know you guys are playing different chords on the chorus, don't ya?"

Kimm and I both looked down at the guitars hanging around our necks, then up to each other. We shrugged.

"What, the G?" I strum a barre across the third fret.

"G?" Kimm says. "D?"

"I don't care, really. Let's pick just one and stick with it."

Kimm hits a D chord, then an open G on his Charvel.

I play a B. *Minor? Major? Captain?*

We both look to Jay.

"It was G on the record," Jay said.

He was the producer of that record, so we go with G.

Played a good set, no major fuckups.

One of the rare nights that we hit the stage with the right amount of alcohol in the bloodstream, a gig loose but not quite messy.

We'd try to achieve that balance each night, of course.

But just one shot too many, twenty minutes too long before we climbed onstage, and we'd be rewarded with yet another sloppy gig.

Kids were slamming in front of the stage, the local punks who would automatically show up for any band that would blow through town.

Some curious types stood further back, just listening.

During "I Didn't Know," a slow song, a normal-looking couple swayed

to the beat, the girl leaning back against her Stetson-hatted boyfriend, his hands dipped into the front pockets of her jeans.
I looked at them while I sang, wondering where they would be in an hour.
Paying off a babysitter, maybe, then kissing their sleeping kids good night.
Or perhaps shooting methamphetamine up each other's arms as they planned the next liquor store robbery.
I envied them in either scenario.
Living out their doomed existence in concert, like birds mated for life.

After the gig we stayed drinking in the hall's beer room, then in the parking lot until they shut the floodlights on us.
Chris and Doug disappeared with a couple of girls who promised to have them back in the morning, Jay wandered off to find a payphone to call his girlfriend.
I stayed, drinking with Kimm.
And when he left, I sat drinking alone.

Jay and Jack were back in the van when Doug and Chris got back to the apartments. A white Datsun B210 pulled up, its wheels red with desert dust, the rear window a quilt of punk stickers: Pistols, Circle Jerks, The Clash, Bauhaus. *Damned.*
I had a momentary memory of sitting in the passenger seat next to stockinged legs, singing along to the Damned to the endless summer night.

The girl driving had white pancake makeup on and pink lipstick, a face camouflaged as confection under a mohawk of green.
I pictured her driving through Albuquerque on a weekday afternoon, out of context and out of time, no longer noticing the little kids pointing at her from the station wagons she passed.
After Chris got out, Doug leaned between the seats and kissed the girl on the cheek, but she didn't take her eyes from the windshield.

Doug shrugged, got out and got into the van.

"Hoo," he said when he got in. "Let's get going!"

Chris got in after him and slammed the door.

"Dang it," Chris said. "What did you do, Doug? She was going to make us breakfast, then she got all mad."

Doug sighed and rubbed his hands together. "Nothing, what? Ah, she said she wanted to go along with us to Denver, I don't know, I might've said she could get a ride."

He pounded at my seat back as if spurring us forward. "Let's go already, what's next?"

Chris shook his head. "Anything to eat in here? You guys already eat?"

I watched the Datsun in the sideview mirror.

She sat there a moment before the taillights came on, her boot on the brake, the car shifted into gear.

I was wondering if she might wait and follow us, take the climbing drive to Denver.

Maybe she would join the band there, and we'd develop a slower, goth-based sound.

We'd attract a small but lifelong devoted pack of fans in whiteface and cotton candy lipstick. We'd marry eventually, she and I.

Live in a black trailer with our two kids, a sullen boy and a feisty girl, Bela and Hazel.

No, Lizzie.

But the Datsun just drove away, and we never saw her again.

Kimm took out the *AAA TripTik* and traced a finger over a highlighted highway. "Fuckin-A, probably five more hours to Denver, huh?"

I was behind the wheel, Kimm in shotgun, the rest of the guys asleep.

Kimm took his calendar from his backpack and opened it on the ice chest between us.

The pages that held our immediate future, the sacred text that Kimm had been painstakingly filling in for the past six months.

The past dates and cities marked with an X, the rest of the squares holding small letters and phone numbers.

Days and nights yet to come, to be stalked and conquered with another X, banished to the past.

He flipped a page of the calendar, pointed at two empty blocks in the middle of July.

"So here, look at this." He circled the dates and tapped at them with his pen. "Two days open. Who do we know around Minneapolis, anybody?"

I knew he wasn't expecting an answer out of me, so I didn't respond.

He looked at the calendar a moment longer, then closed it and put it back in his backpack.

"Fuck, next gas stop I should make a call," he said.

"Michael-chan, Kimm on phone," *Bachan* would yell up the stairs at me.

I'd get out of bed, go to the hallway and drag the black Bakelite rotary back to my bedroom.

There was a 25-foot cord on the upstairs phone, so the phone could reach back to our rooms for a precious private conversation.

My two brothers and three sisters had, at one time, all lived on the upstairs floor and shared the same line with expected conflict.

"Dude. It's noon. Still in bed?"
I could hear the grocery store behind him.
I picture Kimm in his polyester green Alpha Beta apron, finger plugged into his free ear, standing at the payphone in the employee breakroom. A scratchy PA announcement blares in the background: *Flash sale on Birdseye frozen lima beans 39 cents for the next 30 minutes, aisle eight.*
"So what do you think about what we were talking about, upstate New York? Your stepsister still live up there?"
"Half-sister. Yeah, I'll call Barb later. So what you up to?'

"What? Working." I hear his hand cover the receiver as he talks to someone next to him. I can make out the words *cart* and *mop*.
"Gotta go, see you at practice." Then he'd hang up.

We'd have these conversations daily on the phone, and I'd agree with whatever ideas Kimm would run past me with a grunt. I had no input or interest in such things as routing and guarantees, and after the call I would go back to bed or call Chris or Doug, start in on creating the next day's hangover.

Another delicious year of college guarded me against reality, living in the big Cerritos house rent-free and taking lightweight classes at CSU Long Beach to fill in the credits until graduation could no longer be avoided.
Currently I was working through *Intro to Weightlifting* and *Lit 108: American Crime Fiction 1920-1950.*
There wasn't much else to do but go over the songs with Jack and look for a bass player while Kimm juggled his schoolwork, his job, and booking a full summer tour.
We had fallen into our roles in the band naturally, I was head of creative, he the chief of accounts.
I got off easy, ripping off Judas Priest riffs and overwriting lyrics in the

way only an over-earnest English major can.

Kimm had the job to get the numbers from promoters, book gigs, plan our future.

He was fearless on the phone, ringing up Chuck of Black Flag, or the Stern brothers from Youth Brigade for advice.

He'd come away with a list of phone numbers and a hazy plan to get us to the Atlantic and then back home.

Soon, he was plugged into the network of independent promoters, clubs, and shifty venues that played punk.

Tours planned with Bic pen and yellow legal pad, paper maps and landline phone calls.

Soon a map of America hung in the garage, a continent disfigured by Highlighter pen, its body crisscrossed with a tattoo of pink and yellow scars.

It was a tour built on swiped phone calling cards, the black-market secret that could unlock long distance conversation.

A treasure in 16 digits, passed from band to band.

We saw ourselves not as thieves but as pirates, liberating communication from the greedy elites.

A drunken businessman sits at the next payphone, Old Fashioned in hand, tie loosened.

He's desperate to get through to Akron, has a hot lead for accounting: *"The boys at Astro Dynamo, ripe for the picking, I tell ya!"*

He shouts his MCI number to the 800 operator yet again, not noticing the girl with pink hair next to him, scribbling something in the margins of the Yellow Pages.

Cerritos was a planned community, if only a plan that called for plopping identical tract homes atop the dusty shit fields that were once dairy farms.

It was thrilling for us kids.

To move into a brand-new home, sterile as a blank canvas.

Classic '70s architecture with slanting roofs that cut off logical space, cathedral-ceilinged rooms that were impossible to fully heat or cool. The backyards didn't even have back walls, as the builders correctly assumed most of the families would be digging out pools.
The cinderblocks were built out just enough to keep us isolated from the families moving in around us, while allowing the yards to empty straight back into the empty dirt lots that were waiting to be built into another tract of homes.

I could walk straight out the sliding back door into a wonder of dirt and cow manure, old fence posts tangled in rusted barbed wire.
A germy playground with construction equipment to climb over and vandalize, sometimes cows that would wander over from the last few remaining dairy fields.
The children of these homes became instant friends and enemies.
Dirt clod fights would start instantly and inevitably, fossilized cow turds the prized ammunition. We could come home in the blue dusk bloody, filthy, and happy.
The youngest children to older parents too exhausted to care about parenting any more.
New elementary schools and little league fields were constructed just ahead of the bulging population, a futile move to keep the teenagers off dope and fucking each other into their own bewildered parenthood.

I met Kimm before third grade, that puts us at, what? Nine years old? I've told the story enough that it is fact.
We were on the playground, waiting for a chance at the swing set.
He with the blonde crewcut, me under a black mop of wild summer hair.
Think *Tintin* and *Mowgli*.

Kimm was the youngest of five kids as well and growing up together we enjoyed the same freedoms afforded the last kid in line.
Children of divorce, or parents shell-shocked and exhausted after raising an army, the youngest kids always seemed to find each other.

We wore the end of the hand me downs, nursed from bottles never sanitized with quite the same fervor as those suckled by our golden oldest siblings.
We were rewarded with immune systems tough as carbon fiber, and a lifelong fondness for the frayed hems and faded colors of hand-me-down clothes.

We spent our youth playing in those dirt fields, riding minibikes on top, tunneling like convicts underneath.
Underground forts soon spread through our back fields, some connected by tunnel or trench.
A first place of thrilling privacy, only yards from home.
Here, a place to cough on that first cigarette or flip through a shoplifted *Penthouse*, witness the startling first glimpse of pubic hair.
Pet of the Month Jennifer Pascal, she loves to ride horses on the beach and has a naughty sweet tooth - red licorice, mmm!
We'd stare at the mysterious triangle in her lap for hours, as if searching for lost scripture in the peachlike fur.

Kimm and I shared most of the same classes and home rooms, as we both tested above average.
Mentally gifted.

We were branded in placement tests, a curse that corralled us with the other geeks for years.

The early '70s rolled around us.
Kitchen appliances sprouted in shades of avocado and mango, horrible domestic cars roamed the crumbling highways.
A suburban life mirrored by a *Brady Bunch* template, but with all the wordless fucking and drug abuse that happens just out of camera range.
New schools and new clothes in the Fall.
Christmas vacations sleeping on cousins' floors, our parents and their siblings drinking through the nights.
Easter portraits in polyester, the first sunburns of the year after

Memorial Day weekend.
We took our year end exams wearing shredded Keds, filling in the
Scantron bubbles in No. 2 graphite, creating the freckled map that
would place us in the next grade's homeroom.

We spent those long summer days on Stingray bicycles, exploring the
riverbeds that trickled a slimy finger of green water, save the rare rain
days that would flush Los Angeles clean.
Fall, we'd return to school exhausted, an inch taller, hair sun-kissed a
shade lighter.
Kimm and I would always meet in the same home room, get seats next
to each other.
A friendship bonded in familiarity of routine; we became closer than
brothers.
We'd walk to Kennedy Elementary, talking about the things kids talk
about: frogs, *Star Trek*, boobs.

Faye Ross Junior High, on the other side of Norwalk Boulevard, forced
us even closer.
We hid out in the junior high newspaper class at lunch, avoiding the
scary eighth graders who already smoked and came to school with
purple hickies.
Every Friday there would be the front yard fights between the twelve-
year-old Cholos already sporting mustaches and homemade tattoos.
They would circle each other, spitting on the ground,
growling *chingas* and *putos*.
Feinting quick jabs and shuffling their feet like welterweights, a dance
learned from brothers and fathers, violence handed down like a family
recipe.
Then a Portuguese granny would hit the crowd with the garden hose
and we all wandered home, unrewarded by even a single slap.

With each first day of class the teachers would pause after calling my
last name, peer over their bifocals to my raised hands.
I'd be asked if we were related to, *yes, that's her*, one of my saintly

sisters. They would be remembered fondly before the teacher would hope aloud that I'd be *half* the students as they were.

We were closer to our sisters then, Kimm and I, still in the same schools for a year or two before they climbed to the next grade.
But our older brothers were mysterious and scary, a generation older, imprinted by the chaos of the '60s.
Adults in the next room, really.
Already using prophylactics and masking their rooms with incense, blocking out the funk of hashish and quiet sex with their shy girlfriends.

Kimm was not allowed to grow his hair long, and when I started going by his house, I discovered his flattops mirrored his dad's geometric cuts.
His father, Lynn, kept the military hair from WWII, perhaps the last thing he could hold and control from the best days of his life.

Kimm already had one count against him with his name, a girl's name gifted by a man with a girl's name himself.
And to keep your hair above the collar was another strike, a humiliation only reserved for squares or children of dads bewildered by a world gone nuts.
And Kimm became the toughest guy I knew.
Punk rocker and tireless worker and full-time student: living under the roof of a man who longed only for a black and white world and an honorable war.

I'd be at Kimm's doing homework or watching TV when Lynn would come home from his metal fabrication company in LA.
He'd swipe at my head playfully with his folded copy of *The Register*, take off the rubber band and shoot it at Freckles, their farting Dachshund.

They had a closet off the living room converted into a stocked liquor

cabinet. The light inside would automatically come on when the door opened, illuminating the bottles on glass shelves.
The inside of the door was painted with toasts in languages from around the world: *Prost, Sláinte–Bung Ho!* -a kicky idea his mom, Lois, had probably gotten out of *Sunset* magazine.
Not too many years later it would be us hitting that cabinet, refilling Lynn's Stolichnaya with water and drinking the dusty flavored liqueurs no one would miss.

Bung Ho! we'd cry as we slugged Hiram Walker Ginger Brandy.
We'd barf Crème De Menthe into our mouths, croak *Kanpai!*

Lynn would hit the cabinet for a highball, then take to his groaning Lazy Boy. He'd open the paper in front of him with a crack, scan the page for a moment before shaking his head.
Then he'd make a disgusted *tsk*, the sound of a child forced to kiss the corpse of a dead aunt.
"What in the world," he would say.
He'd lower the paper, and if Kimm was upstairs still getting ready, I'd be his lone audience.
"Mike, the world is going to crap, all of it," he'd start. "This certainly isn't what we fought for now, is it?"

And I knew this story, though spurred by Nixon's visit to Detroit, or the threat of gasoline topping a dollar, would somehow end up on the deck of a depot ship moored off Pago Pago.
That water, clear enough to see the ship's shadow playing on the sandy harbor bottom.
The smell of diesel exhaust seasoning the tropical breeze.
His eyes would be alive then, telling another tale of he and his army buddies, during the very best times of their lives.
I got to know their nicknames, picture their scars.
Red, Spats.

Lefty.

"Ol' Lefty, you know how he got that name, don't ya?"

We'd forever be the sons of the men we disappointed; men defined by The War.
And we would have to wonder where we would get our own stories of battle. What grand memories would propel us through the mundane days to come?

Kimm would come down, finally, roll his eyes at me.
I know he'd heard them all before.
Hell, he probably shook Lefty's hand in an awkward exchange.
And those worn stories were probably not told in good cheer, but as a lecture series: *what it means to be a man.*
We would head for the door then and escape, Kimm's pop still telling his story to the room we'd left empty.

olden Colorado.

GI got two wooden nickels after showing ID, went to the bar and cashed one for a fresh drawn lager.

Then I took a seat in the tasting room of the Coors factory. It was a Bavarian style beer hall with long hardwood communal tables, arched windows reaching up to the high ceiling, massive chandeliers overhead made from tangles of elk antlers.

The day had turned dark, with slate thunderheads rolling over the mountains, and the air was charged with electricity, already bitter with the smell of brewing hops.

We'd gone through the factory tour, walked through the lab-like process rooms; saw the automated displays of the fermenting process explained in childlike language.

Stainless steel vats of beer lined the high-ceilinged rooms, a lifetime of spousal abuse and failed careers simmering in monumental silos.

We witnessed a barely recognizable cousin to the precious recipes brewed in Bavaria or Czechoslovakia.

Desperate artisan immigrants enduring steerage class on heaving ships with ale formulas smuggled up asshole and vagina, only for the recipe to be bastardized for mass production and watered down for maximum profit before it touched our lips.

Famously available only west of the Rockies, Coors was the beer that embodied the California spirit.

Final frontier, edge of the New West.

I'd picture drunken pioneers.

They would halt their wagons on a clifftop just before tipping both mule and children into the black Pacific below.

They would dismount then, baptize the fertile ground with their golden

piss, fall to their knees upon the mud and urine.
They'd clasp their hands together at the bounty, teardrops carbonated,
livers fat as Christmas geese.

My Dad, he drank Coors, and then so did I.
My mom kept flats of six packs in the garage, stacked a yard high.
I believe my mother kept so much beer around to keep my father from
hitting the hard stuff with the usual hilarious and costly result.

Sundays, my dad and uncles would gather at the Cerritos house and
watch football.
They'd drink enormous amounts of beer, sucking the cans dry in two
swallows.
They'd chomp on pretzels dipped in mustard; drink more beer as they
waited for *Bachan* to fry up tempura shrimp and onion rings.
Halftime, they would take to the street out front, throwing footballs
with gleeful abandon, running into parked cars for interceptions,
making diving catches that left their palms bloody and their khakis torn
at the knees.
Even after the divorce mom kept the garage stocked, a disciple of bulk
shopping before such a thing had a name.
And after I began my own drinking career she wordlessly kept the stack
level even after we'd take three flats off the top.
I think she knew it kept me close by.

Jack came into the room, alone.
I watched him looking around the hall, this pale, skinny kid with
straight dyed black hair.
He wore a black work shirt buttoned to his chin, a gold crucifix around
his neck: a creepy emo kid decades before there was such a thing.
He squinted around until he saw me, then came over and sat with me at
the table, too shy to try his fake ID at the door.

I slipped one of my wooden tokens to him, and he went back to get a beer.

He got back to the table, took a little sip and traced a finger down the sweating side of the glass. I knew Jack wasn't much of a drinker, but he knew enough to accept one when offered, then nurse it through the night.

"So what ya think?' I asked him. "This trip going ok so far for you?" Jack made a little grunting sound, shrugged his shoulders.

"It's all right, Ok, I guess," he finally said. "Some of the drives… long, huh?"

"Yeah, well… We got lots more of them coming up, so, uh, hold on. I think Jay's working out though, eh? You guys are locking in on the rhythm stuff."

Jack took another sip, spun the glass around on the table.

"Oh yeah, it's sounding pretty good." Here he paused, as if trying out the next words in his head.

"Chris and Doug," he started. "They're kind of," another pause, *"intense,* huh?"

I knew what he was trying to say.

Chris and Doug were in vacation mode, just drinking beer all day and trying to pick up girls at each show.

But they were getting bored on the long rides, cheated without the release of getting up on stage at the end of the day, and they took it out on Jack.

He was "The Kid," as someone always must be, and though he'd already been in the band a year he was the new guy still.

Jack was younger by 4 or 5 years, a half-lifetime to guys of drinking age.

He was along for the music and travel, missing his summer after Graduation for this.

Jack knew enough to keep quiet and do his job, lest he become the easy target for the hazing that was doled out naturally on the youngest and quietest.

He bewildered us when he turned down a line of blow or a proposition from an ambitious gal who hoped to fuck the whole band in one night.

But I'd become attuned to his dry asides, his precise commentary on our absurd behavior that could silence us all for a moment.
Driving, I would look at him in the rearview mirror and he would float his eyebrows, letting me know he was indeed in on the joke, alert as a dog trained for tragedy on the site of a smoking ruin.

Chris and Doug were both oldest brothers I now realized, and effortlessly meted out the teasing as they did on their own little brothers.
"Oh hell, those guys are just full of shit," I said. "Just give 'em another week out here, they'll settle down."
I nodded to Jack and he nodded back, and we touched glasses.
Every little brother's fantasy wordlessly understood between us.
The late-night plans of revenge: first, on our older brothers and then: *the world.*
To grow four inches taller than any of them in the end, the lost baby fat revealing rippling abdomens, our biceps bulging like sated jungle snakes.
And our older brothers, they'd be begging for undeserved mercy as we towered above them in our ragged hand-me-downs.

We were all at the table now, having a great time, the long tabletop cluttered with a dozen empty Pilsner flutes and as many half-drunk glasses.
We took turns walking around the pub, finding leftover wooden nickels from the sensible tourists who only took one of the free samples, probably not risking the steep mountain road drive home after two drinks.

It was nice to relax without a gig that night, a day without the clock ticking backward toward load in and set time, the daylight consumed by miles and hours.

Kimm and Matt sipped at their beers and chatted about cities and dates:
Tulsa after Kansas, an outdoor fest the day after Dallas.
San Antonio, then back to Austin.
Houston cancelled.

The weeks were constantly changing, the maps unfolded again, routes redrawn in a different color Highlighter, a rainbow of backtracks and reroutes.

Doug came back to the table and threw a stack of cards across the table. We all grabbed, hurried to pick them up before they soaked up the spilled beer.
Doug held one up, "Check it, free postcards!"
Postcards, postage paid, to send back home from Colorado.
There was one with an old-timey beer wagon pulled by horses, another with the red Coors logo against the glorious Rockies.
We all patted at our pockets for pens and were soon writing postcards home.
The table was quiet now, and I looked down the row and saw the punkers all scribbling, some of the guys shielding their writing as if hiding test answers from a cheating classmate.
Sending thoughts home to mom or a girl, each of us picturing someone back home taking the postcard from the mailbox and thinking of us for a moment.
I wrote a quick note to mom.
Say hi to Bachan and the girls! I signed mine and addressed it to our Cerritos home.
I grabbed another card and started writing a note to my dad, sentimentally buzzed enough to make note of one of the few bonding devices we shared: our love of Coors Banquet.
But it suddenly occurred to me that I had no idea how to address it.
I did not know where my father lived.

A little girl shyly approached our table then, maybe 11 years old, as freckled and towheaded as the younger brother who held her hand.

We all stopped writing, looked at the kids.

"What is it, honey?" Kimm finally asked her.

She gave us a funny kid smile, a mouthful of empty gaps awaiting adult incisors that would see her to dentures or death.

She turned to look at her parents who were sitting at a table near the door, but her folks urged her on with a wave of hand, and the girl dropped a postcard on our table.

The children turned and ran back to their parents who were now standing, heading toward the exit.

I grabbed the postcard first, flipped it over and saw red ink.

The handwriting, though sloppy, was obviously not from the kids but a note from Mom or Dad.

Dear weirdos!
Nice haircuts, ha ha!
We hope you all burn in hell.

I passed the card down the table, then turned to the windows and watched as the family loaded into a station wagon.

The rain had started now, and they turned on their headlights as they left the parking lot, illuminating their Utah plates.

The guys all took turns then, reading the card aloud in exaggerated southern accents, adding another sentence mentioning cock size and odor.

And though we all laughed it off as hilarious, I, for the first time, saw us as if from afar. Like a spirit floating above its bluing body, being shocked by defibrillator once again.

We looked rough all right, our heads shaved completely or hair sticking out at severe angles, tattoos on biceps at a time when only sailors and convicts had tattoos.

We wore shorts and filthy boots, ragged clothes save the new Coors T shirts that suddenly looked ridiculous.

I became aware of every other family in that place staring at us now,
and how our very being was ruining their day.
Like that moment in a Marvel comic book where the earnest scientist
wakes in his basement lab, just after the inevitable atomic spill.
He inspects the huge lobster claws that were once his liver-spotted
hands.
He clips at the air, his antennae fluttering with realization.
Ah, he thinks, *so I am the villain now.*

***D**enver was an all right gig*, rain pounding outside a small skate warehouse, a small but good crowd of punkers.

People mouthing along to the lyrics, ferocious pit action between a dozen kids who had probably played youth soccer together just the summer before.

After the vans were loaded we hung out at the warehouse, drinking beer and watching the locals skate a plywood quarter ramp.

And though I sucked at doing kickturns I made a lazy pass at the ramp myself.

As I slid to the bottom of the ramp on my knees, I held my beer overhead.

Not a drop spilled, I downed it and crushed the can to the cheers of whoever was still awake.

Jay produced some clippers from his backpack and proceeded to shave the sides of his head, keeping the back and top long, a red mullet mohawk.

I was glad to see him getting into the spirit of things, so I took the clippers next, shaved down close, and then passed them around.

The *snick* of the tiny electric motor kept up its buzzing throughout the night, and a pile of various hair shades soon lay on the ground like bloated roadkill.

Mark from Stretchmarks shaved off his eyebrows, which we then replaced with strips of black electrical tape.

Howls of laughter, tears.

Towards dawn I felt the urge to shit.

My body clock hopelessly confused, my intestines awash with beer and gas station hot dogs, my gut churned and bubbled as I hurried to the head.

There was a closet-sized bathroom, a single bulb overhead activated by

a filthy pull string.
The walls covered with band stickers and marker graffiti, impressionist
sketches of penis and vagina, the bizarre discourse of inside joke
(*Doctor Dracula is making you on acid!*)

A toilet sits bubbling, paisleyed with decades of hardwater and piss,
Dalmatian-flecked with the crap of people probably long dead.
There is no seat, no toilet paper.
I flush in test, but the vile contents just rise higher in the bowl,
threatening to spill over.
This charming tableau we would encounter again and again that
summer, as if the template plan for *Punk Rock Bathroom* was sent
throughout the continent, the authenticity of each venue measured in
direct proportion to the filth of the men's toilets.

I went outside and squatted there in between the two vans as the sky
began to lighten.
A soft drizzle coming down, streetlights mirrored in the puddles, their
cicada-like sodium buzz the only sound in Denver.
Evacuation and housekeeping, a *kamikaze* headband sacrificed in lieu
of Charmin, hands splashed in puddle and dried on jeans.

I went to the roll-up door of the club and pulled up on the bottom
handle.
The door rose easily, and I ducked my head under.
But, instead of returning to the skatehouse, I found myself standing in a
makeshift living room, an Asian family huddled around a propane stove
making breakfast.
Cambodian or Vietnamese I guessed by the guttural clip of their sudden
shouting.

I realized I'd opened the wrong roll-up, and shrugging in apology,
stepped back.
The father bowed and made *Sampeah* gestures, hands together, palms
flat in supplication.
Two little girls screamed, the wife hugged them both with one arm,

made sweeping motions toward me with the other.

"You go now, you leave us alone!" she cried. *"We have nothing."*

She was fierce, magnificent in her maternal power, eyes watering with rage.

A mother raising children in a terrible country of awful people.

I thought of my mother and her family, once terrorized in the place they knew as home.

SIX

Like most Japanese Americans of the Nisei generation, my mom's life was bisected by the time before and after the internment camp.

My grandmother, Bachan, was a girl named Kinuye who came over from Hawaii as a picture bride to my grandfather, Makoto.

Makoto was a serious man with huge ears and heavy jowls, peering out from the faded photos simian and suspicious.

They married, then ran a Chinese restaurant in San Francisco, rumored as a safe house for Yakuza members hiding out in the States.

I picture Bachan back in the kitchen, braising chicken feet in a neon orange sauce.

Upstairs, my grandpop adjusts a table light to illuminate the bleeding man lying across their dining table.

He prepares to stitch a knife wound shut with 4lb. test fishing line.

He chews at his tongue while he works, struggling to keep the delicate lines of an Oni Mask tattoo matched on a bleeding gangster's backpiece.

They started a family, a girl then two boys.

My mom, Teruko, then Uncle Ich and Uncle Sets.

They left the greasy floors and bloodied gangsters behind and moved to Delano, a farm hub north of Bakersfield.

Family fables smoothed by time like a submerged rock rounded by unrelenting currents.

The nasty bits of shame dulled, crimes rewritten as duty or forgotten altogether.

Bachan heard the knocking, only to find it wasn't knuckles upon door she heard, but an 11 x 17 placard being nailed into the clapboard siding of their home.

INSTRUCTIONS TO ALL MEMBERS OF JAPANESE ANCESTORY it began, the print scrolling smaller as it continued down, the words shrinking as their intentions grew more evil.

Bachan stood on tip-toe and looked closely at the words, her nose almost touching the paper.

Sounding out each English word aloud in a whisper, she surely misunderstood the instructions.

By the time my mom came out to the porch and read it for her, their life was already slipping away.

They were told to take only what they could carry, leaving behind their furniture and home, and report to a bus station.

Go somewhere else.

Bachan fretted over the weight of the tetsubin, if she could bring her bowls and cups. Mom assured her they would carry the iron teapot for her, though the lacquered rice bowls would have to stay.

Grandpa took a lantern with him to the vineyards that night, his Japanese ceremonial swords bundled in burlap like a burial shroud. He dug a hole, then dropped the swords into the earth, taking stock of the grave from every vantage in the futile hope he would someday be back to retrieve them.

He smoothed the dirt beside the grapevines he had tended just that morning but would never see harvested, their fruit still green and bitter.

The night before they were to report to the bus my mother lay awake.

She sat at the sound of muffled voices outside, and then raised a corner of the window shade by her bed.

Out in the street were two battered trucks, men standing in a tight circle.

Smoking, spitting.

The glowing red tips of their inhaled cigarettes floating like fireflies, their weathered faces illuminated briefly by match strike.

Mom said it was the Okies, waiting to come in when they left.

To squat in the vacated home, go through the closets and sniff at the strange pantry.

Shreds of dried seaweed are tasted then spit onto grandma's immaculate kitchen floor.

By the time mom and her family were riding the bus to Santa Anita racetrack, the house is already cleared of clothes and hardware.

When they finally lay down to sleep in a horse stable that night, sharing with another family the space usually reserved for one thoroughbred gelding, dusty overalls sit upon their couch back in Delano.

Everclear alcohol splashed into Bachan's prized lacquered teacups, the fine paint already weeping.

But my mom, telling the story again after we pestered her to relive it again, she never really blamed those people coming in and taking their things.

They were just another tribe fucked over and set to wander, though saved the indignity of barbed wire by color of skin and crease of eyelid.

Late summer 1945, as my mother was just finishing high school in Jerome Arkansas Relocation Camp, my father, John, was aboard the USS Missouri.

He'd been cheated out of his own WWII battles, stuck reading the boiler pressure gauges in the hold as the ship steamed toward a war just ended.

He'd boxed for the Navy in exhibition matches, his winning record finally spoiled by a hulking Russian boxer named Sergey.

As they circled each other in the third round, neither fighter has delivered the knockout.

The Russian grins around his mouthpiece, the split decision would fall in his favor.

The sweating sailors, their thirst for battle again denied, cry for blood.

My father kept his right guard up, lest the Russian discover his glass jaw.

He'd often tell me of the fight, making sure I understood he was talking life lesson here.

My dad would inevitably stand and put up his dukes.

"If you ever fight for a championship, Michael… hell."

Now he would shuffle, feint to the left and cuff me on the side of the head. "You see? You must let down your guard, take a chance."

Better to send a telegraphed haymaker in gamble of victory than to play it safe and end up defeated by points.

Your opponent's glistening arm raised in victory by the referee between you, your arm shamefully held down by the wrist.

He returned to Philadelphia in the late winter, taking a job as a truck driver for the Navy Yard.

He navigated the filthy slush of city streets as the grey days turned black by late afternoon, thinking of that crystal blue water he'd swum in the Pacific Theatre.

He married young, had my half-sister, Barbara Ann, resigned himself to the usual career choices of our Irish family there: crooked politician or crooked cop.

Riding home one bleak evening on the PCC trolley, already dark at 5pm, his breath was still visible inside the car.

Exhausted, not by the long day of mindless labor, but by the absolutely normal life that lay ahead of him.

He later told us of looking up and reading the advertisements plastered along the car's curved ceiling.

There, between ads for Burma-Shave and Lit Brothers department store, was a poster of a golden sun setting above a grove of oranges.

Come to California, it read, Summer Lingers Just For You!

The trolley came to his stop, but he stayed on.

He divorced for the first time, took a train to California and enrolled in optometry at USC Medical.

When my mom's family got out of camp, they came back west due to grandpa's health.

The humidity never left Makoto's lungs; the bumps left by mosquito bite seemed to never stop itching.

The family slowly made their way back west, stopping at readjustment camps along the way.

My mother took secretarial classes by day, developing a calligraphic handwriting that would forever make forging her name an impossibility.

She took a job at an egg processing plant in East LA and took her seat among the other Japanese women hired for their supposed prowess at candling eggs.

She spent her shift examining eggs by flame to determine if a developing embryo lurked within its shell, a life stubbornly intent on spoiling breakfast.

My father drove trucks for the same egg outfit. He took shifts after optometry classes, although he already knew he would not be satisfied with tending to just the eyeball and had already set his sight on medical school and becoming a General Practice MD.

As he huddled over stripped cadavers in the lab, his gaze wandered.

From the eyeball down to the body, from jaundiced sclera to the hematoma purpling the corpse's torso, correctly diagnosing advanced cirrhosis.

As he drove the truck at night, he wondered at the greater mysteries held within chest cavities and intestines.

The eggs in the truck bed shuddered gently with each downshifted gear, each deemed safe for consumption by my mother's almond shaped eyes, enchanted by candlelight.

They met, dated, saw plans for a daring future.

My brother John already nestled in her womb, an embryo yet undetected by my parents or candlelight, when they took a long night drive to Las Vegas to wed.

They were turned away, of course, the Irish sailor and the Japanese war criminal denied license or interracial ceremony in 1955.

Reaching the border by dawn, they married in Tijuana and were back in LA that night.

They spent their first married night together at my grandparents' house in Boyle Heights.

They lay together, thinking of the future they'd instigated, regret and hope threading through their dreams.

Just before dawn they hear Bachan rise to fill the iron teapot.

And then they can hear Makoto in the next room, scratching at the phantom mosquito bites on his arms.

PART II

*J*ournal:
June29, Lincoln Nebraska
Boring drive, Doug thinks he has crabs. Promoter guy had some piranha in fishtank.
Small gig at someone's garage. Drank all the beer after and left.

June 30, Kansas City

Daytime matinee gig at a VFW hall, was like a battle of the bands! Played with Whipping Boy and Legal Weapon, good to see them.

I walked past their van as Kat from Legal Weapon was putting on her goth makeup in the Midwestern heat, a day so hot the sun was invisible in the sky.

She looked up when she heard me laughing. "Oh fuck off, Mike" she said, smiling, stabbing toward me with an eyeliner pen.

July 1, Tulsa

I stayed drunk all day and could barely hold my guitar by showtime. I told the crowd it was my birthday, and my sloppiness was excused, a half dozen beers were brought to me.

I would remember that trick. I celebrated my birthday a dozen times that summer.

July2, Dallas

We ate mushrooms before the set.
The lights were amazing.

4th of July, Austin

Firecrackers crackle along the gutters of downtown Austin, bottle rockets launch off the roof of the Club Foot.

Sparks trail across the hot Texas sky, that whistle and *pop!* again and again.

We got off stage drenched with sweat, wet as if we'd climbed out of a well.

The packed club had achieved its own ecosystem, heated by a few hundred punk bodies tribal dancing, walls dripping, humid as a rainforest.

Outside was little relief but we still gulped in the night air, heavy with moisture, seasoned with the sulfur stink of spent fireworks.

Another good set.

One of the nights that the setlist flowed naturally, the guitars stayed in tune.

Jay had started doing great leaps during the set, accenting a chorus crash cymbal with a split kick in midair.

It urged me to start moving as well, and we soon found the crowd packed up against the skirt of the stage.

Coming alive with the movement, the pit behind them slamming with more fury in kinetic response.

I ran from side to side of the stage, dodging Kimm and Jay as they ran to the other, our guitar cords finally tangled in a hopeless knot center stage.

We were playing tight and easy, grooved after the solid run of shows and charged by a big crowd.

We'd practiced these songs hundreds of times, broke them down and rebuilt them under Jay's pre-production. Put them in context of a set list, finding good placement, minding the song's key, or if it started with a guitar intro or drumbeat.

We considered the song's ending, did it ring out the last chord or stop on *four!* with crash cymbals clutched, strings muted?

That runaway school bus, does it fly off the overpass, the children's screams melting into the darkness, or do they simply hit the brick wall?

The Dicks played just before us, and I stood with Big Boys singer Biscuit just offstage watching their set.

I liked Biscuit quite a bit, having met him back home when they played the Whisky with X.

On their closer, a raucous version of "Hollywood Swinging," Biscuit shed his jumpsuit, revealing a pink tutu underneath.

He smeared cheap lipstick across his face and threw himself into the song, into the crowd, terrifying and exhilarating.

As The Dicks played, Gary Floyd roamed the stage restlessly.

Howling his homo radical songs, fucking with the crowd between songs.

Biscuit leaned and shouted into my ear, *Old Gary, he's on a tear tonight. Y'all be sure to step it up, son!"*

He looked at me and grinned, pointed at Gary rolling around onstage now, his belly huge and white, shaking as he humped the monitor.

We all suffered from the homophobia of young straight men, I admit that, and it was startling to see a punk singer shouting out that he was gay, *and you probably were too*, just too chickenshit to admit it.

Biscuit, like Gary Floyd, never made it any secret he was gay.

Instead, they seemed to flaunt it as the ultimate "fuck off" to the norm, about the punkest thing you could be in the ultimate macho world of hardcore.

We'd been staying with the Big Boys on this Texas stay, the dozen of us (counting the Stretchers) spread out between their tiny houses and our vans. Their hospitality was offered without question.

We ended up at Biscuit's house the night before, at the end of a long day sweating in the Austin humidity and a show in San Antonio.

Biscuit came out of his room to wish us good night.

"I had just had a nice cool bath, and y'all are welcome to do the same," he said, tightening the belt on his terrycloth robe.

"And there ain't much in there, I'm afraid," his thumb jerking to the kitchen, "But I'm fixin' to have a PBJ sammy, just let me know how many to make."

We were grateful as abandoned dogs and fell upon the white bread and

Skippy in kind.

Chris had been feeling shitty since Tulsa and didn't want to go out on the 4th.
He stayed behind at Tim and Beth's place listening to the fireworks going off through the night.
Tim was the Big Boys' guitar player, Beth his sweet wife.
We'd sit in his tiny front room listening to records, stroking their big smelly dogs. They collected dark gothic statues, decorated their small place with novena candles and horror movie posters.
Chris told us the next day he lay in the top bunk all night staring at the huge plastic spider hanging in the corner near his face, next to a giant *Die, Die, My Darling* Misfits poster.
When he woke the next morning, finally feeling better, he noticed the spider was gone.

My parents settled into an unsettled married life.
They followed up John Jr. with Tim, Eileen, and Colleen.
Four kids, in perfect balance.
Then, as an afterthought, the unplanned pregnancy met with a slap to the forehead: me.

Five children within a six-year span.
They mated seasonally, like animals intent on the survival their species, all of us dark, cynical autumn children, save spring baby Eileen.
We fell into our roles, JB (For Johnny Boy, son to his father) the mechanical thinker, Tim the musical one.
Colleen was the born cheerleader, Eileen the golden student.
And the youngest kid, as so often happens, becomes a combination of all our older siblings.
An effort to both please and rebel.

We moved to a creaking house in Anaheim, close enough to Disneyland that we could see the fireworks exploding above us each summer night, inhaling the acrid smoke of the big finale that settled upon us like the fog of battle.

Mom raised us Catholic, probably to appease the Irish side of the family.
She was Buddhist, of course, and my father was excommunicated from the church for being divorced and remarried.
We were punished for his sins; sat on pews hard as bone for noon mass in Latin.
The boys in itchy wool pants, my sisters with squares of Kleenex bobby pinned to their heads as veils.
When we rolled into the station wagon after church, tearing at buttons and whining about the Latin high mass, we'd ask yet again *why* we had to do this.
My mom, who was enjoying the only hour of silence of her week, would just snap shut her trashy paperback and turn the ignition, surrendering to the chaos again.
"This religion," she'd say, "you'll come back to it when you're old and afraid."

Bachan and Grandpa lived with us in the big house, and on endless summer days Makoto stayed up in his bedroom, steadily smoking Lucky Strikes.
I'd sit on the floor next to his feet, listening to Vin Scully call a midweek Dodger day game from a small transistor radio.
An old man's world reduced to the easy chair and nightstand at his elbow, the red and white pack of smokes and the Dodgers trailing going into the eighth.
He came across the world to get here, a journey plotted by bewildering forces.
He'd read the *Rafu Shimpo*, the Los Angeles Japanese language newspaper delivered daily, and I'd sit on the floor and watch his gaze following the vertical lines of Hiragana and Kanji.
The English words of local news were print phonetically in Katakana.
He'd point at each character and sound out the words for me:

ドン・サットン

Do-Nu Su-Ah-To-N.
Don Sutton.

He never made the move with us to Cerritos.
The Dodgers at Cubs, down one into the fifth.
Vin uses Alston's trip to the mound to remind us of Farmer John's hickory smoked bacon.
A Lucky Strike burns in the ashtray, a spirit of smoke trails up to the ceiling as Makoto clutches at the newspaper in his hands, crumpling it to his chest.
The lines of print held tight, just for a moment above his palpitating heart, and then he releases.
Bachan kept a shrine in her bedroom for the next forty years, a stick of incense lit at dawn, a small offering of each meal served before anyone could eat.

By the time we moved to Cerritos, dad was already restless with just being a doctor.
To have a job that *literally* meant life or death, even that lost all thrill to him. He'd shuttle back and forth from our house to La Palma Community at all hours, taking late night ER shifts if only for the excitement of sealing a self-inflicted gunshot wound or retrieving a family artifact from a packed rectum.
His westward adventure was stopped only by the Pacific, and when he looked around, he could not believe that life was only *this*.
The wild animal pets started then, as if by bringing the jungle into our home we would somehow become exotic ourselves.

He would come home half drunk (and buzzing on prescription amphetamine, I now realize), a squirrel monkey perched upon his shoulder, a raccoon cooing at us from a perforated cardboard box.
We once had an *anteater* as a pet. I was the fucking king of show and tell.

"Gather round kids," he'd say, the next addition to his menagerie hissing from a kennel crate. *"I know you were asking about a dog but look what one of my patients had instead. Great huh?"*
My mother would just frown at the stripe of monkey shit trailing down his back.
Bachan already fetching a wet towel, happy for something new to clean.

The doctor would focus his attention on this large crew of kids, thinking that surely at least one of us would show a talent for singing, say, or perhaps a savant-like understanding of trigonometry or boxing. He had visions of greatness for this family. I mean, *five kids!* How could we not form a pop band or produce at least one chess master or cello virtuoso?

He'd pull into the driveway with a stack of blank canvases and tubes of acrylic paints crowding the back seat of his gold Cadillac DeVille.
In the trunk, duffle bags of used boxing gear; a de-masted catamaran perched on a trailer behind.
He'd have an odd hippie couple come over and teach us painting in the game room.
Piano lessons after school on Tuesdays.
We also had to learn one other musical instrument, and there was soon a drum set in my room, a baby grand crowding the den.

One afternoon he dumped a fragrant pile of black neoprene wetsuits in the living room.
"We're going to be the first family of scuba diving, what do you think of that?"
He received my mom's frown then automatically redirected to *Bachan*.
"What do you think of that, mama?" he'd ask with a theatrical roll of the eyes.
Soon he was sweating in full wetsuit and fins in our driveway, showing us a new gunpowder-charged spear gun.
"Fields, *FIELDS,*" he'd exclaim. "Fields full of abalone are out there

just waiting for us to pick 'em up! Now, who's with me?" he said, holding up a squat prying knife.

He waved the knife back in forth, mimicked scooping a shell off a rock. "What do you say, mama? Abalone sushi, good?"

Bachan just blushed and worried her hands in her apron.

A month later I found myself floating on the surface off Avalon, helpless as chum.

Too young for a tank, I'd have to snorkel and wade above my dad and brothers, their exhaled bubbles floating up at me from the dark depths. And then we'd always be in that terrifying ocean, or upon it on leaky borrowed boats.

It was as if my dad was fascinated by the void of sea, the final boundary to his journey west.

Soon there were motorcycles and scuba tanks crowding the garage, abandoned canvases haunting the attic like Nazi plunder.

The catamaran leaned against the side of the house; one hull crushed from its maiden launch.

In the backyard, a speedbag hung deflated like a grape withered on the vine.

The piano bench was covered with ironing; no prodigy had come forth.

And as if some target date had finally arrived, my parents divorced the day after I turned 13.

The Big Boys had a horn section playing with them that night, a big hometown show on the 4th, all the stops.

The Austin crowd rightfully treated them as heroes, everyone in the club part of an outside tribe in a Texas town not yet turned hip or ironic. Biscuit and Tim would tell us about clashes with the frat types that hung on 6th Street, beatdowns on both sides.

The stares from people of the old county culture encountering a new type of freak in a town founded by rebels.

It became the common theme we heard all that summer, different versions of humiliations, the threat of physical violence in direct proportion to distance from major city.

Lifelong friendships formed as they guarded their flanks, back-to-back, against their hometown enemies.

Only the accents differed as they told their stories of a brotherhood bonded in defense.

We drank late after the show, eventually hanging out in the parking lot of a funeral home near Tim's house.

We'd be saying goodbye to the Stretchmarks crew after tonight, heading deeper south as they went north and eventually back to Winnipeg.

We made plans to meet again up there, toasting over and over to our friendship, the holiday, just being here on this night.

There were some locals hanging out drinking with us, one girl with a prosthetic leg covered with punk band stickers.

I watched as Doug went over to her with a CH3 sticker, and after she nodded, he knelt to apply it to her hard plastic upper thigh.

Soon she had a crowd around her.

Each of us calculating the van conversation the next day of having bedded down with the one-legged chick, already formulating the jokes and nicknames that would ensue.

Kimm eventually walked off with her, each of them stumbling a bit, hand in hand towards the shadows.

The guys from Youth Brigade were passing through Texas on their own summer tour.

The three vans parked in the mortuary parking lot, along with a few pickup trucks. A dusty old Cadillac hearse was parked there too, shadowed from streetlights by a massive oak.

We opened the van doors and turned up the car stereos. Drinking beers, tossing the empties into the little cemetery next door.

I was standing with the Youth Brigade guys, Mark and Adam, just chatting about the shows past and some dates to come, a plan to meet up again for a Toronto gig once we crossed into Canada in a month.

Mark from Stretchmarks came up then, and I quickly grabbed him in a headlock. *"Go on,"* I growled into his ear, *"liberate yourself from my viselike grip."*
Mark twisted out of my hold then pushed me facedown to the lawn.
He sat on my back and pulled back my head, a classic camel clutch. I pounded the canvas thrice and he let me up.
He wrapped a meaty forearm around my neck and turned to the brothers Stern.
"And this one," he said, "woo, can this boy put down the beer. Wait 'til we get him the real stuff up in Canada, eh?" I shook him off and grabbed a Lone Star out of the case at our feet.

Shawn came over, shaking his head. "Nah man, these CH3 guys. They can drink beer, but they can't hold a drop of hard liquor."
Here he brought up a half full fifth of Jack Daniels, took a swig, and then passed it to his brothers.

The warm Texas night: the summer stretching before us so far that the story had no ending yet.
New dates were added each day.
Only a hazy first day of school as the target, distant as a hand mirror flashing on the horizon, a beacon of distress across an endless sea.
I felt, if not invincible, at least lucky.
I took the bottle from Adam's hand and brought it to my mouth, took the whole thing down in four gulping swallows.
"Ah, fucking Magrann," Shawn said.
I awoke hours later, lying on the hood of the hearse.
I shielded my eyes, looked up at the already hot Texas sun coming through the oak tree branches.
I raised my head for a moment; saw the Blue & White still parked in the lot, though the others were gone.
I lay back on top of the hearse, holding my hand to my forehead, holding the pulsing signal of pain beneath skin.
Feeling like it would be much more comfortable to be lying inside this vehicle instead of on top.

*O**n the way out of town we** stopped and picked up Biscuit. We were heading for Woodshock, an outdoor fest held on a ranch in Dripping Springs, out near a quarry lake. We turned off the highway, then Biscuit took the wheel of the Blue & White after the pavement turned to a rutted fire road.

"Y'all just set back," he told us, sliding the seat back to fit his body. "It's a little bumpy, this old road, but we're gonna get you there."

We bounced along the dirt road, grounding the van a couple times against baby-head-sized stones. The road narrowed at the switchback turns, dead tree branches scratched at the van windows.

I looked back at the guys, we all started laughing.

Framed for the moment in the first act of a teen slasher movie.

The path finally opened to a dirt lot, trucks and vans parked around a small outdoor stage.

It reminded me more of my motocross days than any of the urban alleyways of punk rock: the dust floating above the crowd, the buzz of being outdoors in the dirt, the air electric with something fast and violent about to start.

The crowd was a mix of punkers and scary burnouts, cultish looking types with hollowed out cheeks and toothless smiles, finding kin in the punk anti-society, but way beyond that.

I unloaded my guitar cabinet and stumbled into a tiny man with dreadlocked hair and cloudy eyes standing too close, staring up at me.

"Hey man, you guys a band? You're a band, right?" And here he put a hand into the pocket of his torn corduroy cutoffs, pulling out a dirty sandwich bag.

"So you want acid, right?" He twitched, swiveled his head around like a squirrel alerted to the shadow of a hawk.

"How many people you got here?" He turned around, counting heads aloud, pointing at each of us with a crooked finger.

We played a set on the back of a truck bed in the hot afternoon sun,
only the vocals miked up, the amplifiers calling out to the flat prairie,
nothing out there to bounce the sound back to us.
Later in the afternoon we wandered down to the edge of the quarry.
Below us, I don't know, 30 feet, 80? *400?* was green water pooled in
the void of Earth.
A few punkers were already swimming down there.
Dogs splashed after tennis balls, topless hippie chicks reclined on the
half-submerged tree trunks, sunning their hairy legs.

We all stood near the edge, balls tingling with vertiginous excitement,
waiting for one of us to jump first. The other guys took backward steps
away from the edge, Kimm turning and walking away, muttering "oh,
fuck that."

Only Chris and I stayed at the edge. "Ooh Lordy," Chris said. *"Holy
Moly."*

Chris always talked like a character from an old movie, probably
instilled by the endless reruns of *Twilight Zone*, *Three Stooges*, and *I
Love Lucy* that played throughout his latchkey youth.
He had brought along a bottle of Old Spice on tour, and he would douse
himself with it before opening the van doors to a new town.
He'd jump out with his trousers hiked high, Fred Mertz style, muttering
things like *dagnabbit* and *jumpin' Jehoshaphat!* to the girls who would
later bury their noses into his shoulder, breathe in the Old Spice and be
confused: a twinge of melancholy coloring their horniness, suddenly
missing their dead grandfathers as they fondled Chris's cock.

I grabbed Chris's hand and dragged him to the very edge. He grinned
and gripped back tighter, daring me to be the first one to puss out, but
we took the next leaping step out over the edge.

We fell fast to the water, visions of quadriplegia filling my head as we held midair, pictured a lifetime of begging someone to wipe my ass.
We crashed its surface with a violent impact that surprised me.
I dropped down low, the water thankfully deep enough to just touch the quarry's soft bottom with my toe.

We crested the surface together, then waved at the guys up on the quarry ledge to join us.
I don't think any of the others jumped.
It was a fucking long walk back up to the top.

I first met Chris when he came up to me, lunch time at Faye Ross Junior High.
"Hey Jap," he said, grinning, before looking back at some guys sitting at the lunch tables.
I was working the Slushie machine, green or red for a dime.
One of the perks of being in the "gifted" homeroom was being able to leave class 15 minutes before lunch bell to work the food lines.

I grabbed at his Hang Ten shirt, twisting the striped fabric in my hand, making the little feet logo touch toes.
He laughed and twisted away, turning back to me as he ran.
"They dared me to do it!" he shouted. *"Jap!"*

I surely don't look Japanese, and I've always felt pasty and gawky surrounded by my Japanese cousins, always envious of that cool slant of eyes and flawless skin.
We would go to the *Nissei* festivals in Little Tokyo, dance in the Ondo parades, and I was always the big gawky *Hakujin*– "whiteboy."
I'm ashamed to admit that I would also witness the racist jokes told behind my family's backs, privy to the hatred by looking nothing like them.
I felt like the blue-eyed blonde boy waving farewell to his dark family as they board their final train.
Walking ten steps behind my cousins through the mall, I saw the

60

bucktooth grins, the fingers pushing squinted eyelids up in grotesque apery.
A coward, I did nothing.

Chris and I became friends, of course, and he later told me his friends put him up to that stunt because he did not believe I was half Japanese.
I found out that Chris rode motorcycles as well, riding his father's old 175 Yamaha out in the desert.
Of my father's desperate offerings, only the motorcycles landed with me.
I became obsessed with dirt bikes and my dad encouraged me, though I believe he was forever disappointed that I had no interest in football or boxing, his passions borne of muddy corner lots in Philadelphia and the boiler room matches below the waterline.

I'd already started racing the smooth TT tracks at Elsinore and Perris on a long Honda CR250, though I didn't really have the skill to send the bike sideways on right-handed turns.
I mostly rode the track timidly, far behind the older guys in 250 Novice, only once scoring a small plastic third place trophy when the fourth man in the main crashed out.

We also both had parents going through separation around that time and we communicated our feelings in the ways of thirteen-year-old boys: talking about anything but.
Finding commiseration and comfort in the silences between sentences.
We'd spend long afternoons in his garage or mine, washing the motorcycles, looking at *Cycle News* or *Playboys* pulled from an old milkcrate beneath the tool bench.
We sat side by side, a vintage copy of *Playboy* open to centerfold, ogling a woman probably dead by now.

He once told me that all he wished for when he was a kid was body hair and sperm.

I reminded him of that wish constantly now, his arms as hairy as a primate, always horny as a moose in rut.

Chris's dad was a detective in the LA County Sheriff's Department.
He had the proper moustache for the job, the worried eyelines from too many late nights viewing scenes of horror.
I'd picture him getting off his scary DT360 Yamaha and racing back to the station to grill a suspect in the box, playing the bad cop today.
His buddies take bets on when the perp would piss himself just on the other side of the two way.

His mom was just finishing nursing school, determined to make her young, failed marriage a mere sidestep on the way to her own life.
They had the kids young, Kevin soon after Chris, then adopting a little girl when they just couldn't gamble on the terror of having a third male.
But Chris's folks were a generation younger than Kimm's or my parents, and I always imagined they found themselves suddenly surprised with kids and a mortgage.
Their lives ahead of them in a straight predictable line, yet still too young, unsatisfied.
It was the '70s.
People were using their third and final wish, finally, for themselves.

We'd hang out at Chris's house after school, the place gloriously empty until his mom came home from school.
She'd come in and peek in his room to say hello, then sit at the end of the counter with a pack of More cigarettes and a jug of Gallo, talk on the phone until it was dark and time for us to leave.
It seemed wonderful, this space and quiet, families living like roommates, though I would soon know the stillness of an empty house myself.

My mom and dad would try to keep us all together though they were separated.
A tense family trip to Knott's Berry Farm, a hissing conversation in the

chicken restaurant.

My parents driving us home silently, the quiet infecting the station wagon like an airborne virus, the kids looking out the windows without comment.

The day would end with a muffled argument behind my parents' shut bedroom door, my dad leaving again, dry cleaning tucked under his arm.

I would ride my bike home from Chris's house, dusk settling clear and cool as I pedaled down Norwalk Boulevard.

Past the older homes of Artesia, the Mexican and Portuguese neighborhoods. Their front yards and gardens alive with fruit trees and deep foliage, stones painted in the riotous colors of beloved homeland flags.

A joyous chaos rang from the overcrowded houses, the smell of food being cooked, enough for three generations at the dinner table together.

As soon as I crossed Artesia Boulevard the sidewalks smoothed and brightened.

Through the new tracts, the homes identical behind their rectangles of lawn.

Young trees just planted, slouching lazily against support poles, useless for shade or climbing for a generation to come.

THREE

***J*ay is in the first bench**, window side starboard.
He holds a magazine tilted to catch the last of the evening light
and reads aloud.

"The *candiru*, sometimes known as the *penis fish*, is a small
Amazonian catfish. Believed to be attracted to the scent of urine, the
parasitic creature is reported to lodge itself in the urethra of people who
may be urinating in the water."

I'm at the wheel. I turn down the cassette, turn my head around the
headrest to hear better.
Doug leans over from the back seat to read over Jay's shoulder.
"What? No," he says. "Let me see that."

Jay points at the page but holds onto the magazine and continues
reading:
"In 1891, naturalist Paul Le Cointe provides a rare first-hand account of
a *candiru* entering a human body, but it involved the fish being lodged
in the vaginal canal, not the urethra. Le Cointe actually removed the
fish himself, by…"and here Jay pauses, squints at the next line before
continuing. *"…pushing it forward to disengage the spines, turning it
around and removing it head-first."*

Doug sits back in his seat and turns to Jack,
"Are you hearing this Jackie? The fish goes up your dick. Spines."
He squeezes Jack's shoulder and repeats it slowly: *"Spines."*
Then we are all silent with our thoughts.
To a man, we all squirm, reach down and pat our cocks.

We have a stack of magazines onboard: *Motocross Action, The
Wrestling Revue, Rolling Stone,* and *Creem.*
Hustler.

Some fanzines picked up at each city so far, some Stephen King
paperbacks, a worn *Catcher in the Rye.*
There's also an unopened box set, shaped like a paperback, of Edgar
Allen Poe's *Classic Tales of Horror* on two cassettes.

During the long stretches of highway, an hour since the last gas stop
and three hours until the next chance to piss, everyone is quiet.
The conversation is exhausted.
We've all recounted the adventures of the night before, piecing it
together *Rashomon* style.
The cool bartender, the dick promoter, the girl who dragged Chris into
a dark corner of the parking lot for a timed fourteen-minute hand job.

Then it's back to napping or staring.
Flipping through one of the magazines again:

*Nick Bockwinkel defeats Hulk Hogan by reverse disqualification for the
AWA Heavyweight Title.*
*David Bailey dazzles in Anaheim Stadium season opener aboard the
HRC Honda.*
Exclusive! What porn stars are really like in bed!
I'd take the notebook down from the dash then, make an entry for the
day.
Feet on the dash, hungover or sipping my way to the next hangover, I
would write down the date and a quick note about the day that just
passed.

July 6, College Station- TX?
Lame show, broke string second song. There was a fog machine, fun!
Only got 80 bucks but promoter gave us a case of beer. Chris barfs.
Doug hoses redhead.

The book would be passed around and soon the margins were filled in
with little notes in different handwriting: names of girls, phone

numbers, sometimes cryptic acronyms of filthy things accomplished in the night.

Full passages were written then crossed out with a heavy pen; a heated night's confession retracted in sudden shame.
At the bottom of one entry, like an asterisked footnote swimming along the bottom of a laboriously worded medical journal, someone had simply scrawled *FIB*.
And though we all agreed this was obviously the act of *finger in butt,* no one confessed to authorship, and it was never known if the lucky writer was the giver or the receiver of said digit.

We reported for first day of high school, Kimm, Chris, and I together.
I'd grown astonishingly tall somewhere between junior high and ninth grade, thankfully losing my boyhood chubbiness.
(And I continued growing, confounding the high school basketball coaches who regularly pestered me to join the team though I had no skill or desire.)
Doug went to Gahr High on the other end of Artesia Boulevard, the school district culling the students from the newer Cerritos High campus by street and tract name.
Again, as I navigated the classrooms, raised my hand when called, I was identified as brother to my sisters.
Skeptically regarded in comparison.
But in homeroom, I recognized at least half of the kids from past grades, the *gifted* label herding us into the same rooms year after year.

Cerritos was now bursting.
Achieving the vision, unbelievably, of the men who squatted amidst the cow shit and mapped a city with a stick in the dirt.

A handful of dairy lots remained, but the rest of the farms had been razed and buried under another tract of houses.
Another platoon of families moved in, their kids blinking at the sun bouncing off oceans of concrete.
A shopping mall, of course.

When Toys R Us came to town, the Cerritos city council demanded the usual backward Я in the sign be installed correctly, lest they infect a whole generation with dyslexia.
A wee Par 9 was built on the edge of the riverbed.
The sewage stink on the fourth tee box a charming reminder of the cow fart orchestra that used to season our childhood meals.

We are driving late in the day, Baton Rouge to New Orleans.
Odd show last night.
We got in from Houston after dark, our first gig without the Stretchmarks since we left.
It felt lonely not seeing their green Dodge in front of the club, the boys waving us in to park.
Waiting for us to show up, their set already done.
I'd see them working the kids in the parking lot, shaking hands and slinging their records, doing the proper tour work that would bring them back as headliners the following summer.
I'd crack open another beer from the dark comfort of the Blue & White, hiding out until downbeat, drowning my queasy doubts of commitment and sincerity.

The show was at a gay bar on the edge of town, a lit marquee on a trailer with an arrow pointing toward its door.
BEER BASH FRI
DRAG REVUE SAT
WeD PunkNiteE From HollyWOOD! cH3

I considered the sign as we pulled in, wondering if they had run out of the uppercase, or if they were going for the ransom note font that signaled *punk.*
And why were we from Hollywood?

We found that the gay bars were the only venues open to punk bands in a lot of smaller cities.

Gays and punks aligned in defensive stance, outnumbered by the rednecks who would like to-*literally*- kill them.
We set up quick and played for the 10 or 11 punk rockers, the boys in homemade T shirts, the girls in ripped fishnets.
Southern accents under mohawks.
The regulars watched from their barstools bemused, just waiting for us to get off and for the regular dance music to start back up.
During the last song, the breakdown of "I Got a Gun," Doug got up on stage and started dancing. He took off his shirt, then dropped his shorts, dancing in just his Nike Hi-Tops and bikini brief underwear.
He went straight to the bar when the set ended, collected free drinks and back slaps that lingered for a beat on his glistening skin.

There was a party after, a couch, a washing machine in the basement. We stayed until we were kicked out.

The next day we waited in the van while Kimm used a phone booth.
He cradled the phone between chin and upturned shoulder, the calendar splayed flat against the glass with one hand, pen scratching with the other.

Jay used the booth next to Kimm, another daily call to his girlfriend back home.
His flame red mohawk was sticking straight up like the comb of a preening bird, he wore Speedo shorts and a faded T shirt that claimed *Property of LA Rams.*
He seemed to be enjoying the trip, the daily van rides and nightly drinking, the set list mindlessly easy.
He'd been through all this before, with his bands Simpletones and Stepmothers, after jumping through the incestuous band lineups at the Masque at the very birth of LA punk.
He was a stage vet of Wongs, Whisky, and Starwood, all this while we were still listening to Boston.
But the old Hollywood story: his talents outweighed the missed opportunities that would have rightfully allowed him a life of private jet

flight and backstage riders filled with exotic cheeses left untouched.

He hung up and walked back to the van, arms raised above his head.
"I broke it off. I'm a free man."
We cheered for him.
But when I opened the ice chest and handed him a Dixie, I felt a
familiar ache in my chest.
A deep corner just beneath the right ventricle, darkened by the shadow
of another relationship cancelled.
Somehow it had been comforting. Jay sitting in the back, writing
another letter to his girl back home.
Perhaps his declarations of love dwindled until relegated only to a mere
mention at the bottom of the letter, until a last delicate tether to home
was snipped.
We touched cans, smiled.

At the small gas station on the way out of town they made sandwiches
behind a tall counter.
We got Po' Boys and a six pack of Dixie, then sat at a splintery picnic
bench out in the pea gravel parking lot.
Cypress trees in their disguise of Spanish moss guarded the swampland
behind.
The sandwiches bulged with Gulf shrimp, earthy and firm, juicy under
a shell of fried cornmeal.
Bedded on an aioli slathered, fresh baked French bread roll, shredded
lettuce dressed simply with lemon juice and black pepper.
I took a bite, we all did, the surface tension of the crust giving way to
the roll's inner cloud, the heat of the fried shrimp against the cool of
sauce and lettuce.
We ate in communion, amazed, quiet.

We got on the road to New Orleans then, late in the day but a short
drive and no show to play.
We decided to take the River Road, picturing a lazy country road
skirting the dark waters of the Mississippi, plantation mansions and

quaint roadhouses crowding its banks.

We imagined, really, the Pirates of the Caribbean ride at Disneyland.

Banjoes and hounds on front porches, fireflies dancing.

The serene South, just before the ride rolls down a darkened flume to a land of rape and pillage set to a jaunty shanty.

But there were just a few views of the river on the other side of the levee.

Instead, we passed tiny company towns between huge industrial plants, each corrupting the river with its toxic filth and barge traffic.

No banjoes.

We got into New Orleans in the dark, parked just off the French Quarter.

There was a quick discussion about how safe it was to leave the Blue & White filled with gear on a dark New Orleans side street.

We could see the sky glow over Bourbon Street, the neon signs casting upward, the cooking smell of a roux lazily turning golden brown.

We all turned to Jack, hoping he might volunteer to stay behind in the van and stand watch, but even he was enticed by the shouts and laughter beckoning to us from a block away.

We locked up the van, double checking each door, then turned toward the sound.

At the *Takee-Outee* Chinese food stands they sold 16-ounce beers for a buck.

Their signs all had a cartoon mascot: Chinaman running with a plate of sukiyaki, all coolie hat and buckteeth.

I stared up at the sign as I tilted a beer back into my mouth, Hop Sing staring back down at me.

He is drawn frozen in mid-hurry, delivering another plate of steaming crap, another family recipe destroyed for the palate of the white man.

The street was infested with racist imagery, all offered as charming memorabilia.

Here, the porcelain mammy cookie jar. Twist off her kerchiefed head to get your snickerdoodle.

There, Satchmo as a piggy bank, eyes bulging, lips amplified to inhuman proportion.

A little Black kid comes dancing up to us, bottle caps stuck to the bottom of his Converse low tops making the sneakers into street tap

shoes. He blocks our path and does a simple shuffle with ball change, stumbling a bit but keeping eye contact with each of us in turn. He finishes with flourish, a drop to one knee, arms outstretched.
Then whips off his cap and holds it out to us.
I pat at my pockets, bring out a quarter and nickel, drop it into his hat.
He looks down at the coins and sucks his teeth.
"Aw man. C'mon, big man, you got more than that."

Another *Takee-Outee* is on the next block.
We stop for more beers and drink our way down the street.

The night seems to slow, walking only a block before stopping for another round of beers.
Shots of cold whiskey are doled out in small plastic cups, and we wait in a straight line for our dose like mental patients at pill time.
The air is thick with humidity and sound, the off-tune brass of Dixieland horn on one side of the street, old school funk played from the other side at speaker-rattling levels.
The crowd surrounding us is, for once, as drunk as we are.
Tourists reveling in the novelty of a sloppiness we achieve nightly.

There is a holiday feel to it, 4th of July or New Year's Eve, those drunken fun holidays unencumbered by familial and Christian baggage.
At one stand-up bar they plop down a mess of boiled crawfish wrapped in a page of the *Times-Picayune*.
We poke at the tiny lobsters, take pictures of them pinching our noses with their wee claws. The bartender finally comes up and schools us, showing us how to squeeze the thorax and twist off the tail, releasing the meat with a flick of thumbnail.
She does it all in a few seconds, pops the tiny morsel in her mouth then sucks at the head, winking at me.
We fall upon them then, making a mess and laughing as she brings over another batch, another round of sweating Dixies.
The meat tastes of muddy river water and spices, and another unnamed peripheral flavor, an unctuous funk like the seasoning of music and

light.

We ended up in a small strip bar off the main drag, Jack separated from the pack and pulled in by a fat drag queen in crushed velvet.
We followed them inside and were seated ringside around a tiny stage where a forty-year-old stripper was doing her big finish to Donna Summer's "Hot Stuff."
She whipped off her top and unleashed her huge tits for us, tasseled pasties just covering coaster-sized brown areola.
I put two quarters on the bar rail in front of Doug and went for the front door.
When the music stopped, I could hear the dancer yelling at Doug.
"What the hell? *Fifty cents*?" She lifted at her belly and pointed at the caesarean scars underneath.
"I got kids to feed, ya' know. C'mon, cough it up fellas."

We got back to the van at dawn, untouched as we left it.
Doug and Chris took sleeping bags and lay on the roof, Kimm and Jay snagged the benches.
Jack lay across the front seats, the ice chest in between making a fairly level surface.
Strangely, I was the last one up.
I felt almost sober, this after a long night surrounded by people celebrating drunkenness.
Reveling in being *naughty*.
They would return to their homes in Cedar Rapids, or Chino Hills, and one evening while entertaining the neighbors the husband would point to the mantel.
And there, next to the tiny black negro jockey statue, a picture of them in front of Pat O'Brien's, holding pink Hurricanes in souvenir glasses.
"Oooh boy, now this… New Orleans! What? You've never been?"
And here he would roll his eyes and exhale, whistling.
"I think I'm still hung over! And wild? Honey, you tell them…"

I cleared a space on the van floor under the second bench.
I lay down on the filthy rug, stamped thin and flat, but alive with the quarts of spilled beer and bodily fluid.
I shut my eyes as the sunlight came into the van, and we slept until a cop tapped on the window with a baton.

We had a high school motocross team, of all things.
The races were Saturdays at Saddleback, a proper outdoor MX track carved along the brown hillsides above Orange County.
Chris was riding his 125 Suzuki in the intermediate class; I moved up to the 250 Expert class on an RM250.

I'd learned to relax on the big track.
Letting the bike race beneath me, steering with my thighs tight to the tank, my hands relaxed on the grips. I rode with one finger on the front brake lever, used two left fingers to slip the clutch coming out of corners.

At the starting gate I would stare straight ahead, already mapping a line up the long uphill before it turned left and down, my periphery vision tracking the starter as he ran to pull the gate lever.
Going fast down into the valley of the track now, hitting fourth gear and letting the bike pick its own groove to follow into the rutted hardpack.
The shadows played across the track in the afternoon second motos, hiding contours that would kick the back end up and around.
A moment that would leave me tensed up and breathing through my mouth.
You relax, let the bike pull you up a short uphill with weight tilted forward, still off weighing the front end enough to just skip over the dirt.
Hitting the front brake hard enough at the top to make the back of the bike almost weightless, swinging the rear wheel left for the sharp right 180 and down.

Two laps to go and into lapped traffic, I am leading, but not by much.
As I come to the finish line turn for the white flag, I make the turn and
see the rider on a Maico 250 Magnum charging up the last straight. I
can hear his rear wheel chattering along the dried out blue groove of the
track.
He's braking late and going to make his charge now.

The air-cooled 2 stroke motors overheating and losing power beneath
us, my forearms starting to tingle.
I ride and think only *of* the race by thinking of anything *but* the race.
I'd learned I had the capacity to lose all momentum in an awful
moment of awareness.
Like a tightrope walker who suddenly looks down and can now only
think of the people twenty-five stories below who will soon be wearing
his blood.

We are side by side as we reach the back top of the track, I try to
remember who the musical guest is on *Saturday Night Live* tonight.
He keeps a gear up and takes the outside berm, while I multiply nine by
odd numbers up to 15.
I go straight to the inside line, downshift, brake, pivot and gas it.
We come out even, and I hum the theme of *Courtship of Eddie's
Father*.
When we get to the final left hander Maico Man takes the outside line
hot, one good last try to float around and carry the momentum past me
at the finish line.
But he loses grip, his rear end slides out, and he lays it down easy, just
touching the butt of his red leathers to the ground as I get to the
checkers first.
Nine times seven, that's 63…

The cop tapped again on the window of the Blue & White, then he
took a step back and tilted his cap back on his head.
"What the hell you boys got going on here?" he asked.

He squinted up at the roof of the van where Chris and Doug were still asleep.

"Hell, looks like a goddamned gypsy wagon or somethin', hah! What, y'all gypsies?"

He was grinning, probably used to seeing passed out tourists and hippie campers in the neighborhood.
We were used to our cops back home: humorless, violent.
I crawled off the van floor and opened the sliding door.
An empty Dixie bottle fell out and shattered in the gutter.
The cop looked down at the glass, then at me, shaking his head.
"Well, it looks like you boys are up now, gotta get rolling. We got street sweepers coming, all right?"
And then he just walked away.

We went to Buster Holmes' for lunch, each of us taking a turn in the bathroom to brush our teeth and take a crap.
A plate of red beans and rice was ninety cents, add seventy-five for a half andouille sausage on top of that.
I was charmed by the city, the cheap and exotic food, the dedication to drunken pleasures.
Even the absurd humidity that demanded surrender.
I pictured living here, sweating in a little loft above a nightclub.
I'd sweep the floors for free drinks, learn to play the trombone.
I would thread carnival beads by candlelight, an audience of black cats tracking my bleeding fingertips.

Davey from The Sluts was hanging with us after soundcheck at Tupelo's.
The Stray Cats had been there just the night before to shoot a music video for the song "Sexy &17" and the club was still littered with empty beer bottles and overflowing ashtrays.
Davey pointed out a keg of beer in a trash can of melted ice water.
"Y'all are welcome to kill that keg," he said. "That's what they were giving the kids in the crowd scenes. Might be a little warm but what the

hell, huh?"

We gathered around the keg as if it were a campfire, took turns pumping it and filling up pitchers until it finally sputtered only foam.

We were finishing the last of the keg beer as we watched The Sluts do their set.

Davey had a microphone cord 100 feet long, and spent each song in the crowd, wandering the club, howling the songs and jumping around.

At one point he was outside the club, shouting lyrics to the night sky.

They get off the stage as the crowd shouts for more, and I know we have been challenged to follow up with a good set.

It is that friendly but unavoidable rivalry between bands, old as winking vaudevillians leaving the dogshitted stage after the poodle act, saying, *beat that*.

When we got on stage and plugged in, I already knew it was going to be a good one.

Kids were coming up to say hello before we played, shaking our hands, bringing us shots of whiskey.

We were in a room of people raised on live music.

They were friendly and curious, without the too-cool posture that we'd often encountered in LA.

We started with "Out of Control" and flew through the set list Ramones style, no talking, just end one song and count off the next.

Halfway through the set, Jay came back to the amps and used his forearm to roll each of the knobs on my Fender Bassman head to 10.

Kimm saw and grinned, walked back to his amp and dialed the Marshall all the way up as well.

Now the guitar leads squealed with feedback, the muted downstrokes we played chopped metallic, as if powered by internal combustion.

Beer flew from the stage to the floor and back again.

We slipped on the wet stage but regained our footing with a spin, fell to our knees as if begging for tips.

I tried to remember to breathe as I matched Jay's jumps, running to

Kimm's side of the stage, making it back to the microphone just in time for the chorus.

We were playing just on the other edge of our ability.
It felt like we were racing toward the finish line.

I close my eyes as I sing, but I don't think about the words I am shouting.
I'm thinking of the tiny fish that swam upstream into a warm gulf stream of pee.
I sing to a dozen Hop Sings, delivering poisoned noodles to the fat drunk tourists of Bourbon Street.
We're on the last song of the set, and I'm not even there on the stage anymore.
I am somewhere else, hovering above and just to the left, daring not to be present and fuck up this moment.

Three times nine is 27, I remind myself.
Five times nine, that's forty-five.

FIVE

*C**hris points at the jar on the counter** filled with pink brine, pickled pig's feet.

The severed paws reach upward, like the raised hands of students burning with the correct answer.

"Yech, are you seeing this?" says Chris. "I mean, jeez Louise."

The white-haired lady behind the counter watches us, smiling.

"Y'all boys in the service, honey?" she asks. "My grandboy, that's Jimbo's son, he just enlisted, too."

Chris and I both have straight buzz cuts, after another drunken night with Jay's clippers.

I realize this lady mistakes our shaved heads for military haircuts.

"Umm," I say.

"Yes ma'am," Chris says, stepping up with a sloppy salute to the forehead. "Seventh brigade, calvary... division... unit?" says Chris.

We've stopped at a little store way off the 55: A bit lost.

It's the drive from New Orleans up to Tennessee, cutting through Mississippi and Alabama.

The sky is dark with fat clouds, the humidity heavy enough that each breath feels like a giant tabby is dozing on your chest.

"Oh, that's nice," Lady says. "Y'all out of Hattiesburg?"

Then the door chime rings.

I turn to see Doug and Jay come in, their mohawks wilted in the Southern heat.

Jay wearing his Jackie O glasses, Hawaiian shirt with no sleeves, Converse Hi Tops with no socks.

Doug shirtless, in red and white striped shorts like an old-timey high diver.

Jay comes over to us and looks at the pig's feet.

"Oh ho-I'm in," he says, grabbing the jar. "Let's pick me out a good

one, hmm?"
I watch Counter Lady watching us.
Her eyes track us up and down, up again.
She shakes her head quickly, as if to erase the vision from her eyes.
"Hey, get away from there," the lady says, "we don't want you… your *types* in here, now get!"
But Jay has already fished a pig paw from the jar with the plastic tongs.
He places it in a checkered paper tray, takes it to the counter.
"I will be purchasing this, madam," he says.
There are little cocktail toothpicks on the counter, and now he unfurls a tiny umbrella, spears the meat.
The lady calls into the back room to her right.
"Jim, call the cops, we got some freaks out here. Call Davis but tell him don't send the *nigger*."
She speaks her language of hate with such ease, that's what momentarily shocks us.
We stand before a Flannery O'Connor simpleton brought to life in 1983, but without consequence or context.
Her finger was probably on a shotgun trigger just below the counter, its ammunition decidedly nonfiction.

Jay throws a dollar on the counter, and we all leave the store.
Walking to the van I have the prickly sensation at the back of my neck, imagine a rifle being aimed *right there.*

We jump in the van, tell the others to pile in.
"Go, hit it!" screams Doug.
Kimm gets in and slides the door shut.
"What's happening?" He turns to Doug. "What did you guys do now?"

As we head west down the highway, a cop car comes from that direction.
I watch the side view as he hits his brakes, pulls a U and starts to follow us.

The guys are laughing, filling Jack and Kimm in on the store.

"Call the cops! We got some freaks out here!" they shout with exaggerated Hee Haw twang.
As the guys goof on these simple rednecks, I think of a deeper evil lurking here, like a massive vile fungus that thrives just below the surface, spreading the length of the continent.

I keep an eye on the cop car behind us, fading back as we get closer to the border.
Soon he is just a mere speck in the mirror, but still follows.
We pass a sign that reads *Welcome to Alabama*, and I can just see the car turn again, head back into Mississippi.
Have we really been chased out of the state?

I think then of my mom spending her high school years in camp down here.

I imagine the threats she suffered over her appearance.
And though it has a delicate connection to a van full of idiots who shave their heads on the whim of blood alcohol content, we were simply guilty of being out of place and *different.*

Then it occurs to me she was in *Arkansas*, not Alabama.
I'd confused them, the states: Starts with *A*, in The South.
Casually slighting both, in the way people mix up
Chinese and *Japanese* with a shrug.

The separation of my parents seemed to make us all seek escape as well.
My sister, Colleen, who was just a couple grades ahead of me, was still at home, but Eileen was already in the dorms at USC.
My oldest brother, John, was starting a family on an army base outside of Hanover, Germany.
And my brother, Tim, stayed loyal to my father, doing all the most exhaustive work with him in his ever-smaller offices as his medical practice shrunk with each passing year.

Dad devoted most of his time to shady investments, IRS audits, and his Quixotic battles with the medical insurance covens.

Bachan would wander the hallways, looking for dirty clothes to wash.
My mother would busy herself with daily rituals, spending ninety minutes each morning removing her hair curlers, teasing then smoothing her hair.
She achieved a perfect bobbed shell and left the house looking like a background singer just behind a Motown star.
In the evening she would come home to start installing the curlers once again.
Alone with her romance novels, reading late into the night on one side of a huge bed.

That big house, so full of noise and chaos before, became even larger.
Darker and emptier.
Late at night I would hear the tinny chime of *Bachan* ringing the ceremonial bell for her husband, gone a decade now.
Then the smell of incense would waft up the stairway.
Our house seemed now a monastery in stucco and avocado kitchen appliances.
We honored a vow of silence with nothing to say to each other anyway.

We started spending nights at each other's houses most weekends, having discovered the teenage freedom afforded by the sleepover.
A glorious night of staying up late, eating crap.
We'd show up with a stack of albums tucked under arm, play records in Kimm's room until Lynn pounded on the door after 2am, telling us to *cut the crap.*

Chris would swipe some records from his mom's stack: Carole King's *Tapestry,* Fleetwood Mac and Linda Ronstadt.
I'd bring over some singles my sisters had in their room, music bought because of corny TV shows and dreamy boy singers.
Partridge Family, "I Think I Love You."

Monkees: "Last Train to Clarksville" and "Daydream Believer."
We'd play these as a goof, making fun of the glamour shot covers, but then stopped to listen as the glorious choruses kicked in. Unable to resist the true hooks and craft just beneath the sugar.
I also had records left behind by my brothers, JB's worn copies of Grand Funk, Steppenwolf, Iron Butterfly.
My brother Tim was listening to a deeper catalogue: Savoy Brown, Captain Beefheart, and Zappa.
I had absorbed their music as if by osmosis, music played long into the night and bleeding through the walls as I slept.
Even now if I hear a certain audience cheer, I know it's Edgar Winter's *White Trash Roadwork*.
And when Edgar says, "we got, um, we got something of a special surprise tonight," Johnny will soon be strolling out to the stage, and they'll hit "Rock and Roll Hoochie Koo" together.

Kimm, he already had his own stereo set up in his bedroom and was buying his own records.
Bowie and Aerosmith, KISS.
The Runaways.

We'd play them all, without order or theme, "Kung Fu Fighting" followed by "In A Gadda Da Vida" into "American Pie."
"Sugar Sugar" follows "Strutter," then "Surfer Girl."
A random playlist, a soundtrack spun at low volume beneath our late-night talks of girls and family scandals.
The music worming into our heads, somehow connected, pop hooks and sinister guitar riffs.
Nesting dormant until we'd call on them years later, and name it inspiration.

We pulled into Nashville just after 1am.
Dazed after another long drive, our New Orleans hangovers finally faded into mere headaches.
We pulled into a Denny's parking lot and decided to sleep in the Blue &White instead of paying for a motel so late.

Doug and Chris got up on top of the van again, I snagged the first bench seat while Kimm and Jack went into the Denny's to use the head. Jay lay across the back bench, reading *Inside Wrestling* magazine by flashlight. On the cover- *Bob Backlund Learns the Bloody Horror of Being Champion!* - one guy is headlocked by a balding giant, his face bloodied by tiny razor cuts just above his hairline.
Blinded by blood, he holds a hand up high above his head in submission.
"So, hey," I say to Jay. "What did you do with that pig foot anyway?"

Jay chuckles, and I see by the shadows cast on the van roof that he has put down the flashlight, stopped reading.
"I took a couple bites. Ya know, it wasn't that bad, kinda chewy, though."
We stare at the van roof as we talk to each other, like kids in their bunks at summer camp.
We watch the shadows grow and then disappear with each headlight coming down the highway.
"Oh shit, you ate that whole thing, huh? Ech."
Jay sits up and looks over the bench, grinning.
"Nah, I couldn't. I put the rest in Kimm's guitar case."
We both are giggling then, like children at a sleepover, just before the parent opens the door to yell *cut the crap.*

We went to the Ryman Auditorium the next day.
We sat in the wooden pews and stared at the famous stage, clapped our hands to hear the churchlike acoustics.
There were little exhibits, rhinestone jackets and pearly-necked acoustic guitars behind glass.
One poster showed a radio tower standing high above a map of the United States, the lightning bolts of radio waves blasting out in all directions toward all borders: *The WSM Barn Dance 50,0000 watts!*

I thought of those interviews with rock pioneers, where they'd always namecheck the *Grand Ole Opry* show back in the day.

They would tell of huddling close to the speaker and listening to those moaning country songs.
The music broadcast across a ridiculously expansive territory.

Again and again, these old hicks would wax poetic about being alone in their bedrooms, often on a dusty acre of farmland, with only the icy stars and the sound of Hank Williams to see them through the night.

But there, in the darkness, they were connected to a world bigger than their own and granted the hope of someday seeing it.
Or hell, maybe even being on the other side of that speaker and making the music themselves.

After Nashville, we played at the Antenna club in Memphis.
We splurged on a shit motel, one room with two beds.
We took the mattresses off the beds and put them between each box spring so we could all lay down.
And then we discovered one dedicated grainy TV channel playing nonstop porn.
We lay across the stained mattresses, cracking jokes, trying hard not to get hard.

Lynn and Lois, Kimm's folks, had gone away for the weekend, a little detail I hadn't told Mom as I left for the night.
We stood in front of Lynn's closet alcohol cabinet, eyeing the bottles before us.
We knew enough not to touch the stuff in front, Lynn's daily favorites.
Kimm nudged aside the half-filled bottles of Crown and Stoli, reached to the dusty bottles in the back.

We took the bottle back up to Kimm's room, where Starz' "Cherry Baby" was playing.
We had no idea how much whiskey it took to make you drunk, so Chris poured a bit into the cap and swallowed it.
He turned red and coughed but kept it down. "Whoo, shit!" he said with a cough. "Yeah, we're partying now."

Next Kimm took it, and though his eyes widened at that first burning sip, he smiled after.
"Not bad," he croaked. "Smooth."
I held the cap as Kimm filled it up, gentle as a prospector weighing gold dust.
I took that first sip and felt it course down my throat, hit my belly. It seemed to pull a glowing light through my body.
Starz' *Violation* album was still on the turntable, side one.

Sing it shout it, tell the world about it, they sang.
I didn't cough or choke, and as Chris and Kimm watched me closely I
took the bottle from Kimm and took a proper swig.
And I thought, *ah:*
Here it is.

We started smuggling booze out of our houses for our sleepovers now.
It added a new dimension, the conversation got sloppier and nastier, the
music played louder. Along with the Monkees and Carol King records,
we'd now play Sabbath and Deep Purple at teeth-rattling volume.
The guitars would never be loud enough again.
We exhausted the weird booze at the back of Lynn's liquor closet,
tasting at the sweet brandies and fruit liqueurs.
We passed out with crayon-colored tongues, barfed rainbows.

I discovered a case of Chivas Regal in the attic of our house, probably
a gift from a rich and grateful patient my father had discreetly treated.
Perhaps a pesky venereal wart burned off a cock, or a prescription
for penicillin G benzathine passed underhand.

Chris's mom discovered us swilling the 12-year-old blended Scotch in
her garage.
She wordlessly turned and went back into the house, leaving us to
worry she was on the phone already, telling our mothers to come pick
us up.
But she returned to the garage with a bottle of drugstore brand vodka.
She handed the vodka to me while holding out her other hand for the
Chivas.
"Here, you guys should be drinking *tha*t at your age. You can't
appreciate Scotch yet."
After trading bottles, she went back into the house.
We uncapped the vodka and chugged it. She was right.

With drinking we had stumbled onto something that gave us some
credibility in high school.

That resigned slouch that followed a sip of booze, signaling *I do not care.*

After Memphis we backtracked east for Knoxville.
We got into town at dusk and drove up and down the tree-lined streets, searching for an address written on Kimm's calendar, a map unfolded on the ice chest.

We finally found the right street and pulled up to a big old house.
A wraparound porch with a couple couches on it, some guys sitting there drinking beers.
There were two long haired guys and one dude in a KUB Knoxville Utilities work shirt, probably just off work.
There was also a mohawked punker girl, all ripped stockings and red lipstick, DOA shirt.

"Here we are," Kimm said. "They call it Hippy House? I guess this is the place to stay."
We piled out of the van and went up on the porch, bringing the ice chest with us.
Doug immediately cornered the punker girl, gave her a beer and got her laughing.

I went to the screen door and peered into the house. A chandelier with only two working bulbs lit the room dimly, an upside-down American flag hung on the wall above a stained couch.
An ancient German shepherd slept on a destroyed Lazy Boy, farting and growling through his tortured dreams.

I planned to call dibs on one of the van benches to sleep on, figuring it would be more comfortable than a late night of stoned conversation with the hippies, fighting the pup for a spot to sleep.
But they seemed cool fellas, and we'd been offered sincere hospitality once again.
I guess a crew traveling through town provided some sort of diversion

from another boiling southern summer, and they chatted with us easily.
"So y'all are from So Cali, eh?" said utilities guy. "You know those
guys in Circle Jerks? They stayed here, what? Last summer it was."
One of the long-haired guys sparked a joint and passed it around.
We opened the ice chest and passed out beers, the last of the Dixies
from Louisiana.
Then we sat on the porch listening to the night cooling the Earth, the
faint sound of the cassette playing in the van.
Doug trying some mood music with his new friend.

A kid came walking up the steps, grinning beneath a beaten baseball
cap.
"Hey, yonder comes Camp," said one of the hippies. "Heya boy, what
you say Camp?'"

Camp came up to the porch, tilted his cap back and looked around at
us.
"So, I reckon y'all are the CH3 boys, which one of y'all is Kimm?"
Kimm got up to greet him, tilting his head at me to get up and join him.
"Hi, Camp?" Kimm said. "Kimm. That's Mike."
We shook hands, Camp looking at us up and down and whistling.
"Dang, they grow them big out California way, huh?"
He told us his band STD was on the gig tomorrow, and he had helped
arrange the gig.
Camp looked to be about seventeen years old, mop of curly hair under
a cap, nothing that would signal *punk rocker.*
"So, listen," Camp said, looking back at the old house. "Y'all are
welcome to stay here, they got plenty of rooms. But my folks said you
guys can crash at our house if y'all want. Up to you."
And then he added, "We got AC there."
Our goodbyes were quick but polite.
And as we picked up the ice chest to go, the hippies waved happily and
assured us they'd be at the gig tomorrow.

When we slid open the door to the Blue & White, Doug and the girl were fucking, of course.

999's "Let Face It" blasting out of the stereo, the always-jarring sight of pale white buttocks thrusting under streetlights.

"Who's that, Tracy in there?" yelled the hippies behind us. "Whoo, Trace, get it girl!"

Empty beer cans thrown from the porch clattered on the van roof.

We slid the door closed again and put down the ice chest.

We waited then, in the sultry Tennessee night, for the lovers to finish, the buzzing song of cicadas in duet with the gasps and moans coming from the van.

And another sound: The cassette player playing an old track, something Kimm had included on one of his mix tapes.

At first I cannot identify the melody, but it is recognized somewhere deeper. Like a wolf's howl pricking up the ears of the family dog, awakening the taste for bloody meat.

It is a song of youth, of cheesy pop and drunken nights, now in concert with this night far from home, with fumbling sex in a car.

A song firmly attached to childhood memories but now infected, parasitically, with new imagery that will stay forever.

I hear the melody and think of my sisters playing a record in their bedrooms, swooning over a 7″ sleeve.

I remember sitting in Kimm's bedroom on a late Saturday night, the world an open possibility before us.

And when I hear it now, it also conjures the urgent swaying of the van, the smell of sex under a Southern breeze, and the sound of cicadas urging them on: *Yes. Mate.*

It's the Monkees: "Daydream Believer."

The sand on Daytona Beach felt different, finer than the coarse grains of our beaches back home.

This sand squished soft under foot at the shoreline, like dirt. Like mud. I stood looking out at the Atlantic as the sun set behind me, casting long shadows from the beachfront hotels lining the shore.
It felt odd, this vantage point on the other side of the country, my feet sinking into sensuous muck, the setting sun retreating from the ocean. A familiar tableau but *just* changed, like walking into your house after the furniture has been rearranged and a single tiny family heirloom removed.

The novelty of driving a car on the hardpacked sand was enough to make us detour on the way to the Orlando gig.
We drove the Blue & White along the water's edge, close enough to skirt the foam and feel the spray through the passenger window.
Chris parked on the sand just 10 yards from the weak surf, then we brought the ice chest out and all walked down to the water.
Doug dove into the foam and stayed under for a moment longer than expected. When he surfaced, he held up a quivering sea slug, pink and taut under a thin membrane. It was a condom filled with seawater.
"Hah, look!" he called up to us. "The fuckin' thing hit me in the face when I dove in."
He tossed the rubber up at us, and we scattered, shrieking, like cousins running from a touchy uncle.

It was an overnight drive from Atlanta, on the road at 2:30 am after they shooed us out of the 688 club.
It was a small crowd, a few punks but mostly college types that just came in for cheap drinks and the new wave music they played between

bands.
The hallway outside the bathrooms was lined with posters and flyers for other bands touring that summer.

DOA, Circle Jerks, Black Flag. Their tour flyers listing a dozen different cities without a night off.
These bands circled the continent endlessly, like sharks guided by hunger, forever cursed to keep swimming.

Then, on better poster stock, the newer bands: Hüsker Dü, R.E.M, Replacements.
The bands that were finding purchase on the college radio circuit, touring on the punk DIY ethos but staying at slightly better motels.
They played to a higher ratio of cute girls, and to the budding music journalists who would soon champion them to a wider audience.

Finally, the flyers crudely sketched and cheaply mimeographed by the local punk promoter kid: Youth Brigade and Agent Orange, T.S.O.L., Battalion of Saints.
 Young bands that ventured out of Southern California as if on a dare, often playing for no guarantee beyond a floor to sleep on and a cigar box filled with collected gas money.

Yet even on this level, I sometimes felt as if we were pretenders to the league.
We were just a group of happy drunks who happened to have some instruments in the van.
While the other bands seemed to have a *mission*, promoting a record or uniting the scene, we seemed aimless as hobos.
Distracted by every giant ball of twine or *Real Live Bears!* roadside attraction this crazy country had to offer.
We'd play, then take all of our pay and throw it back on the bar, usually still owing on the tab by night's end.

Two girls came out of the bathroom, talking so intently they walked straight into me.

The girls laughed into the hands covering their mouths, both shrieking *oh my god!* in unison.

They wore new wave outfits, the type of style that had filtered down to college towns from the big cities four seasons too late.
This would soon be a nationwide uniform with the help of MTV and Madonna.
The slashing cut of their T shirts– raised enough to bare just the right amount of midriff, low enough to expose the lacy top of black bra– the telltale signs they cared more about fashion than music.
The typical punker girl, she would repurpose men's shirts with razor blade and staples.
These girls were just in costume for a night out. Fishnet stockings, miniskirt, a garter strap running the delicious three inches between hem and thigh top.
"Sorry, sorry," said the taller of the two.
She had teased blonde hair, eyebrows black and arched like raven wings poised for flight.
"So what, are you guys like the band or something?"

We'd been setting up the stage while the crowd stayed on the dance floor, dancing to Modern English and Go-Gos, Human League.
Doug and Chris stopped hooking up the amps and took off their shirts.
They waved them over their heads, grinded out half-mocking stripper moves as a few girls whooped.

"Yes, that's us," I said, pointing at the wall between us.
It was a badly made flyer, Xeroxed on an office machine on plain white A4.
CH3-From Los Angeles! in a blocky Magic Marker scrawl. Under that, a grainy photo of the *Fear of Life* album cover, the one with Edward Colver's hairy paw holding a pistol backwards.
They both looked at the flyer then, my redhead leaning in close and

squinting in a way that crinkled her nose, destroying me.
She must usually wear glasses, I thought, but had left them home for a
night of new wave abandon.

Tomorrow, I pictured her fumbling for her glasses on the nightstand.
She'd put them back on, a little hungover maybe, but smiling.
Wearing only an English Beat T-shirt and red pump heels, she would
clatter through the kitchen making coffee and poaching eggs as I slept
blissfully in her four-poster bed.

"Wow, Ok. Cool," she said, looking past my shoulder to the stage.
Chris was now holding up one of the tour T shirts and fake throwing it
into the crowd, in the way you trick a dog into thinking the ball held
behind your back has already been launched.
"Can't wait to see you guys." She reached out her hand. "Shelia."
I shook her hand and just said, "Mike."
Then they left, talking again into their hands, giggling.

We got onstage while the crowd was still dancing.
A couple kids on the dancefloor threw up their hands in disappointment
as the DJ cut off Modern English's "I Melt With You," leaving them
lurching mid-sway.
Jay started the throbbing bass intro to "Manzanar," and a few of the
new wave kids stayed on the floor, trying to find a beat to continue
their goofy dancing.
Then the guitars came in with the riff as Jack rolled in tight, a tempo
faster than even the speedy recorded version.
I could see my tall redhead toward the back of the floor, smiling,
raising one of those killer eyebrows to me as our eyes met.
But already, she and her friend were retreating from the floor as the
punkers started a meager pit, and by the time Kimm got to his guitar
lead they had left the club.

EIGHT

There were summer concerts at Anaheim stadium in the 70's, huge
general admission events that featured stacked bills for ten bucks.
You could go the night before, drink and smoke weed in the dirt
parking lots across from the giant Angels halo.
Sometime just after dawn there would be whispers of the gates
opening, and the whole parking lot of stoned, sleepless kids would herd
across Katella toward the Big A gates, shuffling quietly in the cool
morning air like plains animals instinctively drawn to a waterhole.

Kimm had gone to see KISS with his sister, Lori, and called the next
day with tales of the bombastic stage show, Gene spitting blood, Paul
wondering repeatedly if the crowd *was doing all right?*
He described the day in exclamations between hyperventilated breaths,
as if returned, changed, from a religious revival.
During the encore of "Rock and Roll All Night," Kimm told me
confetti was shot by cannon and drifted down like August snow.

Aerosmith was the final summer concert of 1976.
I'd lobbied my mom shamelessly to go: citing my straight A's in June,
flapping my arms at the unfair fact that Kimm had *already* been to a
concert.
Mom resisted still, having seen news footage of the stadium stands
visibly swaying during a goddamned *Beach Boys* concert a few years
before.
Perhaps she pictured me crushed, the infield turned to a sea of jagged
concrete and pink guts.
She'd be out there with a flashlight, searching for an outstretched hand
with my birthmark: a brown stain resembling a kangaroo taking a
dump.

Finally, I reasoned that there was nothing going on anyway that summer, not like we were all going on a *family* vacation.
And then, with the cruelty that only a teenage boy can so easily muster, I wondered aloud what *dad* might think of this whole thing.

Before she dropped us off, my mother slipped me an extra twenty and told me to remember to eat.
She held onto my hand as she passed me the bill, held me there in the station wagon for a moment as Kimm got out the back seat and shut the door.
"No funny business," she said.

We had sprinted down the stands to the field, pushed as far as we could, keeping an eye on the massive stage to see where we might have the best view.
We claimed a square meter of turf as our own, on the destroyed lawn of left field, usually the domain of Joe Rudi during another lousy Angel season.

We were immediately surrounded as the crowd filled in the field liquid-like, a massive round of stoner musical chairs.
Soon we were blocked in, surrounded by bikers pissing in the open, girls sunning in the tiniest of bikinis, jugs of Chianti passing through the crowd.
We looked back to the stands, where people were already filling in the seats in the mezzanine levels, sensibly out of the sun.
But we realized that we would have to stay here, hold our ground if we wanted to have a good view of the headliners still 8 hours away.
To give up this spot, to sit in the cool shadows, would be surrender.

We got into Orlando, then Kimm spent ten minutes in a gas station phone booth scribbling directions in his notebook.
I don't think there was a planned gig, as the real show was in

Gainesville the next night with Roach Motel.

But we'd learned that any gig was better than a night off, where there was no chance of free booze or a place to sleep.

A night off found us lost, even our frail identity as a band neutralized.

On a no-show night I'd hound Kimm for beer money outside a convenience store, Doug at my side, until he'd finally open a worn manila envelope and hand over some bills.

Then Doug and I would go through the store, finding the cheapest swill with the highest alcohol content.

Schlitz Malt Liquor, Olde English 800, Mickey's Big Mouth: The vile liquids that got us through the off nights.

Got us drunk enough to sleep *anywhere.*

We found the party at an outdoor gravel lot, far from the enchanted glow of Disneyworld.

A couple dozen punkers were standing around a barrel fire though the night was swampy and warm.

A plywood stage on milk crates, a single fifteen-inch speaker in a bass cabinet for the PA.

Dogs.

We piled out of the van, still sticky from our swims in the Atlantic.

I felt the grit of fine beach sand inside my shoes, grinding away layers of epidermis with each step. We set up gear quickly and plugged the guitars in without tuning, just a couple of work lamps set down on the stage for light.

I touched my guitar strings to the microphone and heard the crackle of electricity, the circuits ungrounded and sure to deliver a blue kiss of spark to my lips if I got too close.

And then, of course, as we started to play, the rain started.

We played "Strength in Numbers," and a group of guys ran straight at each other, colliding in the center of the gravel lot. Their bodies

flailing, an energy released by music, their hands held up, shaking their fists to the storming sky. Then, as if unleashed by the prayers of desperate, drought-stricken farmers, the clouds emptied.
Great sheets of rain coming down sideways, the fire barrel steaming, the dogs howling, then running for cover.
The kids in the pit whooped, shirtless bodies flashing in the lightning, savage. Somewhere down the line a breaker snapped.
The amps fell silent, only Jack still pounding out a military beat, me shouting out words, the microphone impotent and tossed aside.
It was a ninety-second gig.

It was great.

We hustled the gear back into the van as the crowd shouted and tumbled in the rain still.
Kids patted us on the back, held out beers that we plucked off six pack rings like grapes from a bunch.
We got into the van, hurried by the weather, shut the door and drove.
The sunroof in the van started leaking, no doubt its seal loosened by our walking around and sleeping up there.
Chris at the wheel, me in the passenger seat, we twisted our bodies toward the doors as a steady stream of water poured down on the cooler between us. Guitars, still plugged into cords that were tangled on the seat between Kimm and Doug.
Jack and Jay sat wedged on either side of the bass drum; in the rush it had been thrown out of place onto the back bench.
Chris shook his head, then twisted the steering wheel back and forth in his hands, testing the steering.
"Oh brother," he said. "We got a flat."

He pulled the Blue & White into a closed gas station, parked the van under an overhang as the lightning flashed nearby.
We were probably all singing *One Mississippi, two…* to ourselves when the thunder cracked, causing two Dobermans in the locked gas station to spring from their beds and run to the window.

They snarled through the glass, barking and snapping, their fangs gleaming in the next lightning strike.

Chris started heaving his shoulders, his hand covering his eyes, and I thought for a moment he was finally broken, crying.
Only when he threw his head back did I realize he was laughing, soundless wheezing, shaking his head.
And then we all were.

We held our sides, gasping for air, saying *oh no, oh god* between each burst of laughter, each crack of thunder.

The Anaheim Stadium stage lights finally came on as Lynyrd Skynyrd was finishing their set, of course playing an excruciating version of "Freebird" that had started when it was still daylight.
We were burnt by the sun, dazed by a full day sitting through the opening acts. Suffered the inane emcee patter of both Flo *and* Eddie, who used their stage time to stall and tell corny jokes, urge the ladies to *show your tits, whooo!*
Rick Derringer played his set right in the heat of the day, and as he started the intro to "Rock and Roll Hoochie Koo" I was transported back to my childhood bedroom, to the fitful dreams soundtracked by my brothers' albums.
I scanned the stage, instinctively looking for twinned, white-haired albinos to join in, but that didn't happen.

We took turns going to the bathroom and fetching hot dogs from the concession stands as we were forced to guard our precious space of turf while more and more kids moved down to the field with each act. Weaving my way through the lounging crowd (Here, a naked man passed out, sunburnt a shocking shade of crimson. There, a young mother breast feeding a child who looked suspiciously old to be nursing.), I finally got into the cool of the mezzanine section and made my way up the steps.

I'd been to the stadium before, with my dad.
Awkward father-son trips after the divorce.
We'd sit in the third baseline stands for a few innings, my father drinking several beers and pointing out different players to me, explaining why they were each *bums*.
The Angels always lost when we went, and we would usually leave with the home team trailing before the seventh.
Dad would then drive me back to Cerritos, beer buzzed, one finger spinning the power-driven wheels of his Cadillac.

He would tell me stories of growing up poor, putting in the work to become a success.
He'd drop me off at the curb then and speed away.
A hand held motionless out the window in farewell, his parental duty fulfilled for another month.

The wait for Aerosmith to come on was unbearable and delicious.
As the day cooled, more and more bodies spilled onto the field.

First making us stand up to avoid being trampled, then pushing us even closer to the stage.
Then that glorious moment of houselights extinguished, when the PA stopped playing ZZ Top's "LaGrange" mid-song, and the whole stadium let loose a thunderous cheer that made me jump.

We pushed closer then, as if riding a rip current that sent us into centerfield.
The band made their way onstage, visible in glimpses of the flashlight beams waved by roadies clearing a path.
Some urgent orchestral music, like Bernard Herrmann's shrieking score that accompanied Janet Leigh's bloody murder in *Psycho,* rang through the PA system, lending a kind of air raid urgency to the night.

And then, with the string bending intro to "Train Kept a Rollin'" above a galloping drumbeat, the spotlight found Steven Tyler centerstage.
He spun and dipped, danced to the microphone stand with a straight-kneed shuffle, threw the mic stand down and pulled it back to his face

with a tug of the scarves flowing off it.

"Hello motherfucking Anaheim!" he screamed out to us, and then shuffled off, twirling the mic stand like his dance partner.

I stood, awed through that first song, never quite recovering from the fact someone could yell the word *motherfucker* in public.

Here, in the same stadium I'd sat with my dad, listening to the house organist play nothing more inflammatory than the *Charge!* fanfare.

Before the second guitar solo, the one that explodes after the breakdown, Joe Perry kicked over an amp cabinet and pulled it out as if swiping a tablecloth from under a set table.

He dragged the cabinet to center stage and stood on it, boots to speakers, to play the lead.

Used only to listening to records up 'til now, this was a new and unnerving experience: to hear live versions of the songs that I loved with jealous ownership.

I was hearing those sacred tunes in the moment, in the air.

They changed some intros, played faster than the records.

The wavering soundwaves over open air made it impossible to even identify which song was being played until many seconds into the first verse.

I realized later, of course, that the band was fucked up and they were playing like shit.

But the lights overhead flashed, and the crowd screamed.

And Steven Tyler, who was *right fucking there*, twirled and pointed, screamed into the air.

As if trying to make them pay attention to something only he and I could see.

The show in Gainesville was in a dark warehouse, some colored lights shining down from the lofted ceiling.

No stage.

We dragged in the gear, still rain-spotted from the night before.

The guitar strings had already started rusting, and Jay ran a rag soaked in rubbing alcohol over them, pinching them clean before tuning each guitar himself.

I knew the charm of playing off key and sloppy was getting to him and he was doing his part to make each set better, regardless of how I might end up sabotaging the night.

As we set up the gear, one of the guys in the opening band came up and asked if we had our own microphones.

I assured him we did not, and he shook his head, disgusted, then mumbled as he went to get a beaten SM57 for the wobbly mic stand.

"That's our PA, so be cool. All right?" he said, jerking a thumb to a Shure Vocal Master column.

We hit the first song, played as loud as the amps would go, the guitars ringing out wildly into the cavernous warehouse.

Halfway through the setlist, during a double time version of "Wetspots," the circle pit widened at one point, knocking the PA speaker to the ground sideways.

I saw the owner bring his hands to his head, horrified, as the boots of skanking kids grazed the grill cloth.

But I recognized this cue and walked over to the downed speaker, tested it with one foot, then placed my other blackened Hi Top upon it and stood on top of the speaker cabinet.

I held my guitar high and hit an open E chord, like Joe Perry towering above the thousands in the darkened baseball field below.

PA guy cut the power, but we continued playing a few songs without it, me screaming verse and chorus above the guitar amps until I was silenced by my shredded throat.

I focused on the microphone then.

I shook out of the guitar strap and put both hands on the neck of the Charvel, resting the body on my right shoulder like a Louisville Slugger.

I swung the guitar slowly toward the microphone, testing the limits of the strike zone.

The crowd cheered, started chanting *swing, swing* as I stepped out of the batter's box, adjusted my feet with a shuffle and stepped back in. The PA guy was making his way toward me, shaking his head and mouthing *no*, like a pitcher shaking off hand signals from the groin of his catcher.

I swing, stepping into the pitch, the heavy Northern Ash of the guitar body connecting with the microphone as my arms reached full extension.
It knocked the microphone off the top of the stand, breaking the black plastic holder cleanly in half.

I aim for the gap in left field, just out of reach of a flailing Joe Rudi. He waves centerfielder Gil Flores off, races toward a spot the ball would eventually drop, a base hit RBI that would defeat the Angles once again.

Toward a spot of green occupied by two kids, waiting for the show to begin.

I woke to plaid.
Mildewed shag carpet beneath me, my nose pressed against itchy fabric.

It's the back of a sleeper couch, I think, judging by the tartan skirt of material that touched the floor.

I breathed in the earthy perfume of dog hair and ancient farts, imagined the spilled bong water and Domino's pizza crusts that came together beneath the cushions.

New life forms growing in the fecund recesses, a primordial swamp teeming mere inches from my face.

I heard the squeak and settle of spring and could tell there was someone sitting on the couch.

A TV played, the loopy orchestration of strings and kettle drums, perhaps overture for the opening credits of a light comedy.

The music fades.

Dialogue now:

Halt, stop! Would you...hey!

Show 'em the stick, Theodore, show 'em!

The music swells here, whimsical notes of a Jew's harp telegraphing *western* and *comedy* as horse hooves clop past.

Dang it, Amos, nobody's afraid of no stick...

Now the couch creaks again, apparently someone else has come into the room.

I hear the flint rolled on a Bic lighter once, twice, before catching, then the kettle-like bubbling of a bong.

"Hey," a voice says in a choked rasp, holding the marijuana smoke captive in his lungs. "What's this yer watching?"

"*Apple Dumpling Gang*," says the other voice. "But not the real movie.

Dunno, it's weird."
There is an overlong pause before he speaks again, his meandering thoughts finally connecting like two blind puppies colliding at their mama's teat.
"It's a, what ya call it? A redo? A remake?"

Listening to this conversation, it occurs to me that I haven't watched TV in weeks.
I haven't eaten a meal alone, haven't jacked off.
I haven't reached out for the snooze button on an alarm clock in absurd bargain for just five more minutes of blessed sleep.
And I miss none of these things.

Now there is a great exhalation punctuated with a quick cough, and the room is filled with the smell of weed.
I turn and lie on my back, trying to understand where I am.
I lie in a grave-sized space between the couch and wall.
I am reassured to see an upside-down American flag tacked to the wall: the universal symbol of *punk rock safehouse*, like a quilt-covered window along the Underground Railroad.
A galaxy of asbestos popcorn ceiling above me, marred with a Rorschach pattern of water stains.
I picture a team of tiny huskies racing across the winter landscape of ceiling, an Iditarod upside down, their steaming dog piss yellowing the virgin snow.

The TV continues:
I tell you again, those aren't my kids!
There is a slide whistle and thump, apparently a pratfall.
The couch people laugh, and I hear the smack of hand to flesh.
 I swear to fucking god, it's a knee slapper.
"Oh, oh no," says one of them. "Did you see that guy? What a dick!"

I know out there in America there are people rising from slumber, in actual pajamas, upon clean sheets of a high thread count.

The smell of coffee and bacon wafting up the stairs, a plump wife packing sack lunches.
Freckled kids sit rereading the tiny Stonehenge of cereal boxes circling the breakfast table.
The scene is replicated with only small variants, multiplied by the millions.

Soon the nation yawns out the last of its darkness and stretches its mighty arms, as if to encompass the vast possibilities of this new day.

"Hey," says Couch One. "Is Tim Conway in this?"
There is a grunt, and I imagine a sad shake of the head *uh-uh*, as Couch Two readies a fresh bongload.
Another nugget of sinsemilla is cremated, ingested, and blown to the tundra above.

A beat of silence, though I know-*know*-the next lines of this script.
The wait is unbearable as they sit bleary-eyed in stoned bliss.
The TV performs only for them now.
The world outside races toward purple twilight, lives being saved, millions earned by honest work.
And finally, they speak.
No Don Knotts, neither.
Then:
That's too bad. He's funny.

"Funny, you say!" I imagine myself shouting to them, having popped up from behind the couch like a madman.
They would do a comic doubletake at my scene entrance then, bong water and glowing ash flying in surprise, as the circus music soundtrack crescendos and the canned laughter roars, the unseen audience shitting themselves.
"Try *hilarious*!" And here I would vault the couch's back, landing between the two of them with a pat to each of their knees.

I'd load the bong next and take a flaming hit, turning the room blue with billowing exhaust.

"Now, Arte Johnson, he's no slouch, I assure you," I'd say to my starboard companion.

"And this Ed Begley Jr.," I'd say, turning to port, "the kid has a bright future, boys. *Bright.*"

"But replace Conway and Knotts, remake a classic?"

I would shake my head slowly for my costars, at this world gone mad, in sorrow for us all.

And here I would lower my voice to a whisper, making them lean in close to hear.

"No sir. Not on my watch."

I am tightening the scene, considering the addition of a sassy grandma or buxom blonde to the cast when the room is flooded with daylight, a door opened to the white day outside.

Kimm says *hey* to the guys on the couch, then comes into vision, looks down at me.

"You up? Ready?' he asks. "Everyone's outside, dude."

As we leave, I take a single look back to the room.

They are younger than I imagined, scruffy punks.

Not the Knotts and Conway of mind's eye, gnawing on the scenery.

I wave and they wave, but my guys barely look up at me, their red eyes glued to the hijinks of the rascals on TV.

I leave behind a room filled with pratfalls set to banjo and bugle, where the outlaws are harmless and charming.

We will drive a few hundred miles now, while they sit and let the world come to them.

These fellows float just above us, upon their island of plaid like wise men, untouched by the day.

"Jesus, what was that?" I ask Kimm as we walk toward the van.
The Blue & White sits at the curb. Jay and Doug sit shirtless in the
shade of a willow tree, chatting as Chris is showing Jack how to jump
rope single skip like a boxer.
"What?" Kimm says. "I thought I'd let you sleep in."
We load into the van once again, wordlessly taking our seats for
another day of driving.
Kimm takes first shift at the wheel, I am shotgun.
"Did you know," he says to me then, starting up the motor that will
carry us away, "that you sleep with your eyes open?"

*e eventually **burned out*** on the big stadium shows. Whole swaths of our youth wasted on outdoor sets by Sha Na Na and Rick Derringer (always on the bill, it seemed) while waiting all day only to be cheated again by Steven Tyler tangled in scarves, nodding out between the monitors.

We discovered the great halls of the Southland that stood like castles at each point of a compass rose.

The Forum, of course, for the bands riding the stratosphere of popularity.

That's where your sister would go to see one of Rod Stewart's sold-out shows, returning home with lustful eyes and a glossy eight-dollar souvenir program.

Rod winks from the pages with a leering grin beneath a pink visor, the centerfold a two-page shot of him kicking a soccer ball into the faceless crowd, his ass bared to the cheap seats.

There was Long Beach Arena, maybe a twenty-minute drive for us.

There was a vast oceanfront field across the street to pregame, park for free, drink and smoke before the show.

It was almost better than the concert, sitting in that golden sunset, van doors open, the 8-track blasting.

It was a round auditorium like the Forum, but sized down for the bands grinding out endless tours, maybe a headlining gig before they went back to work supporting the headliners.

The crowd reflected that as well, some in the crowd still in oil-stained work uniforms, devil horns held aloft, fingers crowned with halos of dirty fingernails.

Foghat. Rush. Sabbath. Bands that spoke to sideburned dropouts, drug dealers and their loyal clients.

The only girls in the audience were the ones who rode there in the middle seat, one hand stroking the denim-covered cock of the driver.

Then Santa Monica Civic, wee in comparison, letting only a few thousand fill the room.
Here was a more thoughtful audience, come to see bands on the way up, or those that operated on a fringed wavelength transmitting to specialized freaks. Sparks and Bryan Ferry, Tangerine Dream.
We once found ourselves at a Be Bop Deluxe show there, but unsure of why.

Now, here in the story is where you would normally list the astonishing concerts of your youth, like some wrinkled codger at the end of the bar reliving the Korean War for his eye-rolling audience.
Each generation taking false pity on the next: these goddamn kids who have *no idea* what good music is.
I will only mention being in a seat at The Forum as Led Zeppelin played.
Lakers championship banners hung in the rafters, barely visible for all the blue joint smoke.
The crowd giddy with the thought of seeing those songs that have been burned into memory through endless loops of 8 track tape.
The lights go down and the cheer is deafening, the roll and riff of "Rock and Roll" all but lost in the roar.
John Bonham is still alive, still pounding on the drums like a blacksmith forging a weapon out of glowing steel.
During the encore Keith Moon came out and destroyed the kettle drums.
And as the battle beside the Chosin Reservoir went into a second week, I can only recall the cold that winter, *the bitter cold.*

Kimm and I found ourselves drawn to shows in local ballrooms and VFW halls.
I was immediately taken with the thrill of standing right up against the

stage, seeing guys just a grade or two older than we were up there, our own homegrown rock stars.

Groups with names like Fourplay and Maybee Later, MЭtro Hotel and Secret Sity, their [sic] monikers printed on Day-Glo flyers above a hand-drawn map to Portuguese Hall in Artesia.

The flyers were handed out by shady stoners in the quad before being chased off campus by our beloved narcs.

Mostly those bands played covers, deep tracks by UFO or Rush, Yesterday & Today.

But we could get close enough to see the glow of main tubes in the amps, feel the pulse of air from an Ampeg 8x10 bass cabinet.

Kimm and I would stand right up front, touching the thin felt covering the monitors, diving for guitar picks tossed to the ground.

We knew we'd have to be the ones on that stage someday.

Somehow be the ones tossing guitar picks at the crowd, easy as feeding filthy pigeons with week-old bread.

After seeing Cheap Trick open for The Runaways at Santa Monica Civic, we reported to the Whisky the next night to see their club set. We zeroed in on their odd greatness, that unique stage presence, those irresistible hooks.

It was our first journey down to the Sunset Strip, and we sat in the balcony for both sets that night, drinking enough overpriced Cokes to satisfy the gum-cracking waitress.

Cheap Trick came out on the tiny stage and went into "Hello There," a blisteringly perfect 90-second introduction.

Robin Zander and Tom Petersson up there, the very image of '70s cool, Rickenbacker guitar and 12 string bass, white suits and clogs–*clogs!*

But then, *what the fuck?* The guitar player is a goof jumping around in wrestling shoes, the drummer looking like an accountant behind a desk of drums, chain smoking like it's the height of tax season.

At one point, Bun E. pulls out ridiculously huge prop sticks and *wails.*

We got home at 3am, my mom waiting up in curlers and a frown.
I was grounded for two weeks, but we returned to the Whisky, The
Roxy, The Troubadour often after that.
The lure of seeing bands up close in those storied rooms, the adrenaline
rush of getting off the 101 and seeing the bright lights along the filthy
streets.

Those days on the Strip were a rebirth of the glory days when the stars
of Laurel Canyon would grace the strip and drop a jewel-like song like
a gift from merciful gods.
We *just* missed out on Rodney's English Disco, seeing Jimmy Page
balance twin sixteen-year-olds on his ashen knees.
But those lithe groupies, distressed to be of age now, still roamed the
clubs, weary as brothel madams.
A thin slice of the old guard still crept up and down Sunset, A&R men
in satin jackets, a tiny coke spoon tangled in gray chest hair.
They would ride between the Roxy and Whisky on Peugeot mopeds,
platformed heels upon the stilled pedals, a fledgling porn starlet behind,
clutching at a round waist. We would look up into the VIP section in
the Starwood balcony, get a fleeting glimpse of Kim Fowley or Phil
Spector in the way you might spot a mouse in your periphery, scurrying
across the kitchen floor.
Clubs were packing again with a new music, The Plimsouls and 20/20,
Mumps and Weasels.
The Dickies, The Dogs, The Crowd, pioneers who would outlive the
season.

It was a sparkling moment between the piano-saddled folkies and the
puff metal bands that would eventually inherit the rooms, with their
Troll Doll hair and hatchet-tipped guitars.
It would be a different scene again soon, but the music business types
avoided any of the hardcore punks that inherited those stages next.

Those same wispy record execs staying at a safe distance away from any of the punk bands as if restrained by court order.

We went to the clubs almost weekly, trying to keep pace with the stacked bills of *PopPunkRock* that overwhelmed the clubs.

We'd see Angel City one night, Plasmatics the next.
The Quick, The Pop, The Beat.
We fell hopelessly in love with the music, played loud and live in a small club.
Especially the bands that held fast to the catching melodies that connected us to those days of spinning '70s bubblegum on Kimm's bedroom floor.
We went to see them all, The Babys to The Last.

ELEVEN

I sat in the back row with Jay as we headed further south, traveling down that phallic state like an intrepid crab louse scuttling down to investigate the diseased glans of its gracious host.

We demanded Kimm take Yeehaw Junction, all of us yelling the obvious whenever the sign came into view.

The Florida Turnpike then connected us to 95, the very urethra of the state, if we're still doing this.

We had my old Suzuki acoustic guitar out between us, Jay strumming the battered thing to my right as I watched his fingers navigate the neck that stretched over my lap.

"Here," he said, pointing at a barred third fret, "G is my favorite, really."

And now he ripped off a lead run effortlessly up and down the rosewood neck, bending strings to match the pitch of those below, letting his wrist wiggle beneath a held note, the secret handshake of virtuosos, to tease out the vibrato and sustain of the steel string.

"See?" he said. "The G is a mostly open strings, if you think about it. So, all the strings are fair game when you play a lead."

Then he pointed at the frets casually, his finger tapping out a sequence as if he were reading a filthy limerick in Braille. "That's a major box, all the notes that make sense within that barred chord, you just use the notes in there, move it up and down the neck. Easy."

I clap. "Again," I said.

The mathematics of the guitar neck were still a mystery to me.

He moved up the neck to A, transposed all the notes to that neighborhood. Then again in B.

As he finished the run he tacked on a *shave and a haircut* riff, answered with *two bits* of twin squeaking farts.

Then he passed the guitar over to me.

Outside the van windows the landscape runs deep and green, rich
pockets of swampland almost night black in shadow.
I imagine the clouds of mosquitoes, the prehistoric terror of alligators
just beneath the swamp, only their unblinking yellow eyes breaking the
surface of hell.

I barre the fifth fret and strum an A, then climb over the notes he points
out for me again.
I play each note, and a bluesy scale comes out of the guitar. Grinning, I
reverse the notes and climb back down, until I hit a misplaced note that
leaves us both cringing.
"Not that one," he says. "*Never* that one."

I shrug, and hand the guitar back.

I never really got the hang of playing leads, letting Kimm take
whatever brief guitar lines we allowed into our short and fast songs.
I felt the songs more in the right hand, the urgent downstrokes of the
verse, the soaring power chords of the chorus.
I'd always been drawn to those guitar playing singers who used the
guitar like a weapon: the body a shield, the neck a sword.
Joe Strummer would sing whole songs with the guitar slung behind his
back, forgotten, so lost in his conviction of lyric to even perform his
namesake.
We saw The Clash at The Palladium during the Combat Rock tour.
During "Straight to Hell," Joe knelt center stage, lit by a lone spotlight
as he sang his tale of discarded Amerasian youth.
He hugged his battered Telecaster as if for warmth, the neck pointing to
a far better place than this, never touching the strings once.

At Anaheim Convention Center, during one of the recording nights for
Alive II, I witnessed Paul Stanley prance to the microphone, windmill a
single chord as he let loose a Little Richard-like *woooo!*
Then he took a run across the stage toward Gene, sliding the final two
meters on his spandexed knees while pounding on the body of his

Ibanez Iceman with a gloved fist.

That, I thought, *was how you play the fuckin' guitar.*

Kimm and I learned to play guitar together, starting with one of the community classes that were listed in impossibly small print of the quarterly Cerritos Community Recreation Guide.

I swiped the Suzuki acoustic out of the girls' room, my sister Eileen having left it abandoned when she moved into the USC dorms.

I opened the case, strummed an index finger along the gummed steel strings, surely the same ones that came from the factory in Nagoya.

There was a cleaning felt in the little pocket beneath the neck, along with a tarnished pitch pipe for tuning.

I snapped the case back shut, and brought it to the first class, a free three month weekly called "Guitar for Beginners."

The evening classes were held at our old Junior High School, Faye Ross.

The hallways seemed charmingly smaller than we remembered as we made our way to the band room, as usual the blueprints embedded in memory not to scale and far more drab.

We pointed out locations of our past embarrassments: here, where Kimm split his pants climbing the olive tree, there where I bloodied a tooth trying to French kiss a braced girl the first time.

When we got to the band room, we were surprised to find one of our old teachers, Mr. Misajon, teaching the class.

He was a tall Filipino guy, hair feathered and shells of pukka.

He always gave off a kind of cool island vibe that went over big with the sighing surfer chicks crowding the front rows of his class.

"Hey, it's Mr. Magrann, it's Mr. Gardener," he announced to the class when we entered.

The other students were a collection of bored housewives, retired old guys, and a few other young knuckleheads like us: starting late but with vivid and specific dreams of just how we would wear the golden Les

Pauls we would eventually master.

"Ok, let's get our guitars out, guys," Mr. Misajon started off, "everyone brought one, right?"

And here a murmur of assent, then the clatter of clasps undone on hard cases, zippers unzipped from nylon gig bags.

Soon we were all sitting in a wide circle, holding guitars on our laps.

Most were nylon-stringed classical models, a few were steel-stringed, like the Suzuki I held.

One little grandma held aloft her tiny guitar apologetically.

It was ukulele-sized and painted with colorful parrots with the word *Tijuana!* painted in Old English lettering.

One of the old guys had a beautiful Gibson J-2000, the gorgeously deep wood grain covering its voluptuous curves, the upturned wings of the tailpiece like a whimsical smile.

Even I knew it was no beginner's guitar.

I imagined it being tossed into the pot by a faded country star in some late-night poker game, while my classmate held 3 aces over two kissing queens.

Or perhaps this guitar was last strummed by his son, killed in mortar blast just outside of Khe Sanh.

Mr. Misajon went around the circle, tuning all the guitars.

When he got to Grandma he softly let her know that it wasn't really a guitar at all, just a wall decoration, but she could borrow one of the school guitars for the night.

He got to me and Kimm and winked at us, "So, you guys are finally going to be rockstars, huh?"

Finally, he passed around mimeographed sheets with chord charts, tiny graphs made up of the netting of string and frets, with dark dots showing finger positions.

The strings were lettered down or up, with a mnemonic legend inscribed next to each string, EADGBE: "Even After Death Good Boys Eat," Mr. M. told us. "That's a good way to remember it, right?"

I had an instant and disturbing image of pale, blood-drained altar boys, killed in a votive candle blaze, damned to chew on the flesh of their own fingers for eternity.

"All right class, let's play guitar. Let's start with the E chord, it's like this, here and here."

He picked up his own guitar then and placed each finger on a few strings deliberately, showing us as he walked around the room.

He strummed the guitar, a bell-clear open E, all the while singing, "*E, E this is the E...*" stopping to correct a finger position here, praise a proper chord there. He got to me and nudged my ring finger up from "Good" to "Death."

My fingers felt weak, fat.

Nubby stubs helpless against the thick cables..

I pressed down harder until my fingernails paled and gave the strings a tenuous strum with my thumb.

The strings yielded only a *screech* and awful clunk, like the distant thud of a suicidal clown finally hurling himself out of a fifth story window.

We spent the next hour on open chords, learning E, then C, D, G.

"There," he said, "you have pretty much any popular song, right at your fingertips."

Mr. M., he'd always struck me as a bit too hippy dippy when teaching seventh grade social studies, one of those teachers that sprinkled their lessons with terms like *bitchin'* and *outtasight*.

The type who sat on their desks cross-legged while going over the steps of how a bill becomes a law.

But he turned out to be a great first guitar teacher.

Strange, unused muscles burned in my left wrist and my finger pads were grooved by the wound strings.

I shook out my cramped left hand as if cooling a rectal thermometer, but we were -*finally* – playing guitars.

Soon we were all strumming that first glorious E chord in relative unison, and Mr. Misajon started singing over our playing: *The beat goes on, The beat goes on,* he sang, *Drums keep pounding rhythm to the brain...*

Apparently, that creepy old Sonny & Cher number can be played in its entirety over one droning chord.
We strummed on as Mr. M. sang, now using both up and down strokes, our playing growing louder, we did not want to stop.
I looked across at Granny, she was laughing in delight, letting her thumb brush the strings in time like she was stroking one of the many cats waiting for her back home.
J-2000 man played on, his eyes watering as he played for his son, resting forever beneath a triangle of flag.
We were all embarrassed by our helpless grins as Misajon sang on, accompanied by us, playing the song -*a song!*- on the guitar.
And then we all automatically joined in, as if gathered not under fluorescent lights and upon thin carpet, but under a vault of stars around a glowing campfire.

La de da de de...la de da de da...

TWELVE

S*itting in a Burger King*, South Carolina.
We are spread out, everyone taking in the luxury of air
conditioning and space.
Eating silently, heads down over food.
Like a sad family, the dinner table forever haunted by an empty
highchair at the end.

In front of each of us are heaping mounds of lettuce and croutons,
shredded orange cheese.
A manuscript in wilted iceberg, punctuated by a few cherry tomatoes.
We'd discovered the Burger King Garden Pita, each franchise along the
highway offering a *Build Your Own!* pita sandwich for 99 cents.
For a buck you were given a stale crescent of pita bread in a paper
envelope and pointed towards the meager salad bar.
Eat a Pita! was the inevitable tagline of that summer campaign, some
wag from marketing probably chiming in with that gem as they
discussed a way to bolster third quarter revenues and cash in on the
healthy living fad.

All eyes turn to the Burger King CEO, enthroned at the head of the
polished conference table.
Behind him, through a double paned, tinted window, gleams an empire
darkened only by the twin arched shadows of the true king of burgers.
He chews on the idea for a moment, literally. *Eat a Pita...hmm.*
The Montecristo Robusto in his mouth twists as he gnaws at it, the
soggy tobacco wrap turning as black as his onyx heart.
Finally, he slaps a meaty palm to the table, spits out his cigar.
*Goddamn you, Jenkins, you beautiful madman! This might be just crazy
enough to work...*
It was doomed to fail, of course.
People interested in a healthy lunch were not about to be seen at a fast-

food joint in their garish aerobics spandex, while the fatties in the South dismissed the buffet as *rabbit food* as they waddled past the sneeze guards.

Ah, but it was a blessing for us.

We would simply use a whole plastic tray as a dish, cover its surface with wilted lettuce, then pile on as much crap as possible.

We found a few variations of the salad bar at different BKs, some offering crumbled bacon type thingies, or slices of hardboiled egg.

Garbanzo and kidney beans, a stainless steel cylinder of suspect corn.

We'd meet at the table with heaping trays, a contest of vegetation piled upon filthy polypropylene.

A wee courtesy cup filled with water, salt and pepper in druggy bindles.

Enough nutrition to last us another day, enough roughage to advance our beer-marinated intestines.

The pita bread we used as napkins.

I'm aware of the disapproving looks from the other customers now, overhear *tsks* and fragments of words: *freaks* and the word *California* spit out like an epithet.

An obese woman in a muumuu corrals her filthy kids clear of our tables as she leaves the restaurant, shaking her head in disgust.

Doug is talking to Chris behind me.

"Fuckin' crackers," I hear him say. "I could kick his ass. And his..."

I turn to look at them, "kick whose ass?" I ask.

Doug waves toward some truck driver types sitting across the room.

"Any of 'em. *All* of 'em," he says.

It's three guys crowding a square of Formica: Peterbilt hats, beer guts, Whoppers.

The guy with his back turned to us looks over his shoulder, and stares.

He turns back, slowly shaking his head, as if suddenly burdened with a vision of decency's fiery end.

I hear the mumbled word *queers* float in the air between us.

"Yeah?" I say. "But what if you had to *fuck* them?"
Chris looks up from his food, looks around the room. "What now?
Hold your horses…"

"Yeh, man," I say. "You gotta fuck 'em. I don't know, for a million
dollars?"
The fellas all laugh now.
"Fuck that," says Doug. "I'm no queer."
"Yeah, but for a million smackers?" asks Chris.
Then it's quiet as everyone starts doing the math.
The guys are swiveling in their seats, openly looking at the table across
from us.
Our eyes travel up and down human bodies like judges at a county fair,
standing before a pen of livestock.
Jay pokes at his salad mountain, spearing a cherry tomato and juicing
his T-shirt.
"Is what you're saying you just have to put your dick in one person and
you win?"
I swallow a mouthful of Garbanzo, masticated into hummus, waving a
plastic spork in denial.
"No, no. You have to climax. Inside."
The fellas groan again.
Chris stands now, after saying *whoa, whoa, whoa!*
"Jesus. You'd have to be drunk, at least. Can we be drunk? Or can we
be on acid? Please?"
"I'll allow it," I say. "Perfectly legal."

Jay raises his hands like he's in class.
"I say you have a girl blow you and you're still hard. Then: *boom.*"
He sits back with a satisfied smile, stabs at a cucumber slice.
Now we are all talking at once, strategies involving blindfolds and
masks.
The truckers start looking over, more with concern than hatred.
We stare openly at them, and they look away first.

"Wait," says Jack. His eyebrows furrowed with real worry. "Do they have to fuck us, too?"

When Kimm returns from the bathroom, we are choked in laughter.

"What?" he says. He looks down at us as we cough bits of greenery on each other. "Now what?"

"You have to screw a dude for a million dollars," Jack says succinctly. Kimm just nods and sits down.

"Gotcha," he says.

He is already locked onto the wavelength.

We all are, a coordination of mindset synchronized, like the menstrual cycles of nuns in a convent.

The long days of sitting in a box the size of an industrial refrigerator, inhaling each other's farts to the point we can identify the issuer.

Our talks range from telepathic grunts to long filthy monologues, the silliest and most impossible ideas vocalized.

Kimm recognizes this as another one of my twisted conversation starters.

Stupid, juvenile… anything to pass the time.

"Ok, I'm in. What's the time frame of this little contest?" Kimm says. But he stops and points at Chris "Wait, I'm *not* fucking you."

Chris jumps up now, knocking his tray to the floor. A cherry tomato rolls away, blushing.

"Well, I'm not fucking you *either*! Keep the billion dollars," he shouts back loud enough that the guy manning the deep fryer cranes his neck to see over the counter, burning his hand on a pile of curly fries.

The table we leave is a confused tangle of greenery and half-bitten vegetation, like a garden trampled by mules, decimated by rodents. The truckers are wordless now, unaware of the sexy fate they've avoided as we leave and get back on the highway.

We approached the final months of high school with that sappy solemnity of seniors, destined to write *the long and winding road...* in each other's yearbooks.

I'd already been accepted to USC in the fall, on the spotless coattails of my two sisters who were already in the dorms.

The graduation ceremony was held at night in the Cerritos College stadium, a warm June night.

Kimm was seated on the dais, as he'd served as senior class president. We teased him mercilessly of course, though he really took the job for its italicized appearance on future transcripts.

As far as I can tell, he did his politicized duties without effort or mention, save the day he had to show school spirit *(Go Dons!)* and come to school in Paul Stanley makeup for Halloween. Oh, how I cried. I received my diploma with a sweaty handshake, a singular shout of *Go Michael!* coming from the stands.

I knew it came from my dad, up there in the stands awkwardly sitting next to mom and *Bachan.*

Chris, Kimm, and I spent the night driving from one house to the next, sat three across in Kimm's Datsun pickup, listening to Bowie stutter "Changes" over and over.

Making appearances at each other's' parents' places, eating identical plates filled with supermarket cold cuts.

At Kimm's house Lynn walked me over to the liquor closet, opened the door and spread his hands out toward its bounty.

"Mike, my boy, what'll you have?"

Then he winked and took a dusty bottle of Kesslers from the back and handed it to me.

"I believe this is your brand, no?"

At Chris's place, his mom, Carol, wept and laughed at herself for weeping, hugging us again and again, calling us *her guys.*

We went out to the garage and shared a pinned joint with her while she told us stories of her own recent youth, warning us again not to settle down too early.

When stoned just enough, she told us how, as a terrified and pregnant

fifteen-year-old, she drank two Dr Peppers in quick succession and then jumped on a trampoline hoping to miscarry, this on the advice of her wise sixteen-year-old friend.
But Chris had held tight to her womb and sat here with us now.
Carol reached up to tousle Chris's hair as if he were still that unplanned child on her teenaged knee.
"Hell, you guys. Maybe *never* settle down," she said.

We went to my house last, where I was surprised to see my dad's Caddy parked in his old space in the driveway.
I'd assumed he'd make his appearance at graduation then disappear into the night.
Escape to a room filled with flashing lights and pulsing music.
Awaiting his grand entrance, a dim coke slut in his usual booth, her thighs spread already.
But when I came into the house I could hear my mom and dad, their shared laughter in the TV room.
I looked in and they stopped, mid-remembrance, as if ashamed to be caught in a moment of civility, if not affection.
He was sprawled out in the TV room, his old usual spot on a speckled love seat, my mom on the far end of the matching couch.
We sat with my folks for the obligatory fifteen minutes, then set out on our late-night route of parties, set to take us to daylight.
We wandered the identical tract streets that night, coming together with other flushed kids for a moment.
We contacted like hard shiny objects colliding soundlessly in space before bouncing off in opposite directions forever.

As we neared the North Carolina border we started seeing billboards for the "South of the Border" roadside attraction. The signs were planted with a Burma Shave regularity, inducing a groan at the pun-driven script (*You never Sausage a Place!*) and the wildly racist Mexican imagery, all sombreros and lazy Mexicans sleeping atop donkeys.

We stopped, of course.
And though the signage was enormous, promising an Aztec wonderland, it was just a big truck stop with the usual pen of alligators and tacky souvenir shop attached.
We looked longingly at the menu at the snack bar, which featured Mexican fare spelled out phonetically by some drunken madman.
I patted at my empty pockets, sadly passed on trying one of the *Brrr! eeee! toes!*

We got into North Carolina with a collective ten bucks between us, after our Burger King lunch and topping off the Blue & White's 21 gallon tank.
I opened the Coleman Cooler and swirled my hand through the lukewarm water.
Empty cans and six pack rings, fucking cigarette butts, maybe piss? The water so filthy it obscured the bottom.

It's always go, go, go! we chanted in our best Barney Fife the last 10 miles to Raleigh.
Kimm came out of a phone booth and directed us to Deborah and Sally's place.
They were a couple of hippy punky girls, roommates who welcomed the passing bands to use their bathroom and crash on the floor.
News of their hospitality spread virally along the stolen phone card network, and they were probably as infested by traveling punk bands that summer as by the tiny black ants that trailed from the kitchen faucet to the linoleum floor.
I never quite got the hang of which was Deborah or Sally, though they were physical opposites: blonde and thin here, redheaded and bosomy there.
They also seemed interchangeably cheerful and talkative to the point of never letting a moment of silence enter the room.
"Good Lord," Deborah (Sally?) said, looking up at us when we all lumbered into the tiny townhouse foyer.

"They do grow them big out in California, huh? We just had the
T.S.O.L. guys in through here, what? Couple months back? Those guys
were all over six feet, too."
Sally (Deborah?) looked us up and down. "What they feed y'all out
there?"

After destroying the single bathroom and choking their washing
machine with a fetid load of underwear and socks, they took us to a
local hangout nearby.
We sat on the outdoor patio of Sadlack's Heroes as the day cooled, a
great shadow cast down from the bell tower across the street on the
NCSU campus.
They had fifty cent beers, and with some nifty math we turned our ten
dollars into 18 cups of draft Bud, one dollar tip.
They played *Ziggy Stardust* over the tinny outdoor speaker
continuously that day, side one, then two, back to side one.
After "Rock n' Roll Suicide's" final crescendo there'd be a full minute
of silence before someone inside flipped it and with a scratch started
the record again, the heartbeat of "Five Years" thumping to life.
We sat sipping at our treasure of lager in great spirits, singing along
with Bowie.
We'd shout the chorus into each other's faces, mumble through the
verses that only Jay knew all the words.
And after our cups were empty, local punkers came up to the table and
dropped off more cups for us, stopping to smoke and chat with
DeborahSally. They all promised to be there the next night at PC
Goodtimes, apparently where we'd be playing.

Soon the patio was filled with the friendly freaks of Raleigh, hair of
green and septum ringed.
I had a sudden moment of deep appreciation for this miracle, sitting at
this picnic table with an ocean of gifted beer in front of us.
Ziggy singing down to us from across 150 million miles of cold black
space.

That Kimm had arranged this all, contacted strangers in cold calls that somehow brought us to be sitting here with new friends.

A show booked for the next night, a place to wash our stinking bodies and sleep.

A miracle, really.

I sniffed, alarmed that I might leak a beer-driven tear from my eye, so caught up was I in this sudden love of place and tribe.

Kimm looked at me with a slight tilt of the head, puzzled.

I held out my plastic cup toward him, and he touched it back with his in cheers.

"You ok, dude?" he asked.

I smiled down at my cup, shook my head clear.

"Yeah, yeah," I said.

"So listen up, all of you," I announce to the table.

The fellas all shut up then, and turn my way.

"Suppose you're starving. But you have to *eat* someone…"

THIRTEEN

*W*e're on stage in Richmond*, a long narrow room with the bar running along one side, a few booths to the other. The room comes to an end at the low stage, and as we play people must squeeze past us to get to the bathrooms.

We finish playing "Take My Chances" to silence, then a cough and some guilty clapping.

I watch a fat guy in a trucker cap pass the stage on his way to the head.

I tell him there's someone in there already, but the women's is empty.

Rain pelts the bar front windows.

The night outside is rainy but warm, a long, humid day finally surrendered to the clouds that have chased us all day.

I see only a few people scurrying past on the street, laughing at their suddenly wet hair, shrieking as the street is instantly illuminated day-bright by lightning.

Beer signs light the room, just bright enough to show the maybe twenty people in the crowd.

It's empty enough that the bar smells of sour tap lines, smoke, and sweat still lingering in the air, a mournful funk like the odor of a beloved family pet close to death.

I've come to recognize nights like these, usually Mondays or Tuesdays: an empty bar in a college town deserted for the summer, a damp basement with a makeshift stage before a handful of small-town punks.

These are the real gigs of a tour.

The dates that fall between the Saturdays with guarantees, the big city shows in storied clubs.

We are grateful, though, for any room that will have us, if even just for a meal and a place to crash. We are realistic enough to know we don't have the heat to pull a lot of people out on a work night.

But it's way better than a night off, when we would be spending money on getting drunk, getting on each other's nerves.

The chance to go home with a girl is slim on a Monday.
That sweet reprieve as a girl drives through streets familiar to her, you in the passenger seat and going through her tapes.
An escape from that goddamned Blue & White, from the locker room smells of six guys together.
Then get to sleep on her clean sheets and play with her dog; to get away from the guys for a blessed night of murmurs and candled air.
I stand on stage in the quiet room, and for a moment think back to the night before we left, that ride with the girl in the blue Volkswagen: My hand upon fishnetted thigh, the Damned serenading us.
Windows open to sing and shout into the night, begging the sun to never appear.

We play "Out of Control" now, and then go right
into "Mannequin" without a pause. It's a usual one-two punch that gets the pit boiling.
At the end of the song there is near silence again.
"Hey there," I say into the microphone. "How you good people doing tonight in, uh, *Virginia?*" pronouncing the state as a question, not quite sure if we are in East or West, North or South Virginia.
It's one of the Virginias, that much I know.
The only response is a cough and a scratchy *whooo!* from a drunk trailer park queen in front of the stage.
She has been swaying on the dancefloor in front of Kimm, wagging her gray tongue at him and calling out *Rod Stewart, hey!* between each song.
It occurs to me her spiked hairstyle is remarkably close to Kimm's, and I say as much over the microphone.

After a week of begging, my brother Tim gave in and brought some of his gear down to the garage.
Kimm and I watched as he set the big Magnatone combo on the

washing machine and plugged it into the wall.

He flicked a switch on the back and the jeweled indicator light glowed red. Then a white noise buzz came from the twelve-inch speakers as the tubes warmed, a sound like the electrical hum of powerlines overhead on a dark autumn day.

He plugged a cord into the input and then tested the other end with a thumb, producing a *snik* and buzz of circuit complete, human body connecting spark to ground.

Then he pointed at the guitar cases sitting on the dryer.

"Those," he said, "you be careful with. One scratch and you're dead."

As he went back into the house he turned back to us, doorknob in hand and grinning, as if he knew all about the journey we were about to begin.

In the way a man is gifted his first set of golf clubs upon retirement, damning the rest of his days to an obsession filled with heartbreak and sporadic moments of triumph, we reached out for the guitars.

"Have fun, ladies," he said to us, and closed the door.

Kimm and I opened the first guitar case and beheld my brother's prized Gibson SG.

The guitar sat nestled in coffin plush velvet, the patchouli smell of wood and polish and sweat reached us as we lifted the guitar out.

Dark wood grained with gold hardware, it had a row of three humbuckers dominating its thin body, a weapon-like feel in hand.

In the other case was his black Ibanez, so close in form to a Les Paul that it was famously referred to as a *lawsuit* model.

I imagined exasperated lawyers holding up photos of identical guitars in court, the Japanese engineers in suits bowing, unmoved by accusations of piracy.

We ducked into the guitar straps, me with the SG, Kimm with the lawsuit, turning away from each other to hide our idiotic and uncontrollable grins.

We plugged both guitars in at the same time in the A/B jacks on the amp and stood close together, facing each other, and rolled the volume knobs up on the guitars.

The feedback squeal, the *clang* of guitar strings shaking above the sensitive pickups made us wince in synchrony, as if physically shocked by the guitars.

We took turns strumming open chords, G, C, D, the guitars howling in distortion. We tried the easy up and down strums that suited the acoustic guitars we'd been playing daily, but now those warm familiar tones were translated into something awful and mean.

A howl that ended in a scream of feedback, an animal clawing at the dirt, dragging behind it the steel jaws fatally clamped around its haunch.

Tim opened the garage door again, shaking his head.

"Dummies. Barre chords."

He went to the amp and adjusted the knobs, twisting at *volume* and *main volume* with the practiced touch of a safecracker.

"Here," he said, taking the SG from my shoulder.

He turned up the volume, hit a barred A chord with a Townshendian flourish, did some Chuck Berry string bending licks.

Then he chugged some downstrokes, taming the strings with the pad of his right hand.

He stopped and held his left hand lightly on the strings, gentle as holding a wounded bird, showing us the sweet spot pressure that held the guitar silent.

We spent the rest of the afternoon experimenting with the guitars, playing every song we could think of. We tried the corny songs left us by Mr. Misajon, "Country Roads" and "Baby I Love Your Way," but the tunes were obliterated by our frantic wailing.

We tried the riffs we barely knew: "Rock Bottom," "Same Old Song and Dance," "Just What the Doctor Ordered."

Playing the songs until that inevitable point, at bridge or verse, that we got lost.

Then the song would dissolve and stop, like an unwinnable argument between two weary lovers left at dawn with nothing more to say.

The garage rang with an awful noise that day and we were thrilled.
We stood facing each other with electric guitars hanging from us,
trying windmill strokes, screeching single note leads, spread-legged
rockstar poses.
Enchanted by the roar and power, already regretting the inevitable
moment that my mom would open the door.
And say *that's enough for today.*

There's a couple longhairs at the bar.
They've been watching us play from their barstools, elbows propped on
the bar to their backs, swiveling around in measured intervals to take
another swig off their longnecks or down another shot of Jack.
One wears a classic KISS shirt, the orange to red logo on black. His
partner in a Rush tour shirt, and I can tell even from a distance it was
from the 1978 Hemispheres tour.
We went to that show at Long Beach arena and left early, just as soon
as we heard side one of *2112* and "Working Man."

During one of the awkward silences between songs, in a desperate
goof, I nod to the longhairs and start to play the intro to "Black
Diamond."
KISS and Rush man perk up, get up from their barstools and come to
the dancefloor.
I can get through the intro, Jay and Kimm even stepping up to do
the *ooooooooo* background part.
But then we get to the kick in, and just after Jack clicks off the four
count and I yell, *hit it!* the song falls apart completely.
Jay keeps playing the bass part, but Kimm and I look at each other
shrugging, trying to copy cords off each other's guitar necks; dim
students cheating off another dummy's doomed test.
We are instantly back in the garage, picking at those partial riffs that
we learned from the stoners, of songs we loved but not enough to learn
all the way through.
The song grinds to a halt, and there is a response from the people in the
bar now: laughter and booing. KISS man just says *"Aw. C'mon, man!"*

Then the guy in the Rush shirt throws a twenty on the stage.

He points at me, says, "Play more. Dude… the *whole* song," before going back to his drink.

I eye the bill lying on the stage, Andrew Jackson looking back up at me.

That will surely be the only money to be had tonight, as I can already hear the promoter's excuses of the rainy night and skimpy crowd as he offers Beer Nuts and a sixer to send us on our way.

Jay comes over to me, taking off his bass, and says, "Switch."

He takes my guitar, then turns to Jack and stomps, claps, stomp-stomp, claps until Jack takes up the beat.

Jay turns up the volume knob on my Charvel and starts the familiar intro riff to "Rock and Roll All Nite."

And when I step to the mic I am astonished to learn I *know* the lyrics to the song.

As soon as I shout out *You show us everything you got…* the rest of the song follows instinctively, the words somehow ingrained in a dark recess of my mind right next to the jingle for Oscar Meyer bologna and the ingredients of a Big Mac.

I'd been living at the dorms at USC since September, enjoying a blazing Indian Summer that left the freshmen from the East Coast panting like dogs in the shadows of the red bricked buildings.

My roommate was an acne-ravaged boy who spent most nights in the architecture lab while I drank beer with the other clueless freshmen on my floor.

I'd wake up to find our room filled with startling scale models of cathedrals and banks.

Stumbling amongst the buildings like a hungover Godzilla, I'd lean down to examine his work.

Cut of foam board and assembled with toxic glues, amazing little villages that he'd assembled overnight as I slept.

Meanwhile, I received a *FAIL* on my midterm paper: *Hemmingway and the Religion of Sport* for putting an extra "M" in Papa's name. (*How could you?* the professor scrawled beneath the red F-)

I tried to get into the school spirit, staying over on some weekends to go to the home games in the crumbling Coliseum next door.

The Trojans went unbeaten that season, asterisked only by a tie to fucking Stanford, Charles White whipping off 250-yard games as if he were leisurely jogging the field alone.

I went so far as to attend a couple Thursday night pep rallies in Alumni Park, a crowd of students gathered around a bonfire while coach John Robinson spoke of the weekend's inevitable win.

It felt off somehow. Ominous.

Those impossible cheerleaders in virgin white strutting around the flames, their shadows cast high on the buildings, while a skeleton crew of the marching band played "Fight On." It all seemed more suited to be played out on a plantation lawn under ancient oaks, a deep secret of coded hate lurking just beyond the firelight, than here amidst the palm trees and desert heat.

After, I'd follow my hallmates to a fraternity party, sticking close to the keg until it started spitting foam.

Finally, I was summoned upstairs to a candlelit room, cornered by three grave elders from *Phi Kappa Tau* and asked if I was interested in pledging.

They had been watching me and liked (I swear) the *cut of my jib.*

I had a momentary vision of standing at an actual crossroad, of forked dusty paths that lead away and off into the green hills.

I saw a life of being forever connected to these new *brothers*, pushy lawyers and disgraced bankers, destined toward a third wife named Tiffany, just two years older than my first-born son.

I turned from the chamber and ran down Figueroa, never to visit Frat Row again.

But most weekends I would return to Cerritos, gifting *Bachan* with a sack of dirty laundry.

Kimm was at CSU Long Beach full time and had started spiking up his hair.

He had discovered his fine straight hair took immediately to hairspray and a quick blast of blow dryer rewarded him with a glam punky crown.

He was still living under Lynn's roof and under his *no long hair* regime, so Kimm had found the prickly loophole that left Lynn speechless.

We'd spend most of the weekend in the garage.

Banging away at the guitars, fucking up, learning.

Like shouting ourselves hoarse in a language that we could not quite comprehend.

They're all on the dance floor now, arms raised, singing the words back at us.

KISS guy has Trailer Lady in his arms, twirls her with glee.

I fake it on the bass, but Jay knows the song cold.

He falls to his knees to deliver the Ace solo as the people cheer, and a lone Bic flickers in the dark.

That they are with us, finally, as we play the cover of a hoary old song – and *badly…*

It means nothing and everything.

We are supposed to be punk rockers on a mission to destroy the plexiglass castles built by Kabuki-appropriating millionaires.

But on a rainy Monday night on the other side of the continent we have a dozen people in front of us as we play electric guitars, and they are happy.

Tomorrow, Rush Man will start out on a three day turn and burn, hauling coils of pickled sheet metal out to Everett.

Trailer Park has the opening shift at Publix, a gray morning of choked conveyor belts and wads of coupons to be decoded.

But they each will pull a memory from their hungover heads and smile a moment.

That turn on the dance floor, under the glow of the beer signs, dancing along to a song they've always loved.

When we finished the song I knew enough to shout *Goodnight!* and unplug the bass.

Lights up now, a signal to last call, and the bar is suddenly awash in cruel electric light.

The spell of the darkened room is broken as the bartender barks exit orders, and a tiny old man already steers a push broom over the faded laminate flooring.

We kneel to roll up cords, retrieve dropped picks.

We are wordless, knowing that the night has been saved by a decade old cover song.

The two longhairs come to us once more, Rush Man nudges the twenty that has been laying where he dropped it closer to me.

"Well, hell, that was all right," he said. "Didn't care much for the stuff you guys played earlier, but great closer, man."

And then he holds out a hand to shake and I take it.

I pick up the twenty too, grabbing at it as if it had been left silently on a nightstand, reimbursement for passions exchanged.

F O U R T E E N

*I*t has become elevated to myth: How the Ramones spurred yet another pimply teen to start a band.

Simply typing *When I first heard the Ramones…* into a search engine will fill in the sentence with *I knew I could do that, too.*

But it was indeed the simple three chord genius of "Blitzkrieg Bop," the lead a single note (if there is a lead at all), and Dee Dee helpfully conducting it all with his bark of *one-two-three-fo!* that inspired us all.

And beyond their stripped down music, there was Joey up front: too gawky, too tall - too cool.

I took heart that maybe a dorky tall guy could stand center stage after all.

At first, we made a list of songs we could play together, start to finish. "Blitzkrieg Bop," of course, then the discovery that we could do any number of Ramones songs that were contained within a triad of chords. The simplest of three chord rock songs: Judas Priest's "Living After Midnight," Runaways' "American Nights," Zep's "Rock and Roll." We were slowly decoding the American songbook, learning just how many songs were little more than a rehashed 12 bar blues pattern. Robert Johnson on his knees at the midnight crossroads, he surrendered his eternal soul not just for his own glory but for all future generations of knuckleheads in the garage: stumbling through a medley of "Wild Thing" and "Louie Louie," as if they were the first to notice their twinned DNA.

We soon had a list of songs that we could play from start to finish, and we played them over and over.

Just Kimm and I standing face to face in my garage, or in his game room, holding guitars.

Building muscle memory and learning the grooves.

I would sometimes shout the lyrics, thankfully unheard under the screech of our guitars.

By spring break we thought we were ready for that outrageous evolution, to find a drummer and finally a bass player to join us.

It was a blind date-ish leap of faith, to start a band means bringing your tastes in music and limitations as a player to light.

Like searching the world for others who are also into your shameful fetish for cruel stiletto shoes or lactating pregnant midgets.

We scanned *Recycler* ads, trying to detect sympathetic vibes from the terse haikus.

We met with a few drummers, mostly real players who simply played along bemusedly to our nonsensical repertoire before looking at their wristwatches and remarking on the late hour before packing up and leaving us forever.

We finally found a local kid, from Cerritos of course, a flame-headed marching band drummer named C-

C- had been in a band before, or so he claimed. The pinnacle of their career was a slot at a battle of the bands held at the Cloud 9 club inside Knott's Berry Farm.

C- was an affable goof who was amenable to our antics.

With a drummer onboard, it was far easier to find a bass player.

Larry was maybe two years younger than us but played his Fender tele bass with a sure steady flick of his index finger.

He had a plywood bass cabinet housing a monstrous 18-inch speaker; it was painted Ferrari yellow.

When we played together for the first time I brought an old microphone with me.

We fashioned a wrought iron floor lamp as a duct-taped microphone stand and plugged the mic into the B input of Kimm's twin.

Then we stood for a moment watching it shyly, unsure who would approach it first, as if it were a stunning exchange student standing alone at a high school dance.

I knew all along, of course, *I* would be the singer.

Destined to step up to the battered Shure from the moment I saw Paul Stanley shriek in joy, Joe Strummer wail in pain.

You know already, of course, that the microphone I so casually pulled from my pocket that day had been in my bedroom since I discovered it in the garage at fourteen.

Perhaps it was a relic from a hospital reception desk used to usher the next patient in for an injection or catheter.

I had spent endless hours in front of the mirror, singing into that unplugged microphone, or swinging it lasso style, pretending to be a blind, deaf, and dumb boy suddenly alive with the truth.

The next time we counted off the Ramones classic, I stayed in one place, tethered as I would be for decades to come to the pole in the middle of the stage. We counted off the song, came in together.

C- holding the beat steady up to the floor tom breakdown, Larry adding the bottom floor to our buzzing guitars.

And then I stepped close enough to kiss the microphone, and shouted, *Hey Ho, Let's Go!*

When we all finished the song together, I had to turn my head to hide my idiotic grin.

A band, we finally admitted to ourselves: *we are in a band.*

We practiced in my garage, the same songs over again until my mom flicked the lights on us.

We practiced upstairs in Kimm's bonus room, and the walls shook until family photos tilted and frowned, while a flurry of asbestos drifted down from the ceiling.

Outside, a circle of little kids stopped on the sidewalk, hands still on handlebars as they tilted their heads, listening to the racket we made. They squinted up at the window overlooking Rose Street thinking, *it almost sounds like music.*

PART III

I *walked out of the club into a wall of humidity.*
It still surprised me, the muggy weather, even after being wrapped in it all summer.
Drunk, I waved my arms at the thick night, thinking the atmosphere dense enough to propel me forward as if swimming, or maybe even lift me three inches above the street in actual flight.
I longed for the Pacific breezes that cooled even still July nights, the dry heat of day that obediently dissipated with the curtain of nightfall.

I heard the stage door open behind me, the momentary spill of club noise before the door closed again, then footsteps hurrying toward me.
I did not look back but braced myself, feeling with an odd notion I both dreaded and desired, that a freezing bucket of water was about to be thrown on me.
Kimm grabbed me by the elbow and spun me around to face him.
"What," I said. *"What?"*
He blinked, speechless for a beat, and I could tell he was as furious as I'd ever seen him.
"The fuck was that?" he finally said. "Twelve minutes and you walk off?"
I shook off his grasp and almost fell, taking three backward steps to regain my balance. I was drunker than I thought.
"What?" I repeated once again, this time truly curious.
Kimm shook his head at me, the disgusted look of a man disappointed once again by his shit eating dog or slutty daughter.
"Another show down the drain, what in the hell," he finally said. "We were on that stage twelve shitty minutes before you wander off?"
I sniffed and straightened up, tried to look sober. "Ah, so what man. *Punk rock.*"

We'd pulled into Baltimore at dusk, and then loaded the gear down the stairs onto the Marble Bar stage.

There was no backstage room with iced beers waiting, no drink tickets to be had until showtime.

We were broke and the cooler held only a few empty cans floating in a foot of lukewarm water, yellowed by the squeezed mustard packets that completed a horrific aquarium.

We were resigned once again to wait for the show to start, when we could beg a few beers to get us going.

Then we'd pester the locals for drinks until we were sent packing to the next town.

Until then, we were held hostage in that interminable twilight before show time, the torture by boredom that seemed to squat on the hopeful face of each day.

Kimm went looking for a phone, Jay and Chris started off on a stroll to stretch their legs.

Jack crawled into the back row of the van and took a nap.

I sat on the curb next to the Blue & White with Doug, sharing a Camel unfiltered.

Doug took a drag and passed it to me.

"You know what sounds fucking good right now?" he asked, looking up at the purpling sky. "A goddamn steak."

I pictured a steak, a ribeye crosshatched with grill marks, served on a silver platter.

A flattened flag of a toothpick stuck in it, claiming it for the empire of Medium Rare.

"Ah," I said. "Yes. Ribeye medium rare, still sizzling from the grill, can you hear it?" I ran the back of my hand across my mouth to keep my saliva in check.

"A twice baked potato, please. And a cold beer, hmmm? No, make that two of them."

Doug groaned.

"And," I continued, "It's served by a lonely and bosomy widow named Trixie. She wears pigtails still, Trixie does. Her late husband had a Nazi *Fräulein* fetish you see..."

"What now? *Trixie?*" Doug grabbed me around the neck then, held me in a headlock. "Shut up, you. Quit talking about food and girls." He squeezed harder and hissed into my ear. *"Liberate yourself from my viselike grip!"*

Doug had been in the back of the van that day reading *Catcher in the Rye* for the first time.

He looked up when he came to the passage where Holden wrestles with Stradlater on the cold tiles of the bathroom floor, a scene I'd been known to recreate whenever grabbing one of the fellas in a drunken bear hug.

He read the words aloud and then threw the crimson paperback at me. *"Viselike grip,* huh? Jesus, Magrann, you have any original thoughts or do they all come out of books?"

I twisted out of his hold and pushed him off. "…and Trixie, though the baby has been taken as well, her breasts keep producing milk, you see? Say, have you read *Grapes of Wrath*?"

And then we hear the screech of tires being locked up a moment too late, followed by that sweet millisecond of silence before a crash, before the crunch of metals touching in taboo kiss.

The van shuddered, hit from the rear.

We got to our feet and ran to the back of the van, where a black Trans Am was wedged tight up against the bumper.

The Pontiac driver got out and walked to the front of his car.

"Holy shit, look at this," he said, one hand waving at his shattered front headlight, the other holding the top of his bald head, as if to keep his brains from exploding straight up in a gory fountain.

He looked about forty, black silk shirt opened to showcase the Italian horn tangled in his chest hair.

I sensed low level coke dealer or maybe high school principal, out cruising for the freshly graduated girls he'd been clocking for years.

He crouched at the van bumper and said, "Well, no harm done. Looks like I took all the damage, huh?"

Alone, I may have shrugged and waved the guy off on his way, anything to avoid a confrontation.
But Doug took a step forward, saying, "Nah man, fuck that…"

In Doug I had my bodyguard and cheerleader; he always enjoyed pushing me into a circle of tough looking skins to start the fight he would then gladly finish.

Doug was the oldest of three brothers, raised by one fiery mom, Mary Lou.
She saw right through the bullshit that three fatherless boys can inflict on the world.
Doug was already working full time swinging a 20 pound sledgehammer, while middle kid Duane was working on being expelled and transferred between every school in the ABC school district.
The youngest, Darren, would come to rule his own gang of underclassmen, the junior high boys who already worshipped the less melodic and more ferocious sounds of the East Coast, calling themselves the *DC Boys*.
I always thought Doug and his brothers had been drawn to punk for the mayhem, mainly.
The music was merely a soundtrack as they destroyed a kitchen, stole a girlfriend, or punched the face of a bewildered stranger.
If it was not punk it could have been cock fighting or rugby, I imagined.
They seemed suited to an earlier time, perhaps in an industrial town in the gray north of England, dedicated to a failing football club and nonsensically fighting for it with endless and vicious passion.

Doug egged on my heavy drinking and got a kick out of my cruel wit when unleashed by that drinking.
But he was there to back me up when my insults landed, his chest jutting out like the prow of a ship braving a horrific storm.
He'd push me aside and wade into an argument that I had taunted into a fight, his fists tensed at his sides, poised for drop like battleship anchors.

Now he went straight to the Trans Am guy and got close to his face.
"What the hell man, *you* hit us! Didn't you see us, huh?"
The guy licked his thumb then wiped at the Blue & White's bumper.
"What, where? This? Not a scratch here, huh? But look at my darn car, sheesh!"
Doug sputtered then, grabbed a handful of silk collar. That's when the van door slid open and Jack crawled out.
He shook his head awake and looked back at us. "What was that?" he asked. "We get hit or something?"
I ran to Jack, hugged him to my chest. "Oh, mother of God, the baby was in there, asleep!" saying this, for some reason, in an Irish brogue. "Are ya ok, Jackie?" I held him at arm's length then and winked.
"Uh," Jack said, "wow, I don't know… feeling kinda weird here."
Trans Am looked down at Doug's hands on his collar, then to me as I stroked Jack's hair, whispering, *"there, there, boyo."*
"Whoa, whoa," he said. "C'mon guys, we can work this out."

Five minutes later we walked back into the Congress Hotel bar just above the club, Doug fanning his face with four twenty-dollar bills.

We ordered a round of drinks, then another, when the rest of the guys came back and found us upstairs in the bar.
We told and retold the story a half dozen times, Doug miming the guy rubbing at the van bumper, then cowering at his raised fists.
Jack telling how Doug followed the poor guy back to his car and demanded he open his wallet and grabbed the bills before sending him on his way.
And when we ordered a round of Jack Daniels, I said the line I'd always longed to say since hearing it uttered a hundred times in a hundred old Westerns: *Leave the bottle.*

I was *fucked up,* of course, by the time we hit the stage.
I sauntered on, holding the bottle of Jack, then drained the final quarter inch and tossed the empty bottle over my shoulder. Jack easily dodged

it as it hit the back wall but did not break.

I got on my guitar, but was unable to plug it in. I stared at the input jack with one eye then gave up.

I started into the microphone then, complaining about the shitty drivers in this shitty city, describing the lovely, pigtailed widow who'd just run into our poor van. Then I recited a detailed recipe for pan searing a ribeye steak.

The crowd laughed, then hissed, then fell into the embarrassed silence that meets the fool in the morning, unaware of the jaunty penis Magic Markered on his forehead.

In my mind I was Andy Kaufman up there: taking the crowd on a whimsical journey *a la comédie absurd*, when I was really the drunk uncle who commandeers the microphone at the reception and tells the story of how the horrified groom once shit his pants during a screening of *Jaws*.

I started to sing the Japanese children's drum song acapella:

Okina Taiko don, don... Chiisana Taiko ton, ton, ton!

Ok, now everybody!

Doug was onstage next to me, shirt off and waving it around his head. "Yes, yes!" he barked into Jay's microphone. "Go, Big Daddy, *go!*"

Kimm had heard enough and started playing the intro to "Take My Chances." Doug remained onstage and sang the intro *whoa, oh, ohs,* then took a leaping stagedive, landing exactly in the spot of concrete the crowd cleared for him. He jumped up and touched the blood on his temple, then raised his fists above his head. "Yes!" he shouted again. The years of practicing the same songs, singing the same lyrics, it builds a sort of muscle memory. Even in that drunken state I was able to hit most of my cues, remember most of the lyrics.

I slashed at my unplugged guitar, pointed at people in the crowd as I sang, accusing them of sabotage.

But after just four songs, following the secret logic that is whispered only to the inebriated (or, perhaps, those upon their deathbed), I

shouted: *"Goodnight, Virginia!"* and walked off the stage.
I walked out of the club into a wall of humidity.

We started letting people sit in on practices, my mom and *Bachan*
politely listening for two songs before excusing themselves to go wash
the rice or get a root canal.
We'd invite friends over to watch; terrifying recitals that would leave
Chris crying tears of embarrassment for us.
And finally, we dared to play at an actual house party thrown by my old
motocross buddy, Dave.
An actual party, *a gig.*

We didn't have a guitar tuner, so we brought our guitars up to Kimm's
bedroom and tuned up to Led Zeppelin's "Custard Pie," that riff a
perfect key of A.
We tuned the guitars and took one more look at the casual outfits we'd
spent a week assembling.
Kimm had on creepers, his hair spiked to impressive height and
volume. I had on my *Never Mind the Bollocks* T shirt, though I had to
wad it up to erase the evidence of *Bachan's* careful ironing.

We put the guitars in their cases with trembling hands, went downstairs
and past Lynn, who eyed our stage wear, then militarily saluted us with
his highball of brown liquor, barking, *"break a leg, ladies!"* as we left
and went to Dave's.
Dave had cleared out the service porch that was off the side of the
kitchen, pointed out electrical outlets, got us some beers, which we
immediately tore into.
Doug and his brother Duane acted as our very first roadies, shooing
people out of the way as we loaded in.
Chris stood off to the side, his eyes shining at the prospect of our
immediate shame or triumph.

We set up wordlessly, my tiny amp on the washing machine and
Kimm's combo assembled on the kitchen counter.

Larry dropped his boxy yellow speaker on the floor and went out to the backyard where people crowded the keg, taking turns at the pump.
He was as free of stage fright then as he would always be, and I envied this, watching him jostling with Duane at the beer line while I wondered at the bubbling in my gut and thinking I might need to shit.

We kept our backs to the party, fiddling as more drunken kids packed into the hallways.
When I turned to face them my head was flushed with blood, my ears burned.
I wished to be, if not far away, then at least on the other side of this microphone.

We rolled on the volume and I hit a chord, a ringing open E.
The alien sound of a live guitar played too loud in an enclosed space commanding all attention, as it should.
The faces watching us, these were kids we knew.
Guys we played kickball with on baking asphalt playgrounds, girls we wrestled with in high school dugouts, negotiating that first pet of silken pubis.
The party hushed in anticipation, ready to render judgment, the sibilant start of the word *suck* already staging on their tongues.
We kicked off: 999's "Let's Face It."

We'd practiced the song endlessly, but here we played it too fast, barely recovering from the sloppy 8 count that started the song.
Larry caught the groove with the rolling bass riff, though, and the guitars caught up, stayed in tune.
I remembered all the lyrics, though I rushed and mumbled through them like rolling off a hurried Act of Contrition at the end of a rambling and awkward confession.
But we played it all right and when we finished, all on the beat, there was a delicious moment of silence.
And then the party cheered.
People clapped and yelled: *Yeah!*

The rest of the guys came out of the club and found me and Kimm
shouting at each other by the Blue & White.

A little galaxy of broken headlight sparkled behind the back bumper, an
asterisk footnoting a sentence, redacted by a skid mark.

"So, hey," Jay said, "we done or what? The promoter guy is asking in
there."

Kimm turned back to me then. "Let's get back in there," he said,
through teeth clenched tight.

Doug, drunk as I, came and slapped me on my back. "That was fucking
great! Leave 'em wanting more, Big Daddy! Hah!"

I suddenly felt that terrible power of a single person in control of the
night, the driver of a car full of sleeping passengers, aware of the
moonlit ocean just beyond the guardrail.

"I don't think we shall be returning to the stage tonight, thank you."

Kimm came close to me, eyes sparkling with fantastic rage. "Fuck that,
let's go back in there and try to save this fucking thing, get paid."

I looked around at the guys then.

Jay shrugged, having been in enough bands to recognize a ruined gig.

Jack weaved a bit, a goofy smile on his face. We made him drink a lot
more than he was used to, his reward for being in on our earlier
windfall, and he seemed to be having his best night so far.

Chris shook his head grinning, those eyes wet, tears forming at the
awkward standoff.

I felt Doug's hand still on my back as he pushed me into Kimm's face.
"Forget that shit," I said. "Fuck those clowns in there. They hit us man,
the van!"

Kimm, exasperated as a mother with a shrieking child rolling in the toy
aisle, shouted:

"Are you fucking nuts? *Who?*" He looked around at the van, and the
fellas. "What is all this?" He waved his hand at the night, at the city, at
us. *All this.*

I was without response then, though an ember of cruelty was fanned
deep in my gut. I swallowed in a vain attempt of extinguishment.

Then he adopted a lower tone, as if crouched down on knee to speak to the hysterical little girl in the toy store who will not release the Malibu Barbie.

"Listen to me, I am the one who sets this shit up, ok? I've been talking to this guy for months, he's been promoting a show, ok? We have to play a full set and get paid. I'm the one with his ass on the line here, me. All right?"

I grabbed at Kimm, wrapping him in a clumsy headlock.
We danced a bit, the night whirling as he held me up at the same time trying to shrug me off and get away.
But I did not speak the words of Holden grappling with his roommate on the eve of his unraveling.
No, I speak different words.
Words that shame me even now, as I sit here decades later.
"Yeah," I whispered back to Kimm, mouth to his ear. "But *I* write all the goddamn songs, and I sing them. They're here to see *me*, not you."

C- left the band when we wouldn't let him sing lead on any of the songs.
He suffered from a malady we discovered common in many drummers. It seemed that a lot of them were frustrated front men, and suddenly felt cheated with the realization that they would be forever seated in the back row, cursed to a lifetime of watching our sweaty butts and chained to a seat, hidden.
We immediately replaced him with W-, beginning an endless parade of drummers who joined us for doomed honeymoons that lasted from a few weeks to years.
W- had a large kit that he wheeled in on a homemade plywood cart, a redundancy of double kick drums and second *and* third floor toms.
He took a full hour to set up, and we soon heard rolling triple fills and windchimes inserted into our Clash covers.
He used *all* that shit, a justification for the wall of toms and cymbals that hid him as if he was squatting behind a duck blind.

We started thinking of names then, had long *band meetings* after practice that we attended with hilarious seriousness.

We talked of stage clothes and *image*, nicknames that would someday be captioned under our quarter page photos in *Circus* or *Creem*.

Larry was on our wavelength from the start, knowing punk rock and its streamlined aesthetic would be the fastest route to getting out of the garage and getting onto an actual stage.

W- thought perhaps we might go a more progressive route, maybe write some original songs based on *Tolkien* that would feature, oh, maybe a gong or the RotoToms that he'd just gotten for his birthday.

We replaced W- with S-, who was then replaced by Burton.

The punch Kimm threw was technically a jab, though I would've liked to see full elbow extension and a proper twist of wrist, really.

But he snapped it off quick enough and it landed with sweet contact to my nose, flattening several capillaries under my eyes and tearing the cartilage that guarded my septum. I pictured a tiny lightning bolt splitting the tissue there, which would heal into a faint second bump, just above the original one earned tumbling down a mountainside at Mammoth Motocross track.

As soon as he threw the punch, Kimm's eyes widened.

He was as surprised as I was, I knew, and though it had certainly been a long time coming (and from my point of view, certainly deserved, if not welcomed), we had never ventured into this territory of physical violence before.

Years of being best friends, as close as brothers, and yet we never consummated our relationship as brothers truly do: by beating the shit out of each other.

We now stood at a new possibility, becoming one of those bands where the members fucking hate each other.

At least gigs ending in historic onstage fist fights would live on; normal gigs were as forgettable as a torn ticket stub in a back pocket.

Doug was suddenly sobered, seeing an actual *fight* blooming between us.

After I regained some balance and touched the snow-crunched surface of my nose, he came to me. He rubbed my shoulders, like a trainer wiping down his fighter between rounds.

Between him and his brothers, and their lives being so intertwined with a survival level of violence, he sensed the natural rhythms of a fight starting, and would be disappointed if we did not bring this to its natural conclusion.

"C'mon, Big, you gonna let him get away with that, mmm? Hell no." And then he pushed me back toward Kimm, who was already holding his right hand and looking at the bloodied knuckles in wonder.

"Fuck off," Kimm said then. "Just get away from me. All of you." And then we were circling each other on the street, looking all the world as if we were going to fight.

As always, my mind was elsewhere.

A cartoon song about conjunctions re-imagined as trains cars, the multiplication tables by fives.

I then recalled my dad's words, words about dropping your guard and aiming for the fences. Also: words about fertilized eggs and Philadelphia trolleys, shitting monkeys. Dunno.

I swung a roundhouse right, a classic haymaker that I telegraphed clearly, as if I was willing Kimm to duck safely out of its way.

He did step back, of course, and I followed my wildly swinging arm past him, pulled off my legs as if pushed from behind. I went tumbling down to the asphalt, falling first to my knees, then elbows, and finally, once again, on my battered nose.

There was quiet, then the shuffling of feet backing away from me and retreating back to the club.

"Jiminy Christmas," I heard Chris say.

"*Aw, man.*" That was Doug.

I lay there for a bit, turning over onto my back when it was apparent I'd been left lying there in the street alone.

What? I said once more, to no one.

What, the word of the night.

I lay on my back for a while, let the blood seep back into my nose, and then the rain started.

A few halting drops, this followed by fat drops that smeared the blood on my face, left my Sex Pistols shirt stained forever after with a crimson continent.

I stared up through the water, at the stars wheeling above in the black cloudless sky.

T W O

I ***woke*** as bright sunshine hit the van.

Pain announced itself, renewed as the light flooded through the windows and found my face.

This was not a familiar hangover with its known lifespan and cure.

I shifted on the bench, lifted my aching head a few inches up before dropping back down again.

A mere hangover, *that* I would have welcomed; my familiar old nemesis who respects the unspoken ethics of our daily-fought battle. This was different.

An ache that reached deeper and attached not to my head or stomach but to my heart.

And it took a few minutes to correctly diagnose it as shame.

After the gig, I lay on the back bench as the guys loaded in the van, an arm over my eyes, my wrist flat across the swelling bridge of my nose. There was a brief conversation about who had the van keys, if there was room for a girl named Mo.

I felt eyes on me, then Jay whispered, *he's still out*, and then we drove. I tracked the shadows of trees growing then fading on the van roof as we drove along the Baltimore streets, listening to the noises around me. The creak of the suspension as we dipped through intersections, the baritone thrum of the exhaust pulsing just below my body. I rode back there as luggage, separate from the guys.

Chris up there driving, following directions Kimm called out, the crinkle of a hand drawn map held up and rotated.

A street name is repeated three times in question, then finally as a statement. Then a U-turn. The van comes to a stop, the engine is turned off, and I can hear the sliding door open as an empty can falls into the gutter.

I opened my eyes as Jack peeked back one time to make sure I was still breathing.

He raised his eyebrows in question, but I dismissed him with a wave.
He nodded, gave me a thumbs up and turned forward, leaving me
alone.

I slept on and off, riding twisted dreams.

I'm standing with my hands weighed down and useless, while endless
jabs connect with my nose, delivered from out of the darkness by a
faceless attacker. My nose grows larger with each strike 'til it
resembles my dad's wonderfully blossomed nose which spread on his
face like a willful spore, sprouting impossibly out of a block of granite.
Then: a black Trans Am is bearing down on me, my legs unable to lift
as if sucked into mud. With the dissolve and refocus of dream logic I
suddenly find *I* am at the wheel, headlights aimed at Kimm as a second
grader, flat-topped and innocent, frozen in fear.

The brakes give freely to the floor, I pump at them impotently, and then
I wake with a start just before the collision.

My heart pounding, my nose weeping blood once again.

We played party after party, growing our setlist longer, practicing
three days a week.

I'd leave the SC campus right after class to make it back to Cerritos,
return to the dorms later that night with my ears ringing, carrying a
duffle of clean clothes and a Tupperware of *tonkatsu* for my
overworked roommate.

We'd play in that garage until my mom would flash the garage lights
and invite the guys to stay for dinner, thrilled to have the long dining
room table filled once more.

We were learning something, some understanding and ease just beyond
definition, like the subtle groove forming on my left shoulder where the
guitar strap would hang forever.

After playing as *Forcible Entry* for a few weeks, (not a bad name,
really), we somehow decided to rename ourselves as *Channel Three*.
It is a name that has haunted us for decades, countless flyers featuring
visual puns of television screens, endless interview questions on the

origin of the name.

We simply wanted a neutral name, and that was the one channel on the dial back then that yielded nothing more than static buzz.

Sometimes I tried to reverse engineer a more interesting story (*It's based on the third channel of consciousness, famously theorized by Edelman…* I once blabbered to a junior college journalism student, as she scribbled the nonsense on her notepad), but in the end it was just some words that became the band.

It seemed there was another party every weekend, and we were astonished to find we were suddenly in demand.

Cerritos seemed absent of all parents that season, homeowners gone for the weekend and their suburban tract homes left in the care of their devious children.

Phone calls were made, maps drawn and copied, a circuitous route through cul-de-sacs and right angles hand-drawn like the busy schematic of a circuit board. Couches were moved to the backyard, old blankets thrown over heavy mahogany dining tables to guard against cigarette burns and telltale rings.

We'd bring in the gear, set it up in a living room or enclosed patio.

We'd play until the cops would bust it up, or a hysterical girl teetering in her mom's sluttiest heels would beg us to stop as kids destroyed the home in her trust.

Couches were thrown into pools, rails of coke were cut into those fine heirloom tables.

Kids fucked and vomited in every room of the house.

I wonder, now, at all the inevitable Sunday evening scenes:

Parents arriving home, cranky and hungover after a weekend in Palm Desert.

Dad, still holding a suitcase in either hand, sniffs at the air and says, *"what's that?"* while mother notes the shimmer of something shattered on the floor. On her knees now, she picks pieces of an *I Love You This Much* figurine out of the shag carpet, tears already rolling down her sunburnt cheeks.

Scratches and dents soon come into view.

Upstairs, bedspread stains are guessed at.

Neither parent willing to utter the obvious, though each beholds the spectacular paisley of dried cum with a tinge of wistful envy.

The girl is sent to her *goddamn* room, where she suddenly stops weeping and smiles as she touches the hickey swelling above carotid pulse.

She thrills at the thought of homeroom tomorrow and the scandalous points credited to her social status: her new identity as the girl who had the *punk band* play her wild party.

There was another band playing those parties, *The Hated*, made up of way cooler surfer dudes.

They played a similar set of covers as we did, though their frantic lead singer, Steve, effortlessly copped a Lydon-esque sneer, and so they played a more Pistols-heavy setlist to our Clash-y and power pop bent.

We'd go to see them play; they'd come to see us.

And then, with only two garage bands in town, a natural rivalry emerged.

Kimm and I were still remembered as honor students from Cerritos, guys who rarely were invited to the cool kid parties. And now were seen with suspicion, as if we only started a band to finally gain admittance to those parties.

Like the goofy Narcs on campus, their cover quickly blown by passing out cigarettes a little too easily and using slang three months dated.

But we had our own fans, the girls who liked our Beat and Plimsouls covers, loner kids who saw a geek rock glimmer of hope, urging them to go home and learn the guitar.

We played a ragged take on Elvis Costello's "Mystery Dance" that got 'em shaking every time.

Larry was our true third now, committed to the band to the point of cutting his curly hair down punk short, wearing darker colors, finally adopting a cool overcoat and fedora ska style that suited his frame.

Burton stayed on with us, though he kept to his own jock friends outside the band, perhaps keeping a wary emotional distance from us knowing our penchant to cycle through drummers.

But he had sparkling red drums.

And he hit the center sweet spot of those drumheads with his gym-muscled arms to produce shotgun-like blasts that propelled us forward.

Chris became our early hype man, dressed like a 1950's aluminum siding salesman in plaid and saddle shoes.

He would dance alone in front of us with such awkward jerking moves that he soon urged a crowd to come join, all thoughts of coolness and appearance abandoned.

Doug and his brothers Duane and Darren would plow through then, jumping off balconies into the middle of a crowd, turning a group of kids dancing into a sudden slam pit there in the sunken living room.

Linoleum was bloodied, stair railings busted and bannisters ruined, now unable to hold even a single Christmas stocking.

But when we would regroup on Tuesday in my garage, Kimm would come in with an offer for yet another party to play the upcoming weekend, sometimes two.

It was all we ever dared dream of, being in a band that people requested, and it ruled my every moment of thought.

I'd sit in the classroom, studying ol' Shakespeare now, hacking away at the ancient language while my foot kept a steady tap under the desk.

I'm hearing "White Riot" while the professor channels Lear.

Blow, winds, and crack your cheeks! he intones; *White people go to school, where they teach you how to be thick*, answers Joe.

I'd sit at the dinner table, just me and the ladies home now.

I'd watch as mom and *Bachan* picked over a stewed fish with their *hashi*, thinking only of a gig that weekend, a backyard party in Artesia.

We might try to play the 999 song "Boiler," I'd be thinking while their chopsticks would be clicking with surgical precision as they picked the corpse clean.

I'd turn in bed, sleepless, thinking of the possible shirts I might wear.

I sat up on the back bench when the guys finally came out of the house and loaded into the Blue & White.

Kimm took the passenger seat, as much distance between us as we could afford within the 40 square feet of the van.

Jay turned back and filled me in on the party, the girls who teased them until dawn, a bottle of Creme de Menthe being passed around, Chris vomiting emerald across someone's prized Persian rug.

The promoter miraculously paid us the full guarantee, apparently telling Kimm it was *one wild gig*, and to be sure to hit him up next time we were coming through.

Though my mind nibbled at this morsel of justification, I had the sense not to make comment on this. We rode along the Parkway quietly, everyone in their own pain, sunglasses on.

We pulled off, filled the tank and went through a McDonalds. McMuffins were tossed through the van, tall colas sent back.

We drove without any music, save the symphony of working mouths, chewing salty fast food and the squeak of straws searching for a last swallow.

I had dodged, if not a bullet, then at least the shame of forfeiting our pay.

And it would be a nice enough story if we -*I*- learned a lesson from the ruined gig, but there would be a score of similar drunken debacles sprinkled liberally throughout our career.

It's a truth that the disasters-the sloppy messes, the onstage fistfights, the nights where bartenders and bouncers outnumber the paying customers-these are the gigs that are remembered.

Memories are burnished to a warm yellow glow by the retelling: ragged nights are forgiven, sloppiness accepted in the name of *Rock and Roll*.

Fans proudly claim attendance not at just a regular tour stop, but on the night of the fire.

It took decades for me to consider the guy holding a stack of cherished vinyl to be signed, after driving fifty miles on a worknight to see us play, only to find I'd discovered the Jameson in the green room after soundcheck and was now rolling around onstage, fly undone.

I'd finally connect, as a damp pervert might trace a childhood diaper disaster to his fetish for piss porn, a day at Anaheim Stadium years earlier.

Hours of waiting in the brutal sun.

It's me there, fifteen and thrilling at the moment when the house sound is cut. The stage lights come on and the siren wail of "Train Kept a Rollin'" cries out, raising visible dots on my arms.

I am there, but so is Steven Tyler, shrieking the wrong lyrics, smacked back and incoherent.

And the disappointment is instantly recalled, like the bitter taste of a charged 9-volt battery, terminal to tongue.

But then, who am I but a fan boasting of that day to you now: claiming to have *been there*.

We were tracking back down to D.C. for an early show, then we'd head back north to NYC.

Soon the exits for D.C. came into view, and Chris pulled off on Capitol so we could drive around the downtown area before load in.

We peered out the windows at the white buildings gliding past, no one really in the mood to get out and walk or get a closer look.

The guys made a game of incorrectly naming the buildings that had graced our textbooks for years.

Here we have the Capitol Dome, where Reagan sleeps diapered next to Nancy. There, the Nixon War Memorial; Treasury just behind the rose garden.

That tall, pointed thing? Maybe the Smithsonian, Fonzie's leather jacket kept in storage up at the very phallic tip.

I kept waiting for patriotic inspiration to swell in my breast as these historic buildings came into view, a sensory awakening at my proximity to the brittle Constitution.

But I felt nothing.

I looked upon them as if passing just another bank or library, another futile exercise in limestone.

The past fires of battle, the blood spilled in misery, it meant so little to me.

So wallowed in my own self-pity, at war with myself, in the back of a van as history passed out the window.

After we loaded in to the club I went up to the balcony with Jay to watch the opening bands.

A band finished setting up, then stayed onstage for a good five minutes screwing around with their gear, the band members wandering offstage then on again. The guitar player noodled by himself, playing shrieking metal riffs at full volume. The drummer ran ridiculous figures around his set, paradiddles and triplets that surely wouldn't surface in any of their 90 second hardcore songs.

"See, don't do that," Jay said. "You get onstage as a group. Test the volume on your guitar once, don't make another sound until the downbeat." We watched some more as the band kept it up, the guitar player eventually stepping to the mic and asking the singer to *please get the fuck up on stage.*

"We've already made up our mind on this band, right? They suck, and they haven't played one song."

I nodded, thought, then nodded again.

Then we got up there.

Not a beer on stage between us and hangovers just faded, we plugged in and played it tight.

It was an all-ages show, this in a city known for earnest attention to the bands and a high regard of the straight edge lifestyle. We played the set fast, with hardly any stops between blocks of songs as I wasn't inspired to come up with any stage banter beyond a few *thanks* and *thanks for being here.*

As we played, I saw Ian MacKaye down on the floor, in the back, watching.

We'd just played with Minor Threat back home in April and I had chatted a bit with Ian beside the roller rink stage, but to see him here in his hometown, watching us, was like having to pee in a cup as a probation officer sat just over your shoulder.

My swollen septum kept the tones in my head, helping me to scream in tune. I looked to my left and saw Kimm slashing away at his guitar, his knuckles still speckled red with abrasion, but his pick held true.

We caught each other's eyes through the frantic middle section of "You Lie," a stage diver threading between us before jumping off stage into a boiling pit. We shook heads and somehow grinned.

After, as we found ourselves alone on the stage, on our knees and coiling cords, I looked over and said, "hey."

Kimm looked back, shrugged. "Yeah," he said.

Just two syllables between us, and all the apology and forgiveness that was required.

Like two estranged brothers who simply nod at each other across their cruel mother's casket, a terror resolved.

Then Ian came up to the stage to congratulate us on a good gig.

THREE

***O**n the night drive to New York I dozed*, struggling to keep awake as Chris drove. I sat shotgun, everyone behind us crashed out.

My eyelids lowered as we traveled north on the NJ Turnpike, pulled downward by the same gravity that dropped my chin slowly to my chest.

As I drifted in and out of this twilight, I was soon aware of a sonorous voice that followed me onto both planes.

I saw black and white scenes in my head, half waked dreams of ancient movie stars, maybe Vincent Price and Peter Lorre, up to no good.

Basements lined with human remains and lit by torches that cast sinister shadows on the stone walls.

I finally shook my head to fully wake and discovered Chris had opened the box of Edgar Allen Poe, and we were listening to a reading of *The Cask of Amontillado*.

"What's this?" I asked. "The Poe?"

"Yeah," Chris said, not taking his eyes from the straight highway. "You just missed the pendulum one- *Whoa, Nelly*."

I heard Jay stir in the back and say, "*what the hell we listening to?*" only to be shushed by Doug.

"Hey, what was that he said?" Doug asked from the dark back of the van. "Rewind that, is there bones on the floor?"

The other guys woke now too, pulled awake by the deep voice reading words of revenge and perfect murder.

We listened, entranced as children, as the final stone was set into place, sealing the tomb.

The story ended and we drove on.

Each of us wide awake now, each not quite sure if we

were *Montresor* or *Fortunato,* on which side of the masonry we'd stand while the mortar dries.

Manhattan came into view.

Black towers, windows sparkling, as if lit from within by torch and vengeance.

The plan was to spend a week at our friend Jack Rabid's place on the Lower East Side.

We had a couple shows in Manhattan and would travel out and back to gigs in Boston and New Jersey, each night returning to Jack's two bedroom *(one bathroom…!)* walk up off Houston.

The week was the centerpiece of the tour, with a guarantee of a thousand bucks for a show at Gildersleeves, then a return to CBGBs a few nights later.

I had told Jay, Chris, and Doug about the wonders of New York for weeks now, of the people that did not give a fuck, the bars that stayed open 'til dawn.

We'd been there the winter before when Larry was still in the band.

We stayed on the East Coast most of winter break, playing last minute shows at CBGBs and A7, wandering the city, meeting a new species of fast talking, no bullshit punkers that we liked immediately.

I was thrilled to finally be in that city, a place that played as a central character in so many books and movies.

I walked each block with a tingle of anticipation, feeling with a silly English major notion that I would be murdered or fall in love at any moment.

Jack's roommate was Doug Holland from the band Kraut, and he introduced us to a head spinning collection of kids each time we hit the street.

We followed his lead on Alphabet City protocol, as he guided us through the streets named mnemonically for their level of danger ("A: yer alright, B: you better go back," he'd lecture us in his Bowery Boys bark, "C: yer' crazy… D: *dead.*")

We'd get up around five in the afternoon, after sleeping through the cold gray days, rousing in the dusk and bumping into each other in Jack's cluttered foyer. Every wall surface was covered with flyers and posters, handwritten notes Jack wrote to himself for the upcoming issue of his fanzine, *The Big Takeover*.

We'd sit around and bullshit for a while, listen to Holland and Jack argue like a couple of old vaudevillians, go down to the bodega for tall cans of beer, and slowly get ready to start the night again.

We'd get out on the street as darkness fell and softened the filthy slush that piled around each intersection. Night seemed to awaken the city, a palpable energy humming as we'd cruise around the Lower East Side, finding out what was happening and where, grab a couple slices at St. Marks Pizza before hitting the clubs.

On a couple off nights we would simply make up a flyer in Magic Marker announcing a gig that night at A7, where Holland was bartending.

Run off 50 copies, and hand them out to the crowd on St. Marks Place. We'd play at 3 in the morning on a weeknight to a crowd of night creatures unfathomably energized at such an hour.

It was all so different from Los Angeles, where a bouncer might snatch a full beer from your hand at 1:30, clearing the bar for last call.

We'd straggle back to Jack's with the morning sun, after a sumptuous breakfast of cheeseburgers and pirogis covered in caramelized onions. *Why the hell didn't we have anything like this back home?* We kept asking each other.

We emerged from the Battery Tunnel and made our way up FDR, well past 1 a.m. now, but seeing the city wide awake on a Saturday night. Places started coming back to me, and I would point out buildings and street corners as if I was a local, incorrectly pointing out the Brooklyn bridge as we passed the Manhattan.

But no one cared. We'd made it to fucking *New York*, as far from home as we could manage, and had a couple of our biggest shows coming up.

We pulled up in front of Jack's apartment, where Kimm and I got out and yelled up to Jack's open window.

Soon a bundled sock was thrown down, Kimm missing the catch as it fell to the gutter, then I stooped to grab it and retrieved a key.

The city steamed in late summer now, all the neighborhood windows open as shouted conversations joined the cacophony of blasting stereos and overworked air conditioners. The block had that ripe funk of immigrant cooking and baked garbage, the pulse of so many lives concentrated here, each a story behind triple locked doors.

I stayed down below while Kimm went up to get Jack, and shortly they came out together.

We hugged, then Jack Rabid got in next to our Jack, was introduced to Doug and Chris, then he turned to Jay.

"Well, it's Jay Lansford, as I live and breathe. Welcome," he said, grabbing Jay's hand.

On the way to A7 Jack asked Jay about all the bands Jay had been in, talking about the Simpletones and the Stepmothers, along with a few other obscure ones I'd never known about. They chatted about the very early days of LA punk, scandalous nights at the Masque, obscure songs that Jay had a hand in writing or producing. I sat listening to them, proud as the owner of a prized hen at the county fair.

Jay was in our band now, and we got him to New York.

When we got to A7, we parked by Tompkins Square Park, and after the matinee show and 250 miles, Jack was glad to volunteer for van duty while we hit the bar.

We got out and practically skipped into the club, stopping to hug Jimmy from Murphy's Law, who was working the door.

"It's the CH3 boys! Oh shit!" Jimmy shouted as we came up to him. He blew a cloud of marijuana smoke into the air and offered a fat joint around. "You fucking made it," Jimmy said.

Doug Holland came around the bar and hugged us all, even Chris and Doug, and brought out a grip of dripping Bud longnecks to toast our arrival.

"Fuckin' Magrann, you madman," he said, keeping me in a hug.

Holland was wiry and redheaded, fair as a vampire from his nocturnal life.

He was a wickedly urgent guitar player who seemed to play with a current of energy running through his body, intercepted between amp and guitar.

"Cheers, big ears," he said, after releasing me and tapping his beer bottle to mine. "Hey, so we're going out there, to LA tomorrow, ya know. Remember?"

They were set to do some shows in LA that summer with GBH, and in a neat little trade off they'd stop by my mom's house while we were out here in New York.

Davey, the singer from Kraut, was there too, and came up and kissed me on both cheeks. "Mikey," he said. "All right then, what's happening, tell me how it's been, this tour. You know we're playing in LA right?"

"Yeah man, you're all set," I said.

Holland went back behind the bar and started setting up another round of beers. He stopped and sniffed at the air and slapped a hand on the bar. "All right you fuckin' animals, who farted?" *Who faughted* is what we heard, and we all raised our hands with a cheer.

Jack Rabid had Jay corralled in conversation still, Kimm was talking with a couple of girls with familiar faces.

One of them looked over to me and raised her eyebrows toward her spiked pink hair, perhaps to remind me of a drunken January promise still unfulfilled.

The bar was as small as a rumpus room, reggae music throbbed loud enough to chatter the glasses.

Jimmy G was behind the turntable now, headphones on his shoulders, joint in his hand. He took up the microphone and shouted "C-H Three boys in the house! *Ho shit-hide the booze yo!*"

We stood shoulder to shoulder at the bar, our heads happily swimming with the booze and shouted conversation.

We drank, as promised, 'til the sun came up, a wicked sliver of gray creeping into the bar when Jack cracked the door at 7 a.m., asking about breakfast.

Holland locked the bar behind us, and we stood in morning light, the day already damp and hot.

The Blue & White was parked across the street, as the shadowy figures in the park started to move into the bushes, ready to hibernate through another sweltering day.

The season of Cerritos house parties tapered off.

The punkers had migrated to proper gigs at the Cuckoo's Nest in Costa Mesa while the New Wave girls discovered the Knott's Berry Farm Cloud 9 disco with a wider menu of boys.

We found ourselves out of time, a backyard cover band with fewer backyards to play.

Neighbors attuned to the first squeals of amplified feedback reached for their phones, the police showing up some nights before we even finished setting up.

The sleepy bedroom community was perched on the edge of a darker chapter, an epidemic of stolen car stereos in place of the harmless toilet paper pranks of a Saturday night.

The cops found not just joints and filched cigarettes in patted denim pockets but bindles of white powders, paper tabs of LSD.

And concerned citizens, wondering just what was going on, became alerted to the cars suddenly parked at every empty curb; packs of kids walking past their lawns, some stopping to piss or puke on the azaleas. Perhaps they'd part the blinds, just after their call to the police. They might squint to the end of the block, spy a blue and white van there, black speaker boxes being carried from its lit belly.

That's us, loading in the gear for another backyard party, and in moments the quiet night will be shattered, another living room will be destroyed.

One of the last Cerritos parties we played was not in a large backyard or cathedral-ceilinged living room, but in a smaller condo, together with The Hated.

Andy and Lisa somehow had a place of their own just on the other side of the 91 freeway, the river of asphalt that separated the large tract homes in Cerritos from the newer condominium complexes.

Andy was already prelaw, Lisa a smart party girl who was destined for a life of teaching others to think.

And, like us, they shared a determined penchant for getting fucked up on the weekends, as if already aware of a life of responsibility that lay ahead.

Andy was a close friend of The Hated crew, Lisa a friend of ours, so on this night we came together to play our sets.

I pulled the van up to the party and parked.

I cut the lights but sat there a while, finishing a can of beer that I'd been sipping on the way over.

I watched cars pull up, clumsily parallel park, abandoned still a foot away from the curb after a third attempt.

Interior lights would flash on as girls did a last review of their makeup, tiny flames flared as hash pipes were lit.

In a moment the car doors would open, and kids would walk to the party in couples or threes, holding packs of beers or bottles of wine by their necks, cigarettes and joints cupped in hands.

I'd seen those corny old spring break movies, where college-age boys already dressed like insurance salesmen picked up their Connie Francis girlfriends.

They drove to the country club for the big dance, an unfiltered Lucky Strike between index and middle finger on the steering wheel, Connie's hair kerchiefed against the convertible's vortex of desert wind.

They mimicked their own parents cutting lose on a Saturday night, mirroring what it meant to be an *adult*, grasping at brief desperate pleasures in a world that urged only work and death.

We pulled up to the parties, not in slacks and blazers, but in shorts and thrift store bowling shirts, boots made for combat. We tore up perfectly good clothes, spray painted over brand new Hanes tees our moms had just bought us.

We costumed ourselves not as the adults who raised us, but as the

impoverished of the inner cities, or perhaps those furious UK kids, hopeless and on the dole.
Our drink of choice not a smart Old Fashioned, but beer-bonged 40s of Colt, sucked down in haste to oblivion.
We were college-aged kids ourselves now, at an age when our fathers wore *real* uniforms and traveled around the world to fight in a glorious war.

Larry pulled his Baja Bug in behind me and we carried the gear into the party.
We set up and played first in the cramped den, the room close enough that the microphone knocked into my mouth each song as the kids danced into us.
Our set was faster now.
We'd culled the setlist of the odd Judas Priest and Runaways songs, the goofy takes on Devo and the Monkees.
We played frantic takes on The Germs and Dickies, *Dead Kennedys*.
The Ramones remained.

Though instead of the peppy "Blitzkrieg Bop," we played Dee Dee's love song to heroin, "Chinese Rocks."

We finished our set with "I Fought the Law," Chris dancing in front of us with birdlike flaps of his arms, Doug and Duane slamming into each other like rams delirious in rut.
As I knelt on the ground rolling up guitar cords, Steve from The Hated walked past and snapped his fingers in front of my face.
"Not bad, kid," he said with his perfected sneer. "But don't you get tired of playing those *covers of covers*?"

The Hated played then, but I didn't recognize any of the songs until they played "Bodies" by the Pistols.
"Here's another one off the demo tape, suckers," Steve, the singer, shouted into the microphone. "And we got tickets for the Nest on us, hit me up and I'll make you a deal."

I realized they were playing *original* songs now.

And were about to play at an actual *club*.

I felt my face flush with the realization that they had beaten us to the next step: they were writing songs.

I stood in the tiny kitchen, the band just visible over the bobbing heads and swinging arms. They played eight or nine original songs that night, and though I could identify a wiry copped riff from Dead Kennedys or the melodic alarm of a Pistols song here and there, those fuckers had done it themselves.

As if from above, I suddenly saw the folly in what we were doing. We were using punk as a shortcut, simply copying what had been created, and this in a musical form that championed originality and boundless style.

Andy was out there in front of the band, dancing with his friends, the cooler kids who had easily identified The Hated as the proper flavor. And their chosen band was the one playing now and moving forward. Lisa came up to me in the kitchen and said something. I shook my head then leaned down to her mouth.

"I said, you guys sounded great tonight. Why don't you play the Batman song anymore?"

I saw the room shimmer, as if the music gave off waves of heat, felt the concrete foundation shift with the force of a dozen teenaged bodies jumping to the beat.

Hands on crotches, the hallway lined with bodies waiting for the bathroom, a tiny jar of drugs being slipped from hand to hand. Saturday night in America.

I felt Lisa's warm breath in my ear as she spoke.

I imagined a quick lick of her tongue and the dark room wrestling that might follow.

We would not marry but move to Paris and live in a freezing flat in the Latin Quarter, parent a dark-eyed child who would eventually destroy a million lives in the name of a God only he heard.

Then she floated backward a few steps before turning and dancing back into the party.

And I thought to myself: *that* could be a song.

FOUR

There's a photograph that pops up now and then of the Blue & White parked on a dark city street.

It appears on social media without reason. Perhaps some evil algorithm has reminded the user that it has been exactly one year since it has been seen.

It drifts back into my life like a stubborn ghost immune to exorcism. Old prints digitized, rendered immortal by a series of zeroes and ones: that we even took photos during that summer is either sheer luck or a curse.

Kimm had the last-minute foresight to pack a simple Kodak 110 camera along, and somehow kept track of the little cassettes of exposed film, protected them all summer like unhatched eggs.

The constant digital capture of every mundane moment now, a high-resolution digital camera in everyone's pocket, makes these print images seem ancient and noteworthy by comparison.

The unfocused grain gives the old photos a historical gravitas, like those coppery tintypes from the Civil War.

So the embarrassing little moments of my past live on, photos showing the shocking hemline of OP shorts in the early '80s, say, or some horrid shots of the disastrous experiment in cowboy boots and teased hair we experimented with as that decade ended.

But when this one photo pops up I always stop and look at it again, and smile. It is filled with motion and sound, and I see those photos and feel the city sweat, hear the pulse of reggae, taste the thick perfume of weed.

The van is parked on a street, shredded newspaper piled up to the windows, some of it still airborne as the picture was taken.

Chris behind the wheel, Jay in a straw cowboy hat.

Jack peers out from the dark recesses of the Blue & White.

Kimm is on the ground, his eyes closed at the moment of capture, but I

know we are all laughing.
The sliding door is open, a yard-high pile of torn newspaper spilled
from the van to the gutter, Doug spread atop it, his feet sticking up like
a hamster upturned on its bed of wood shavings.

And when that photo appears once again, people come across it and
comment (*What the?…*), then ask for details.
A hot night in the Lower East Side, I tell them, if I am in the mood to
respond beyond a wan blue thumbs up.
The middle of a long tour, drunk and happy.

The big NYC show was at Great Gildersleeves.
We ramped up toward this show, anticipating our heroic return to the
city.
In the back of my mind, I dreaded the weeks after this pinnacle, our
route curving back toward the west and, out there, the end of this tour.
Like the day after summer solstice, the sunlight just a breath shorter,
the first day of school now visible on the horizon like a charging beast.

We played a stacked bill with Murphy's Law, Adrenalin O.D.,
Whipping Boy, and Even Worse. The cover charge was seven bucks.
The room was only half full, due to the Bad Brains deciding to throw a
last-minute free gig down the street at CBGBs, supposedly in protest to
the high cover charge at our gig.

As so often happens, such an anticipated gig was destined to be just *off.*
Kimm's guitar amp blew, we flubbed some intros, we played too fast.
We took our guarantee though, and went straight to Danceteria, where
we promptly ran up a bar tab of three hundred dollars.
We bought rounds for anyone in earshot, pointed at primary-colored
liqueurs behind the bar and ordered shots.
We wandered from floor to floor like kids riding a department store
escalator on a Saturday afternoon.
Busting through the dancefloors, jumping around to early rap, techno,
and gay disco anthems with equal goofy abandon.
We ended up at the Park Inn, a tavern a couple blocks from A7.

It was a spare room with dim lighting and concrete floors, a bunker for getting seriously and steadily drunk.

A mix of reggae and soul played bass heavy, loud enough to emulsify the alcohol into your bloodstream. The room held a mix of punkers and mysterious Rasta dudes, their red-yellow eyes peeking out suspiciously from beneath a blind of dreadlocks.

Ike was the old guy running the place, a Black man who seemed just as perplexed by the mohawked white boys as the island medicine men, all drinking Red Stripes together at the bar, shoulders touching.

He treated us all with equal disdain, kicking someone out on the hour, shouting: *You ain't good enough, punk!* as he 86'd another soul into the night.

When we finally piled out of the club, we saw stacks of the morning paper piled on the sidewalk.

And without word, we each brought a bundle into the van and started tearing at it, making our own confetti to celebrate the night.

Paper flew as the stereo blared "Complete Control;" tiny strips of origami took flight.

The headline in the *NY Times* that morning was TOXIC BLAZE UPSTATE LEAVES LINGERING CLOUD OF CONFUSION, and these words flew about separate, out of context and somehow prophetic, *TOXIC-CONFUSION-BLAZE.*

We left an impressive pile of shredded newspaper in front of the bar when we finally drove away, like the collected ticker tape after an astronaut is paraded down Broadway. As we pulled away Ike came out to the curb, and seeing the trash in our wake started chasing us down the street, furious at the rubbish.

I could see him pointing after us yelling into the night, and though he appeared to be lip syncing along to Joe Strummer's voice over the shuddering Blaupunkt, I knew what he was really saying: *You ain't good enough, punks!*

I woke up in the van, windows closed, blazing hot.

I sat up on the front bench and saw that the Blue & White was parked in front of Jack Rabid's place on Eldridge.

I heard a groan behind me and looked back to see Doug stretched out with an arm across his face, shielding his eyes from the daylight.

We threw open the doors and gasped for air.

Doug and I walked to the corner bodega for a jug of cold water that we gulped as we sat on the sidewalk, sharing the small shadow thrown by the Blue & White.

The air already heated, fragrant as bus exhaust.

"You know, we had a couple ladies in there," Doug said, gesturing toward the van with the plastic jug. "You wouldn't wake up, man."

"You're fucking kidding me," I said. "How'd you manage that… it was almost light."

I tried to think back through the night for a gap in the plot, but I had the full document intact: no blackout.

"Couple hookers, Black gals," Doug said. He shook his head and grinned to himself. "*You too drunk honey,*" he said in a high southern accent, "that's what they kept saying. Hell, I couldn't get it up anyway. I think the other one was patting you down for money."

I shrugged, felt at my pockets then, though I didn't recall holding any of the money.

I tried to imagine a woman, her skin glistening with sweat, hovering over me. Trying to discover commerce or willing organ, disappointed in either case.

We spent Monday afternoon slowly regrouping, taking turns showering in Jack's single bathroom between shifts guarding the van.

The gear sat visible through the back windows, vulnerable to the junkies and thieves who sensed a new treasure parked in their neighborhood. We started to recognize the same two or three guys who circled the block all day and nicknamed them "the hyenas."

I went with Jay and Chris up to 48th Street to drop off Kimm's blown
amp at a music shop, and then we walked through Times Square.
It was still filthy and great there, just before the Disney store and the
corporate family restaurants ruined the grimy fun zone.
After standing under the giant billboards for a while, we walked
towards 8th Avenue, pulled to the sleaze of that block.

We walked along the peep shows and porn theaters, the barkers
grabbing at our elbows trying to usher us into black hallways, hinting at
the dark delights just beyond. We finally relented, going into one huge
theater, its bulb-framed marquee lit up even in the stark light of day.
Show World, its blazing signage read, *69 Raw Films!*
Live Girls! it promised.
25¢ was in dominant font on each side of the marquee, apparently the
price to witness either.

We pushed through a second door and found ourselves in front of racks
of filth, display cases filed with complicated looking gadgets, tools
frilled and curved toward unholy crevices, specialized and horrific as
18th century surgical instruments.
I pointed out an 18-inch dildo, black and shiny, scary as a police baton.
"What in the Sam Hill...," said Chris.
Jay came back to us with a handful of quarters he'd just changed. He
pressed some coins into each of our palms, then nodded to a turnstile at
the back of the store. He shook his fistful of coins to his ear like dice,
said, "Shall we?"

I stood in a darkened booth, the only light coming from a lit coin slot
below a framed panel. My hightops felt weighted to the sticky floor, as
if on a planet with a slightly greater gravitational pull, releasing with an
audible *schmick!* each time I shuffled my feet.
It smelled of Pinesol and cigarette smoke, and just beyond that, an
infused funk: the timeless smell of *pussy* and generations of spilled jizz.

I fit a quarter into the slot and a panel suddenly lifted in the frame.
My window looked into a round room, its radius vast enough to spare

you a view into your neighbor's window.

The room was filled with women, in lingerie and bikinis, some naked save for fluffed slippers or 5-inch pumps.

It was like peering into the girl's locker room, but here the team uniforms consisted of track marks and cesarean scars.

A heavy blonde woman suddenly appeared at my window and peered in at me. "Hey there, cutie," she said between sideways chomps of chewing gum. "So what's it…" and then the screen lowered again, shutting her off in mid chomp.

I stood in the booth and considered escape, but she knocked at the window. "Hey, where'd ya go? Put all your coins in the slot, babe."

I fed another quarter into the slot, the panel raised again, then she watched patiently as I fed the remaining coins into the slot.

"Ok, babe, that all ya' got? So, top or bottom?" she asked.
"Pardon? Top or bottom what?"
And here she sighed, turned away to roll her eyes at a co-worker.
I heard a voice from the booth next to me, unmistakably Chris.
"Giddyup, sister!" the voice said. *"Heavens to Betsy!"*

"Top or bottom?" Then, more forcefully: "Tits or ass, buddy? What's it gonna be?"
I hesitated, too long for her liking, apparently. She suddenly thrust her naked chest through the window into my tiny room. Then she reached in blindly, grabbed my left hand by the wrist and guided it to her breast.

"Ok, buddy," I heard her muffled voice say from just above my view, "go to town. No pinching, huh?"

And so I stood there, on a Monday afternoon in New York City, with a woman's warm tit in my hand.
I moved a thumb slowly across her nipple, unyielding as a callous or scar, then stopped.
For some reason I thought then of *Guys and Dolls*, that glorious intro scene with all the cartoon colored grifters strutting about Times Square. Frank Sinatra and Marlon Brando sitting a block away at Mindy's, their

depravity glorified by a catchy Frank Loesser score.
Nathan, Nathan Detroit... I may have audibly hummed while I simply held the heft of her breast in my hand, motionless, feeling the mammary gravity in my sweating palm.

I thought of the scores of men around me, desperate for human touch, or perhaps just drunk businessmen killing time after a 3-martini lunch. Their loneliness extinguished momentarily, like a peckish hunger held off by a saltine cracker.

She stepped back and lowered her head back into the window. "Hey, what the fuck, you ain't even got your cock out yet? C'mon buddy, let's go."

She reached in again, her hand sweeping the booth now, grabbing at me as I backed away towards the door. I began, for some reason, laughing. And among that circle, the men silent and intent as monks flagellating away on their own personal vows, my laughter enraged her.
She swatted her arms through the air, and it gave me an animal thrill. I dodged her, both of my hands guarding my groin where, to my surprise, I felt the tightness of arousal.

O sweet Jesus, I heard Chris croak from the next booth.

As the panel started to lower again, she pulled her hands back away from me and looked at me one last time.

She lowered her head with the closing door, keeping her eyes on me, and just before it shut completely, I heard her whisper *"freak."*

I walked out to the street where the blue evening was dropping down on the city again.
The marquees and lit storefronts kept the street bright, an unnatural glow like a summer day recreated from a shattered memory.
I stood out there waiting for Jay and Chris and I suddenly remembered Doug's story of hookers in the van.

And it occurred to me I'd disappointed two sex working women within the same day.
Failing them both in the simplest of transactions.

The first songs I wrote were stolen, of course.
Or *homage* to the songs we'd learned and covered in the band up until then.
Like an infant burping up those first syllables of *ma* or *da,* we were simply repeating the 3-chord language we had heard.
Those greats of rock and roll who so selfishly used up every combination of *A to D to E* so that every song after would be a mere cover.
I kept to the dots on the guitar neck, writing almost every song in friendly major keys, and none of this minor crap.

Kimm and I knew we liked short songs, simple songs, with short or, better yet, no guitar solos.
And melody.
The first song was "You Make Me Feel Cheap," a straight rip of Aerosmith's "Mama Kin." It's unremarkable, except the dude in the song is the one who is left used and abandoned.
But I could at least point to that and say, *there*: I did that, it's ours.

We spent the next few months in the garage trying new songs on each other, sometimes playing through one of our beloved cover songs then sitting down and trying to figure out just what it was we liked about them.
Looking for the elusive riff or hook that grabbed us, an autopsy in search of the mysterious cause of death.

I took the Clash's "Safe European Home" apart and salvaged the pulsing verse for "I Got a Gun."
The falling melody against a held chord of the Plimsouls' "Now:" that's the chorus bridge in "I Wanna Know Why."

We justified the theft, covered our crime by changing key or tempo, easy as switching license plates on a stolen car.

We were writing fast now, reenergized by the thought of replacing songs in our setlist with originals, racing to get up to ten of our own, as if we were on a deadline.
Kimm came in with "Waiting in the Wings," a song whose genius was in its simplicity, like an outtake from The Jam's "In the City."
We wrote songs that made us crack up at inside jokes, wrote some so terrible they were played once and never mentioned again.

I would write awful, sincere lyrics, of course, double checking the spelling on "obsequious" before placing it in the lyric like a coin dropped in a septic tank.
Shameless, I copped "I Wanna Know Why" from Hemingway's young boy who sat by his father's horse-trampled corpse, starting the song with *…In our time,* from the story collection.

Other times, I would read the comic page and take the first lines off one of the corny old serial strips when I was stumped for an opening line.
I hope you know this ain't a social call, some tough holding a gun threatens Rex Morgan MD.
We've been through this before, a concern out of context, a bubble above Mary Worth's worried brow.

Our collection of songs grew quickly and mirrored our love of pop and punk, heavy metal.
We used the fierce tempos of the punk songs we loved, yearned for the heart-aching melody of those '70s bubblegum classics.
We wrote a pop song for every thrash song, still unsure if we might end up a punk or power pop band.

Kimm came in one day with a climbing riff, played in a G flat (E sharp? Dunno; it's one without a dot) followed by a logical verse and chorus pattern.
We learned to play it and found its urgent energy, structured around that irresistible riff, then released to a soaring verse.

It was probably our first original-sounding song, and I was inspired to go beyond ripping off a class syllabus or the funny pages.

In the Cerritos house the kitchen sat on the west corner, and in the early summer evenings the room was bathed in the glowing light of sunset. A twilight moment of final brilliance, as if the sun was a flickering light bulb flaring up just before burnout.
I sat in the TV room just off the kitchen, doing homework while watching a rerun of *Twilight Zone*. A young boy takes command of a party, ordering the grownups around, wishing the doomed into the cornfield.
Mom and *Bachan* were busying themselves in the kitchen, still cooking enough for eight, though it would be just the three of us eating.
On my lap Vonnegut's *Slaughterhouse Five* bookmarked to the firebombs raining down on Dresden.
On the TV, the boy silences the party with a squint of his eyes, threatens the cornfield treatment with a wave of his hand.
I must admire the easy cruelty of this child and wonder if he will become a prophet or politician when he grows up.
I am aware of another sound beyond the TV, the *swish shwisha shwish* of my *Bachan* washing the nightly rice.
She stands at the sink, running water over the grains.
Running her hands through the rice in a practiced figure eight, a precise tempo, a muscle memory of seventy years.
I think of the daily preparation of the family's *gohan*, a comforting constant throughout her long life.
The days of happiness with a young family, the nights of worry in a prison barrack.
She will clean the rice and empty it into the cooker, wait for the chime that lets her know it is ready.
The first tiny bowl is served to her dead husband as she burns another stick of incense on his shrine.

I am angered suddenly, mad at the planes for dropping napalm on those beautiful European cities and innocent flesh.
Mad at this tyrannical brat who transforms a man's cervical spine into a

loosely wound spring.

Furious at the thought of my grandmother herded into a stable like cattle.

Saddened by the thought of my young mother on a bus north, holding onto her last shred of grace as if it were a piece of floating detritus in the wake of a shipwreck.

I write, then name the song "Manzanar."

I get out of the shower at Jack Rabid's place and stand dripping in the tiny bathroom. The walls are an unnatural shade of blue, brushed thick over countless layers of leaden paint.

I consider the families that have lived and died within these rooms, the tiny triumphs and crushing heartbreaks endured by generations of immigrants huddled together four floors up.

In the mirror Johnny Thunders peeks over my shoulder, a Heartbreakers poster pasted to the opposite wall.

Johnny wears a fedora with a syringe stuck in the band.

Cool and tragic, the instrument of both his inspiration and demise hovering above him like a halo.

The window cracked open just enough to peer out at the rooftops alongside, shimmering as the day's heat is returned to the evening sky, tar paper and brick surrendering their energy to the night.

We were headed out to New Jersey for a Tuesday night gig, nobody really moving too fast or saying much about it.

Kimm was on the phone as I dressed, shaking his head at me as I sniffed at T shirts and socks pulled from my duffle. I knew by his look that another gig had been canceled or postponed, adding yet another loopy backtrack to our journey.

I left the apartment then, Kimm holding up his pen in farewell, phone still pressed to his ear.

Down on the street I found the van locked.

I looked around for Chris and Doug, knowing they couldn't have gone far from the gear.

I discovered them sitting in the small park just up the street, sitting on a bench, holding quarts of beer.

They were talking to some old women while the neighborhood enjoyed the shadows of the evening.

I went into the little bodega and grabbed a quart bottle of Miller myself, went to join them.

We sat there on wooden benches, sipping at the sweating beers.
The ladies didn't say much, just grunted laughs at our silly conversation and kept their eyes on their men playing dominoes on the picnic tables nearby.
It would be fine, I was thinking, to just sit here all night.
Chatting with the neighbors, hearing the clack of the dominoes, taking turns complaining about the heat.
We could take turns going back to the bodega for more beers, getting some slices for dinner later; I had no desire to get back into the van.
But then Kimm came out of the apartment, Jay and Jack trailing, and he waved us over to the Blue & White.

We finished our giant beers, bowed to the ladies, and got back in the van.

Everyone was pretty quiet on the drive down to New Jersey, the glow of NYC behind us as we rode the turnpike south yet again, Chris reached up to the visor and pulled out a cassette, shoved it into the Blaupunkt.
And then the song came on, Misfits' "Where Eagles Dare."

I sat in the passenger seat and listened to the song as if hearing it for the first time.
I was aware of the communion, all of us soon singing along when he came to the *goddamned son of a bitch* line, of course, but also of the singular connection.
A song somehow energizing us, leading us from the malaise of a hot summer evening to the stage door.
The thrill of music, a transformative ritual in two minutes nine seconds.
Someone sat down, in a bedroom or at a piano in the living room and wrote that song.

Kimm leaned up between the seats and turned down the stereo, right in the middle of the glorious outro, everyone still singing along at full

186

blast.

"You know, Glenn said to swing by and pick him up," and here he nodded to the stereo knob he still held between thumb and index finger. "Danzig. *Him.*"

Kimm, on one of his black-market card calls that day, had rung up Glenn and invited him to the Jersey show.

"He said he'd come to the gig but needed a ride. Why?" Kimm said, noticing my silence. "Is that weird?"

"I dunno," I answered. "I guess it never really occurred to me you could just...*call him.*"

I met Glenn once when Misfits were out playing in Santa Barbara, but I was still astonished to be in the same room with the people who wrote *those songs.*

And whenever I did find myself backstage or at soundcheck chatting with our heroes I was struck mute.

We were fans just a year before and now we shared a stage with these people.

I was always prepared for someone to tap me on the shoulder and ask to see some pass or wristband that would prove us worthy to be there, before being escorted through a maze of hallways back to join the other *fans.*

We pulled up at a regular old NJ suburban pad, and after a polite knock that rattled the screen door, who answered but Glenn Danzig.

He invited us all in and we followed him down to a basement room.

And though I'd imagined some sort of dungeon lit by torches (when we pulled up to his house Jack admitted surprise; thought Glenn would live in a haunted castle or at least a trailer on the edge of a graveyard), it was just a tidy rumpus room turned office.

There were tables covered with T shirts, boxes of vinyl, rolls of posters.

Everywhere the Crimson Ghost mascot grinned down at us.

He offered us glasses of water, passed around EvilLive T-shirts for us each.

We gave him a copy of *After the Lights Go Out* and one of the last remaining tour T shirts, then we stood and chatted a bit in quiet tones about people we knew in common, clubs to avoid, shitty promoters that still owed.

I listened to Glenn and Kimm talking shop, but my mind was back in the van with the Blaupunkt blasting "Teenagers from Mars" and "London Dungeon."

I thought of those songs that captured melody and rage, remarkable in context, written in fucking 1978 while we were still juniors at Cerritos and just discovering our beloved Cheap Trick.

And now I was there, probably in the room where the songs were written, sipping New Jersey water from a mason jar.

I knew it was connected, and though I rejected any notion of destiny, I felt marked in that place and moment, experienced a slight tingle of spine, like a faint electrical current seeking ground.

Then he shook his devil lock free from behind his ear and brought it down over his forehead and pointed to the stairs.

"All right then," he said, summoning his chesty roar for the first time, "Let's go." Just before he shut the screen door behind us, in the same familiar baritone, yelled back into the house: "Bye, Dad!"

We insisted Glenn sit shotgun, and he pointed out local landmarks (*here's where Jimmy got clobbered, that there's where Jerry flipped the Camaro*), as we drove in the twilight towards the club.

When Glenn suggested we make a stop before the gig, I naturally assumed we were going to some dark bar.

Maybe a horror-themed speakeasy with Amazonian bartenders who dressed like Elvira and served smoking drinks out of tiny skull goblets.

But when we pulled into a strip mall parking lot, we got out and discovered ourselves at, of all things, a video arcade.

A goddamned *arcade*—and no beer taps in sight.

Glenn jumped out, looked into the flashing parlor, and then motioned back to us to follow.

And yes, that is how we prepared for the gig: not in our usual search of intoxicated momentum, but in a *bleeping booping* video arcade, quarters in hand.
And then we each wandered off, into the maze of flashing machinery, called back to the liquor stores and pizza parlors of Cerritos, to the screens that filled so many summer days.

I rediscovered my love/hate relationship with Centipede as Doug challenged all comers to Ms. Pac Man.
Jackie and Jay took on the local junior high kids in a fierce air hockey game as Glenn and Kimm went into the old school pinball gallery.

On the way out we encountered the new Dragon's Lair game in the corner.
An animated game that incorporated movie graphics in a rather clunky choose-your-path sort of plot, it was really a groundbreaker back then. We gathered around it and watched, amazed.

I saw Glenn staring at the game and could imagine his thoughts.
The world of dark fantasy where he roamed merged with a new technology, bringing the gaming experience ever closer to the cinema that he loved.
I saw then, all those old movies probably watched in that basement den, the Saturdays spent with some corny old TV host, the cheesy horrors films, the classics starring Marilyn when she was already visibly shattered on screen.
These, *this*. This is where songs come from.

We played a great set in front of a constantly churning pit. We played well due to the lack of alcohol in our systems and having Glenn crouched on the side of the stage, watching.
Glenn jumped on stage during the closer of "Wetspots," shouting the chorus into Jay's mic.

We dodged the stage divers who started crowding the stage.
They took turns jumping back into the pit like kids awaiting their turn at the high dive into the urine-soaked community pool.
And after a moment of surprised recognition, Glenn was promptly dog piled on, the kids keeping their hometown legend in check, all in good cheer.

We dropped him off at his curb, all of us sweaty and sober, smiling at the unexpected night we'd just had.
We said our goodbyes and drove away, leaving Glenn standing at the curb, his arm raised in farewell.
I watched for a bit in the side view as we pulled away, and then he turned to go back into his house.
Maybe to sit and write his next song, somehow inspired by a night out with a bunch of California knuckleheads.
I slipped the cassette back into the stereo and the chugging intro to "Hollywood Babylon" blasted from the speakers.
Then all of us sang together again.
Who came along for the ride....

The last week of winter break, as the year turned to 1981 (without John Lennon or Darby Crash-both punk souls lost to Christmas mayhem), we recorded a demo tape.
I was now working alongside Kimm and Chris at the Wild West clothing store by the mall, mainly to avoid the disapproving glances from Mom.
I had found a daily routine of sleeping well into the afternoon, only to descend the stairs and eat the huge meals *Bachan* prepared for me before returning to my room to work on songs and staying just ahead of my schoolwork.
Then, practice. And then: get drunk.
I luckily got assigned to the small shoe department at the back of the store, spending my days dusting off the outrageously priced cowboy boots and retrieving boxes of cheap Keds for frazzled moms.

I'd toss boxes of half sizes on the floor, leaving them to lace up the
shoes for their sticky brats.

The shoe department was under a faux wooden awning, the shoes
shelved against a wall painted like an old west saloon front.

Hammering the *Olde West* theme home, a few weathered barrels were
used as display tables, and a sign on the wall promised *Root Beer, One
Nikkle* next to a set of fake saloon doors.

The store was filled with such western hokum to the point our
nametags were shaped like little sheriff's badges.

Sometimes I would put on one of the stiff cowboy hats no one ever
bought (we traded almost exclusively in OP and Hang Ten surf wear)
and I'd waddle bowlegged over to hectic "Trouser Gulch," where
Kimm would be inevitably re-stacking his ruined piles of corduroy.

I'd point to my badge and give him a lazy tip of my hat.

"We're going after Bart, that rascal," I'd say. "I need ten good men to
ride."

He'd flip me off, and I'd mosey back to finish my lazy day in,
yes, *Boot Hill.*

Chris got a job at the *Checkout Corral*, the lucky bastard, and spent his
shifts flirting with the girls coming through the front.

We were encouraged to greet the customers with "Howdy," which I
never did, except to one woman.

She was large framed but beautiful, maybe thirty-five, with meticulous
makeup and hair.

One of those stunning college beauties who battled the extra fifteen
pounds gained in birthing her lousy husband's snotty kids.

She'd come in without fail every Wednesday that I worked.

"Howdy, ma'am," I would greet her in my best Eastwoodian growl,
and she would simply nod to me and finger the strand of pearls spilling
down to her cleavage.

She'd then point at the same pair of Candies (Rose Gold Stiletto Heeled
Mules) each time and say "nine and a half please," our only words

spoken.

I would fetch the shoes from the stockroom, pulling them out from behind the dusty boxes of Tony Lama ostrich boots where I hid the same pair after each of her visits, lest one of the other guys actually sell them and end our little charade.

Then I would bring them out with a flourish, drop down onto a little stool in front of her where she already had a perfumed, stockinged foot bared and resting upon the inclined ramp that pointed right to my crotch.

I would take a shoe from the tissue paper, and, holding her firm ankle in one hand, guide her silky foot into the heel I held in solemn presentation. She would look down at the shoe, twisting her foot back and forth to get a better view, lifting her foot up and flexing her ankle so the heel would shimmy inches from my lap.

Then she'd bring her other foot to the stool where we repeated the ritual, slower this time, my hand sometimes daring higher to her plump calf as I fit her into the matching shoe.

We would sit there still, she never standing to appraise the shoe further, me never asking about the fit.

Then she would sigh, simply shake her head, and put on her own shoes and leave.

I would retreat to the backroom to hide the shoes until next time and will my raging hard on to settle down before going back out to the Wild West for the rest of my shift.

A demo tape is just that: a demonstration of a band's ability.

Hope and dreams all smashed onto a C60 cassette.

These would supposedly then be sent out with all the desperate hope (and approximately the same chance of success) as a letter in a bottle, flung into the foam by a shipwrecked lunatic.

We truly had no intentions of sending it out, it was just another thing you did as a band.

We thought it would be fun to get that perspective.

The chance (as everyone does, without fail, when hearing their own

voice on a tape recording) to ask: *is that what I really sound like?*
Kimm and I pooled our meager part time pay checks (minimum wage,
$3 point 35 fucking cents an hour!) and reported to the
tiny *Stabbaj* studio in Bellflower where all the local bands did their
hopeful demo tapes.

It was our first time in a studio, and we loaded reverently into the tiny,
converted garage, careful not to knock over the exotic looking
microphones on crane-necked stands.
Joe, the studio owner and engineer, was a dead ringer for Jerry Garcia
and wore a perpetually bemused, stoned smile beneath his shaggy
beard.
He kept a huge Nazi flag behind his office desk, not for any crazed
affiliation, but just for the Lampoon-ian shock value.

He dug the thought of a punk band visiting his studio, and helpfully
pointed out where to set up amps, asking if we had a favored speaker to
mic up before baffling the cabinets away in tiny cubicles to prevent
bleed over.
We waited while Joe coaxed a passable drum sound from Burton's
drums, plugging cables into different outboard boxes like connecting
calls on an old-time switchboard.
He made adjustments that were imperceptible to me as Burton
continued to smack the snare for twenty solid minutes.
Finally satisfied, he had the rest of us go out into the studio and put on
actual headphones, strap on guitars.
We tuned, then tuned again, then looked at each other.
Burton was hidden behind a nest of microphone stands and blackboard-
sized baffles, Larry in front of him with his quarantined bass cabinet,
Kimm and I on opposite sides of the room.
We counted off *take one* and then slashed away at our instruments,
finding the weird signal of our amps: compressed and isolated, jarringly
featured in detail.
A sound barely recognizable through the headphones.
The song seemed to come at us a millisecond after our strumming, like

a badly dubbed movie.

But Joe assured us he was getting a good signal and after tuning the guitars yet again, we tracked five songs within an hour.

"I Got a Gun" and "Manzanar," of course, then our pop songs, "Make Me Feel Cheap" and "I Wanna Know Why."

Ahead of schedule, we decided to lay down one more song, "Mannequin," which clocked in at a nifty 88 seconds.

We did a quick pass looking for places to put in guitar leads, punching in only a few brief seconds in half the songs.

We listened to the basic tracks, amazed at the cleanliness and separation, each drum and cymbal, guitars and bass coming together in rough mix.

The songs shook the beers in our hands as Joe put the tracks through the gargantuan attic speakers and pushed the master sliders all the way up.

We listened, each of us with closed eyes and head down as if in prayer, waiting for a glaring mistake that would ruin the track.

Joe set up a single condenser microphone in the studio, the mic guarded by what looked like a small circle of pantyhose.

It looked like a de-tasseled dream catcher, a device that supposedly kept the popping P's from ruining a vocal take.

I took my place-*alone*-in front of the microphone, put on headphones, and flipped through the lyric sheets I had neatly typed up on my mom's regal IBM Selectric.

I checked the microphone, leaning close enough that my nose brushed the silken fabric, giving me a brief groin tingle as I was suddenly reminded of those lovely stockinged feet pushing into my crotch.

We went through the tracks, and I sang the songs in one or two takes, amazing Joe when I insisted on moving on without listening to playback.

I did not want to let up, did not want to think about where I was or what I was doing, but instead out of body and hovering just above.

Effortlessly, like a teenager from a red planet 200 million miles away,

floating through blackness.
Like guiding a bucking motorcycle around a track with just a gloved
fingertip.
Or seducing a lonely housewife without a word.

*O*ur last day in New York, I got out on the street early.
I left Doug in the van across from Jack Rabid's place, sleeping face down on the front bench, his legs sticking out of the open sliding door.

A few remaining strips of newsprint fluttered around the gutter.

The neighbors had grown accustomed to the Blue & White parked on the street, one or all of us hovering nearby, watching the gear, drinking beers in the park with the doors open, stereo loud.

The street people wary enough now they would cross the street to pass instead of hovering nearby, brick in hand.

I walked up 2nd Avenue, stopping first in front of St. Mark's church.

I peered up to the cross crowning the steeple, splined against the white morning sky, a weathervane unmoved by neither breeze nor dedicated horror.

Beneath, in the ancient nave, poetry was praised each New Year's Day.

I cut through Union Square, getting grabbed three different times by the elbow, whispered offers of weed, blow, blowjob.

There were sidewalk merchants, glittering junk and books offered hopefully on blankets along the tree lined edge of the park.

I slowed to browse; my head tilted to read a few titles.

I stopped and picked up a paperback copy of *Indian Journals*.

An old Black woman sitting on a milkcrate watched me put it back down, saying, *"Ginsberg, ooh that dirty cat!"* as I walked on.

After slashing diagonally up Broadway, I turned left on 23rd, the ship-like prow of the Flatiron threatening to crush me in its wake.

I pivoted west, then came to the Chelsea Hotel.

There I stood, smoking a cigarette under its striped awning, waiting for something wonderful or tragic to happen.

Behind me, Sid stood, the fated imbecile, as Nancy bled out.

Room 100 soon awash in blood as he presses his hands to the slash,
trying to stop the flow.
Her final heartbeat pumps a trickle down the hall, past Dylan Thomas'
room just as he finally succumbs to that good night.
A finger of crimson finally reaching under a doorsill where William
Burroughs sits in a hard backed chair.
He suddenly thinks of his own murdered wife for the first time in
twenty-seven years.

I ended at McSorley's after cutting through the Village, barely glancing
up at The Bitter End where the fucking hippies or beatniks saw fit to
revive folk music.
I drank two tiny mugs of dark beer beneath the chandeliers of spider
web and wishbone, desperate charms thrown overhead by departing
soldiers, men on their way to die overseas.
I suddenly had the sensation of physically shrinking, the floor dropping
as the ceiling rose, the vertiginous trick of Disney's *Haunted Mansion*
lobby.
The magnificent weight of history looming both before and after me,
the cobwebs and bleached bones stretching further into the heavens as
the wooden floor sunk, heavy with the weight of spilled alcohol and
doomed tears.

I knew then I could never understand this city, though its filth and glory
would continue to draw me back.
Perhaps I had found the American history that had escaped me in D.C.
The buildings of poetry and murder, the avenues and streets awash with
bodily fluid, alive with stink and smoke, steam rising like spirits
escaped from Purgatory.

That night we played our last show in the city, at CBGBs.
Estranged twin to the Whisky, CBGBs had that same storied lore that
was reduced to something smaller at load in, the houselights
illuminating the filthy corners and dog shit on the floor.
Empty and damp, like a morgue waiting for bodies after a local

disaster.

Ready for the characters and the music that would transform the room into the *club*.

We played after a stacked bill: Government Issue, Urban Waste, Jimmy popping up yet again with Murphy's Law.

It was a Saturday night set with no expectations, but as we got on stage and plugged in the amps the crowd was already jumping and yelling.

We were exhausted from our week in that crazy fucking town, humbled and buzzing still, yet not quite ready to leave.

We stood upon those creaking boards for a moment before launching into a grand set, then used that filthy toilet and drank until closing with that crew of fiends.

Both the kids born of those streets and the freak transplants drawn to the city, destined to walk those same streets reverently, seeking their own history; following a migratory pull to that place, deep as marrow.

Our final act in that city was watching Doug fight a crazed bum in an abandoned lot just past the Park Inn.

After stopping by Stromboli for some farewell slices, we stopped back at the Inn.

Ike threatened to kill us for the newspaper mess (seeing us walk in, he jumped up from his barstool and said, *"Uh uh, no way, fuckers, nope!"*), but we put two twenties down on the bar and he set up a row of icy Red Stripes, shaking his head.

An hour later I hurried from the bar at Jack's urging because Doug was getting into it with some dusted Black dude down the block.

When I got to the dark lot, I saw Doug throw a solid left at the guy's liver.

His opponent didn't flinch, just threw his head back and cackled into the night. Both shirtless, the dirt sticking to their sweating torsos making each of them a dusky matte in the streetlight, black and white neutralized in filth.

Doug delivered a roundhouse right to the bum's head, then ducked a counter before they both fell to the ground, grappling, clawing at each other's faces. The bum stumbled to his feet, rising with a bottle in his hand.

He brought it down toward Doug's head, but it deflected as Doug nodded to the right, the bottle thudding audibly into his shoulder.

The bum yelled again, a feral howl, and as Jack and I came closer to them I could see his eyes were unfocused, crazed.

Doug backed away, but the man was still taking practiced jabs at the empty air. His footwork shuffling in the dust, showing skills etched in muscle memory, perhaps a past in Golden Gloves that survived still within his madness.

He swung at the demons surrounding him on a distant plane, a terror both a million miles away and there inside his head.

They came together and traded punches again, the smack of fist on flesh ringing out, grunts with each blow given and received.

Doug came up finally with a 2 x 4 and cracked it across the bum's shoulders, sending him down facedown to the ground.

He lay still, but still mumbled threats into the dirt.

As I helped Doug out to the sidewalk, brushing dirt off his back and checking for any deep wounds, a cop car pulled alongside.

A NYPD cop leaned out the passenger window, waving a flashlight into our eyes.

"What the hell," the cop said, as his beam traced from Doug's dusty form to the bum laying behind us in the dirt.

"He," Doug said, jerking a thumb toward the bum, "started it."

The cop looked at his partner, shook his head, then they both laughed.

"Oh, I'm sure he did. Hear that, Ed? Good ol' Smokie started it, he did." The flashlight beam hit me square in the eyes then. "Listen, where you fuckin' guys from?"

I spoke up then: *"Uh, California,"* I said after considering: LA? Cerritos? Disneyland?

"Ok, Hollywood, you guys get the hell out of here, and don't mess with these whackjobs. They're fucking crazy. What, you don't know that?" Then he shut off his torch, leaving the night to the yellowed streetlights again.

As they pulled away, the cop leaned out his window again.
"Hah, *California!*" he shouted.

We were still going to shows, Hollywood to the South Bay, but the
shows were bigger and more violent; thrilling.
The suit-jacket-wearing pop groups overshadowed now by hardcore:
Black Flag, FEAR, Circle Jerks, along with their legion of scary fans.
Bands playing to a more immediate code, songs stripped of all
pretenses of intro or solo, as if the urgency in their screamed message
could not be diluted with melody or lyrical innuendo.
A metamorphosis in reverse: like a butterfly changing into something
earthbound, uglier and wriggling in the dirt.
We went to see Black Flag at the Fleetwood, a dark warehouse packed
with mostly males, the testosterone buzz of battle palpable in the musty
air.
It was the first time I felt a real danger at a show, and I stood just on the
shore of the surging pit, willing myself finally to be swept in.
The pit was a living entity, wet and steaming with body heat.
I remembered the lifeguard's adage to swim along the current, parallel
to the distant shore when caught in a riptide.
And, elbows up, I would let the swirling mass of humanity carry me
along until I was back to my original spot.
Dez was singing for Black Flag then, and he stared out at the crowd
with a dark intensity.
Like De Niro in *Taxi Driver,* a loner wound tight, ready to explode.
I watched him command the crowd with ease, losing the microphone
into the crowd at one point, and getting it back with a single point of
his finger.

The Starwood in Hollywood became our favorite place to see bands,
and between sets you could hang out in the little side disco and request
songs from Rodney Bingenheimer himself.
Rodney was on the air on KROQ Saturday and Sundays, playing glam

and punk songs, sometimes premiering songs that would leak onto
daytime airplay.

We would gather at Kimm's house on Saturday nights, a pile of beers
on the dining table pyramided between us, and simply listen to the
radio.

Rodney would come on the air to the strains of MFQ's "This Could Be
The Night." Then he'd welcome us to the show in the most *non*-radio
voice, a charming and stilted everyman croak, before unleashing
another *amazing* playlist.

It was rumored that he would play a song on his show, unheard.
That a hopeful band could knock on the studio door, and he would
answer, accept an offered demo tape.

And the song would be on the air, gloriously ringing out the car stereo,
the jubilant band not even back to the onramp of the 210 Freeway.

He played Bowie and Monkees, Germs, Pistols-*everything.*
And that's when radio could truly come to life in a way that connected
all of us drunken brats, from the Valley to the tip of Orange County.
You couldn't believe you were hearing this on the radio, the vitality
and truth, guitars out of tune and singers shouting, the joy crackling.
And then Rodney would come back in with a friendly "all
right!" or "amazing!" and we could only smile and nod in agreement.
Like kids of the '40s, I imagined, lying on the living room floor in front
of the Motorola, enchanted, seeing the Lone Ranger ride the dusty
plains of their imaginations.

One night we went to see the Adolescents at the Starwood, copies of
our new demo tape in our pockets just in case Rodney was spinning
records in the disco room.

The Adolescents were getting daytime airplay from their
song "Amoeba" off the *Rodney on the Roq* compilation album.
It was wonderful, really, to hear a punk rock song played over
commercial radio in the light of day, a band of kids from nearby
Fullerton crafting a song of melody and energy.

A success for the tribe.

During one break in their set, a gentleman in suit jacket and tie came on stage to present them with some sort of plaques, probably commemorating their unlikely success.

But Tony, the singer, tossed the trophy across the room and chased the man off the stage.

We assumed it was just another punk rock moment, the denial of any of the standard rockstar trappings, or perhaps some backstage record deal gone sideways.

The band went back into their set, playing the songs off the Blue album, and the pit boiled once again.

We drove back home from Hollywood that night quietly.

Two copies of the demo tape still in each of our pockets, cued, heavy as unfired pistols.

As we passed the lights of downtown LA to our right, signaling the return path to the quiet bedrooms of Cerritos, we had a new goal in sight.

Both of us sharing parallel visions, yet not quite sure how to express the audacious hope that we too might someday play on one of these stages.

The Starwood was denied us forever of course, the club soon shuttered for good following some nasty business involving murder and porn stars, mismatched accounting, and piles of coke.

But on that one night, standing at the foot of the stage as Tony and the brothers Agnew, Casey, and, of course, *Steve Soto* played their timeless songs, we felt such proximity to a greatness happening *now*.

That man who came up onstage and was berated by the band, that was Robbie Fields.

Posh Boy, of the namesake record company that put out those glorious compilations.

And that we would have our lives entwined with all the characters listed here (and quickly, perhaps within the brief season a lowly grub might sprout gossamer wings to take flight), it's a part of this story that

I am tempted to pass over.

Unbelievable and happenstance, false as a fairy tale.

SEVEN

*W*e had a show in Boston* after leaving New York. While we loaded into the Rathskeller, Doug lay groaning in the Blue & White, touching at the various bruises and cuts along his body.

The doctor's son, I prescribed four beers and a half pint of Seagram's before heading back into the club.

We played two matinee sets, a doubleheader of sweat and mayhem in the dark basement, the day notable mainly for being fined fifty bucks by the mobbed-up promoter who claimed the second set was ten minutes *too short*.

Kimm took the cut pay (after realizing that, no, the unsmiling man in the office was *not* kidding), and we left for Upstate New York in the late afternoon.

As we reached the Connecticut River, the water dark under the long summer shadow, Jay reached between the front seats and pushed his own mix tape into the Blaupunkt.

When he originally brought out this cassette in the first days of the summer we rejected (and ejected) it after the first few songs: ZZ Top's newish "Gimme All Your Lovin'," Brownsville Station (and not the assumed "Smokin' in the Boy's Room," but the seven-minute space opus, "Martian Boogie!"), Undertones' fey "Teenage Kicks."
And then: Hall *and* fucking Oates.
Rather, we played our beloved Misfits mix until the tape stretched thin, went through *London Calling, Machine Gun Etiquette, Rodney on the Roq* I and II, on a nauseatingly regular rotation, before finally giving Jay's mix another listen somewhere in Tennessee.

Jay would point out the production value of the ZZ Top track; have us consider the punk spirit of Brownsville's weird song in context of 1977.

He asked us to *just listen* to the stuff, and on the long midnight drives along shattered back roads we finally did.

And then, forgive us, we even conjured a tender spot for *fucking Hall and Oates*, reaching for the volume knob when the malicious beat of "Maneater" came on. Next, "Sara Smile," (which I admittedly always thought was a soul standard from the '60s, perhaps sung by a Black man whose heartbreaking vocal came from being cheated a lifetime of royalties).

The crown to the trinity then: the pop perfection of "Kiss on My List." Great fucking songs we all had to finally admit to liking once our punk sneer was thawed by melody, by the unseen mastery and craft.

I opened up the Coleman and fished out two iced cans of Bud.

We hadn't had our beloved Coors since Colorado.

And though we enjoyed the novelty of the regional suds-the *Yoo-hoo* redolent *Shiner Bock* of Texas, those dirty ol' *Dixies* down South, the fun of ordering *Yuengling* aloud in Philadelphia- we were reduced to drinking musky Budweiser most of the time.

Budweiser, the lowest common denominator in every market across the country: the fucking *King* of Beers?

More a ruthless dictator self-crowned right there on their ubiquitous bowtied cans.

I popped the top of one and handed it over to Chris, but he took a squished look then shook his head before turning his eyes back to the road.

"Nah, man," he said. "We got any water onboard?"

"Water, hah," I said. I sucked down the offered beer in three long pulls, then crushed the can with a theatrical flair and tossed it into the well.

"Nasty stuff. What's that they say about water, that's where fish shit? Or is it where they fuck?"

I opened the other beer and took a taming sip off the top before settling it between my legs. "What, you hungover still?"

Chris kept his hands steady on the wheel, eyes on the turnpike heading west. Finally, he shrugged. "Jeez," he said, "are we going to drink every day? Like, *every* day?"

I felt my head jerk back a fraction with a momentary bobble of incomprehension.

"Well, I goddamn hope so, pal. I mean, isn't that the point?" And here I brought the can of beer up again and took a long swig, catching the eye of a nine-year-old boy sitting in the back of a wood paneled station wagon we were just then passing.

"Ah. I dunno'," Chris said.

He looked into the rearview, then said, "Doug and me were talking, maybe about laying off the booze for a while."

"Yeah, right," I said. But the van was quiet save the hum of the radial tire upon asphalt.

"Hey. What, you're serious?" I said.

I looked back into the van myself then. "You and *Doug*?"

Jay and Jack were on the back bench, each asleep and leaning their heads to the right and left, their bodies only touching at the waist like disgruntled Siamese twins.

Kimm was behind me with sunglasses on, head tilted straight back so he snored gently at the ceiling.

Doug was next to him, rubbing at his temples, looking rough.

His knuckles tracked with raspberry abrasions, the saffron hint of a ripening bruise along his jaw.

He made eye contact with me, shook his head, then crossed his arms and closed his eyes.

He lay his head back, joining Kimm in jerky slumber.

We got off the turnpike and skirted Albany's sober pile of administrative buildings, then took increasingly smaller highways toward Voorheesville, finally turning onto a shady two-lane road that passed open fields of green.

Everyone in the van roused at the smell of evergreen trees baking in the fresh air.

We were blinking at the vast lots, pointing out delinquent deer arching for crabapples.

After our slow climb up the industrial spine of the east, through the tangle of intense city streets, those canyons of soot-veiled buildings, the sudden oceans of green stirred us all awake.

We pulled up to my sister Barbara Anne's place just as the sun dropped behind the hills.
Chris parked the van in front of the two-story house, porched and latticed, nestled like an egg atop the riot of nature.
Barb and her husband Larry came out to the porch with open beers and lit smokes in their hands.
I ran to Barb, gave her a hug, slapped at Larry's back
"Michael! You made it," Barbara Anne said.
Then, pushing me back to arm's length, she looked me up and down.
"Jesus, are you *still* growing?"
Larry put a cold light beer in my hand, gave me a backhand tap on the shoulder. "Whatya' say, Miguel? See the game last night? Yanks made your goddamn Angels look like chumps!"
"What is this, ya fuckin' hillbilly," I said, "light beer? *Really?*"
The rest of the guys joined me on the porch then, shaking hands and hugging all around, all of us relieved to be in this green open space, breathing in the fresh air.

Barbara Anne was a *half*-sister officially, halved by different moms.
But we shared the same wild memories of Dad.
I always considered her as just the oldest kid, another one of the giants surrounding me as I raced to catch up.
We were distanced by enough years that I had fuzzy memories of her when I was young.
She was left behind in Philadelphia when my pop decided to make his own separate peace and reinvent himself out west.
I remember her staying with us in Anaheim, Mom loving the freckled Irish girl as one of her own.
She became a flight attendant for American, met good old Larry when they both worked the redeye LaGuardia to Tampa Bay.
They shared the same love of corny, pun-driven jokes and smoking, mastered a skill for constant (yet measured) beer drinking whenever

grounded.
They married, worked out of Queens until they found the sprawling pad
upstate, and found happiness in their life among the trees.

We ate a dinner of barbecue chicken quarters and sweet corn in their
backyard.
The night turned deliciously cool and quiet, only the occasional doppler
whine of a mosquito teasing my ears.
Their lot emptied straight out into lush dark forest and when the
fireflies started dancing, we were charmed.
The guys jumped from the Adirondacks to chase after them.
I sat with Barb and Larry, drinking can after can of light beer, wearing
Yankees batting helmets in guard of falling acorns.

We watched the guys running wild as dogs finally unleashed, swatting
at the flecks of light swimming the air.

Chris and Doug made good on their vow of sobriety and drank only
water and iced tea that night. They each took long, soaking showers,
retired early to grab the upstairs bedroom with twins to themselves.
They claimed the luxury- the first in weeks- of a night alone in a bed
and fell back onto sheet and pillow as if into a well-deserved coffin.
Kimm went in to make calls, cheerfully carrying his calendar along
with two cans of beer to the spacious kitchen counter.
Jack and Jay played lawn darts until it was dark enough to be lethal,
and then carried great bundles of mildewed clothes down to the
basement.
Larry followed them down to demonstrate his collection of gag toys
collected from layovers across the continent, each figurine a visual
riddle that would inevitably squirt the handler in the eye as punch line.

Barbara Anne and I stayed out back, drinking beers, smoking her
cigarettes.
We chatted about the places I'd seen, mom and her suffering kindness,
the rest of the family.

Not surprisingly, she knew more about the family than I, and told me how my brother, JB, was soon moving his young family to a bigger house.

Eileen and Colleen, each now engaged to men in *banking*, would soon set up homes orbiting centers of finance before being relocated yet again on the whim of the market.

We then, finally, considered dad: his remarriage to a towering southern beauty queen, his quixotic battles with Big Medical Insurance, the dodgy investment schemes.

My brother Tim kept alive dad's neglected medical practice, still made up of a shrinking number of aged and devoted patients.

They waited hours for a brief audience with my distracted father and the good doctor's free hand with the prescription pad.

"Oh, dad," Barb sighed, a cloud of smoke carrying her words as if we were in a cartoon panel. "If that man would only be a *doctor,* right? Do his thing and make his money, go retire to a golf course. You know?"

We sat quietly for a while, looking into the dark, each of us thinking of past things.

"What about that big monkey that dad brought home," Barb said. "The one who used to hang herself by the neck all day?"

We both spoke at the same time, nodding. "Brigette."

Then she turned her head to me. "Your mom," she said, "is a *fucking saint.*"

She reached into the cooler, handed me yet another watery low-calorie beer. "How funny, isn't it? You out here, in a *band.*"

"Ah yup," I said. "A band."

It all seemed ridiculous, now, sitting there.

The stars above were brilliant, flicked on and off by the Pines swaying invisibly overhead.

I felt a momentary tickle in my heart, a flicker of doubt as if lost in the middle of a sentence.

I wiggled my empty beer can to her.

"Hey, you got anything, you know..." I said. "You know, *stronger?*"

She went into the house, shaking her head and smiling, and came back with a bottle of Jameson.

She set it on the table between us with a single glass.

I poured myself a full glass, tilted it to her in question. "Ya want?"

Barbara Anne shook her head. "You haven't learned about the hard stuff yet, huh? We Magranns can't handle whiskey."

At that I drained the glass, held it aloft in triumph.

Barb lit another smoke, coughed out a laugh.

"Oh, we can damn well drink it all right," she said. "We just can't *handle* it."

Robbie Fields -Posh Boy– came into the garage as we were practicing.

We were in the middle of playing a new one Kimm had brought in, "Waiting in the Wings."

I watched as mom ushered him into the garage, then Robbie turned to thank her with a worldly bow.

I stopped playing; dropping out of the second verse, but Robbie made a circular motion with two fingers, *keep going,* so we continued the song.

It was an easy three chord banger, just the right balance of simple, chopped verse and anthemic chorus, a natural addition to our growing setlist.

Robbie looked around, and, not finding a proper chair, jumped up to sit atop the washing machine.

As we played on I watched him take in the room, at the workbench covered with cords and guitar cases, milk crates of old motorcycle sprockets and chains shelved underneath.

He turned to look at the posters spanning the bare studs of the garage: Aerosmith and KISS, The Clash and Factory Honda.

Marty Smith jumping a red Honda in stylish cross up, Paul Simonon eternally frozen, spread legged, bass held overhead just before glorious impact.

I could imagine *Bachan* fuming in the house, her beloved Maytag

temporarily blocked by the jaunty Englishman sitting on it, sly as a hookah-smoking caterpillar atop a giant mushroom.
He wore a paisley tie, half-Windsored above a royal blue shirt, all under a jacket of tweed.
That, along with a mop of unruly hair and the brown leather satchel he held in his lap, gave him the harried air of a college professor forever rushed between classes.
And though I can't imagine his blazer held any crest upon its breast, whenever I think of that evening I can't help picturing it there. Perhaps two clawed eagles guarding crossed swords, a scholarly shield that marked his tenure as mentor to us students.
The roles that we would naturally fulfill long into our own adulthood, encompassing the whole of our career.

Posh Boy Records was on a *roll* that year, Robbie hitting that rare intersection of culture and market.
This new punk rock, like a mutant variant of a pesky virus, was a hardcore unique to Southern California.
Robbie focused upon the sound like a fascinated child holding a magnifying glass upon a sizzling ant.
It was a time when legions of kids were shaving their head daily, abandoning their Vans slip-ons for chained engineer boots.
I imagined tufts of shorn bleached hair tumbling down the empty shoreline like tumbleweeds dancing along the windswept prairie: the surfer kids all gone, content to snort black beauties at the Cuckoo's Nest and ride the swells of the pit.
Posh followed up the *Beach Boulevard* and *Rodney on the Roq* comp albums with T.S.O.L.'s ep, a stunning 12″ platter that captured the hectic moment in five urgent songs, 464 seconds.

After we had mixed our demo tape (Joe bobbing his woolly head to "Mannequin," his new favorite song) we duplicated it and passed it to friends, made our parents listen to it in awkward recital.
"Really good," my mom said. "Do you have to use *that* word, though?" as *Bachan* got up wordlessly to do another load of wash.

Kimm's folks sat as the songs unspooled in the den, Lois nodding politely to the manic beat.

Lynn's brow furrowed like an umbrella over his highball glass.

"Sounds like two cats fucking in a burlap sack," he said, rising to the liquor closet to freshen his drink.

We had no other plans for the tape beyond a drunken fantasy of somehow slipping the tape to Rodney over the back door sill of KROQ. Then we'd wait in the parking lot for *our* song to drift out of the van speakers, riding the FM airwaves above us, invisible as Santa Ana winds.

But with the cliched plot device of *chance*, of a course nudged just two degrees off, resulting in a wildly unexpected destination, the tape found its way to Robbie.

Through the years several people have claimed credit (and sometimes, sheepishly admitted fault) for getting the tape through.

But it has been agreed that the tape traveled the path of *a friend of a friend.* Received and passed along, perhaps in the ladies' room of a club along with capsules of amphetamine and fake IDs, like wartime contraband.

And on a trip up the coast toward San Francisco and its repurposed Mabuhay Gardens, a young lady dared to slip the unnamed Maxwell C-60 into Robbie's cassette player.

When we finished the song he gave us a few claps, saying "bravo."
"What was that one?" he asked.

He took a legal pad out of his satchel and looked at some notes. "That song wasn't on the demo tape, was it?" he asked in his mannered English accent. "Well, that's a good one, that'll work."

He jumped down from his perch then and walked among us, taking in Burton sweating behind his gleaming Slingerland set, Larry still finger-diddling his Telecaster bass.

Kimm and I, he looked us up and down as if measuring us against an image conjured by the songs he'd heard.

He shook my hand and looked accusingly into my eyes. "So, was it you I talked to? Kimm?"

I disengaged and nodded to Kimm. "He's Kimm. I'm the other one," I said. "Mike."

He then turned his unnerving attention to Kimm, giving me a moment to raise my eyebrows to Burton and Larry. They shrugged back, the language of children in the presence of a grown up.

"Ah, of course," Robbie said, "You're Kimm," and here he looked back to me, "and you're Mike."

He brushed back a curtain of curly hair, taking us all in with clear vision. "And you," he said, collecting us all in a sweep of his hand, "are Channel Three."

I noticed then the door was cracked a discreet inch and felt sure my mom was on the other side, shushing *Bachan*, listening.

"And" he said, without a trace of question, "you want to make a record."

*I*t's going on three hours* at the Canadian border.

The Blue & White sits in the inspection turnoff, emptied down to its threadbare carpeting.

The amps and drums, all our bags, stacked alongside the van like the collected detritus of a failed marriage left curbside.

We wait for someone to deliver the proper papers to the border, for the proper call to be returned.

Stuck in some twisted bureaucratic dance that will *perhaps* allow us beyond the bolsters guarding those emerald plains.

Kimm stands at a phone kiosk, one finger plugged into free ear, handpiece pressed to his face.

He listens more than he talks, though I do hear him say, "yeah, but we're already here!" whenever the connected party allows him to speak.

Jack has found a shady place to nap in a small greenbelt, unconcerned with the yellowed evidence of dog piss mottling the lawn.

The kid has been sleeping a lot, I realize, maybe like those prisoners who pass the time by sleeping eighteen hours a day, anything to escape the terror of captivity.

Jay sits at a picnic table, one hand shielding his penpoint from the sun, writing a letter. I wonder if it is a homesick note of apology to the ex. Or perhaps a naughty note to that girl he met in Memphis, the one who sent him back to the waiting van holding a single red patent pump.

The shoe sits proudly upon the dash of the Blue & White, presently being inspected by latex-gloved Mounties.

Doug and Chris skip rope under a wide awning, reinvigorated by their vow of sobriety.

That morning at Barb and Larry's I woke to the sound of Doug and Chris grunting and panting in the next room.

They were doing morning pushups and sit-ups, but it sounded all the world like they were buttfucking, a detail that Larry made smirking mention of several times over breakfast.

We sat in the kitchen as Barb brought out heaping plates of scrambled eggs and sausages. She watched us devour each platter in amazement before turning back to the stove to make more.

Beside my plate Larry had placed the sports section of the *Albany Times Union*, folded to the American League West standings. He had taken the time to highlight in canary yellow the Angels: wallowing down in their usual basement home, no chance of a playoff spot yet again. I pointed to his beloved Yankees in fifth, also bound for early vacation, before tossing the paper over my shoulder.

We spent the morning cleaning out the van, hovering around the washing machine.

Barb made me call mom, and she reported the Kraut guys were there the day before.

She made them a huge dinner of ribeye steaks while they splashed in the pool, *Bachan* happily washing every bit of laundry they would surrender.

They would not, mom reported, try the guacamole, though.

"The one skinny guy with red hair," mom told me, "he said he wasn't gonna eat anything *that* green."

Before leaving we spread out on the lawn, sucked in lungfuls of restorative air before another stretch in the van.

Like submariners shirtless on deck, taking in the last bittersweet glimpse of sunlight before diving back down to the dark ocean floor.

We recorded the CH3 EP at Brian Elliot's workmanlike studio in North Hollywood.

Brian's claim to fame was penning the Madonna hit "Papa Don't Preach," that melodramatic dance track that suddenly had all the pro-lifers on board with slutty Madonna, claiming it as a moral anthem. That the song was written by a grizzled music vet out in the Valley - *and a man!* – was never widely publicized, but I assume Brian was content with the tremendous royalty checks.

Robbie was not going to be there to start the session, but he had given Kimm the address and some specific instructions in a quick phone call that Kimm later relayed to me.

"So, what's the deal?" I asked Kimm on the way up the Cahuenga Pass. "We're actually making a record today, right? I mean, like it's gonna be an *actual* (and here I held my hands up as if holding an invisible 12-inch globe) record?"

Kimm assured me that was the plan. Robbie had given him the address to the studio and schedule: load in at 10 a.m., meet the engineer, David Hines, record four songs.

He'd also given Kimm the exact songs he wanted: "Manzanar," "Got a Gun," "Mannequin," and the one he'd heard in the garage, "Waiting in the Wings."

Robbie had picked the hardest and fastest songs, passing over our poppier offerings.

In his calculated wisdom he was packaging us as the latest *hardcore* band in his stable.

He made a couple specific preproduction notes as well, telling us to cut out a clunky intro and climbing middle break to "Manzanar," and telling us to replace the quaint line, "I just want to fuck your mom" in "Mannequin" with something more subtle.

And:

No drinking in the studio.

"And please," he told Kimm lastly, *"tell Mike no English accent when singing..."*

We loaded into a recording studio, incredibly, for the second time within six months. It was a plain, open space, bordering on dingy, a proper working studio.

But those rooms held a religious majesty for us, and like heathens approaching an empty vessel, we set up with hushed reverence.

David Hines came out of the control booth and introduced himself with quick handshakes, then we waited around while David set up the mics, got some tones.

He cued up a thick 2-inch reel of tape, which spun at such a dizzying speed it added a sense of budgetary urgency to the session.

He hit the talkback button, checked to see if we could hear him through the headphones.

David seemed slightly bored, or perhaps hungover, probably up this early on a Saturday to do this session in exchange for studio time for his own record (we soon learned Robbie was a master of the barter economy that kept all the independent record companies going, and he swam among the terrifying current of Hollywood backstabbers with ease).

Satisfied with the sounds, David asked us to name the first track and to count off.

We looked at one another, conferred briefly on which song would be easiest to pull off with our shaking paws, and decided to
tackle "Manzanar" first.

Larry set off with his throbbing bass intro, I mirrored that with my trebly Rickenbacker 425.

Kimm coming in then, the humbuckers in his Ibanez Destroyer channeling a fatter signal through a Marshall combo.

Burton rolled into the riff, and we were off.

We played it faster than we'd ever played it before, surely speeding up after the first chorus, but it seemed to work, giving more urgency and anger to the track.

We finished the take, David holding up a hand to shush us 'til the final tones died, then he pushed the talkback,

"Sounds good to me, is that the take?"

We turned to each other and shrugged, all of us relieved that we'd gotten through it, none of us wanting to object and go through it again.

I was getting familiar with the exquisite torture of recording a song, the fine negotiation between *good enough* against the possibility of just one more take. The perfect track was always *just* out there, floating like the specter of fortune forever haunting the degenerate gambler.

Robbie appeared in the control booth just as we were finishing the last of the basic tracks.

I watched from the studio while he and David talked, silenced by the glass separating us.

It was like deciphering a scene in a silent movie; reading lips and exaggerated gestures before the title card appears.

David nods toward us, and I imagine his words: *Man, where'd you find these clowns?*

Robbie looks down at his notes, then makes a mark with a pen before answering: *Quiet, you. Six letter word for pamper. Starts with C…*

I then pictured Robbie stopping the tape, ripping the reels from the machine. *Whoa, mistake. I meant to sign the other band, The Hated!*

Kimm nudged me. "So, let's do the other song, don't you think? We gotta be ahead of schedule."

I waved a hand to get their attention, and after hitting the talkback button, Robbie called on me. "Mike. Yes?"

"Is it ok if we lay down one more song?' I asked. "It's a short one. Quick."

They talked a bit more, checking the amount of tape left on the spool, then David came back on.

"All right, we got some space here. Robbie says no guarantee it will make the cut, though, cool? What's the title?"

"Wetspots, " I said.

A torrid slash of a song, all of 55 seconds, we put it down in one take.

David and Robbie both looked up in surprise at the abrupt end, the song over while they were still twisting at their candy-colored knobs.

I waited for, and was rewarded with, the inevitable, *Is that it?*

A song so slight it was forgotten on the original track listing.

Only after it was pressed and sent out to the galaxy was it discovered the song was a horny little ode to precum.

I stayed out alone in the studio for the vocals.
I had the lyrics neatly typed out, double spaced, on snow white
Hammermill 20lb.
I paged through the words as David set up the condenser microphone
(and again, that sensual disc of pantyhose at nose level!) and was
suddenly horrified at the triteness of the lyrics displayed nakedly upon
the page.
Out of context of the roaring guitars and frantic beat, the words jumped
out at me.
Precious and overwrought, like a brat waving her arms and
shouting *Look at me Mama! Papa! Look!* as she threatens to jump into
the shallow end of the urine-laden community pool.
I took a pen and started crossing out words when Robbie came through
the talkback and asked for a level.
Posh took control of the session now, the vocals his point of interest,
and we went line by line in search of a satisfactory take before moving
on.
He stopped me again and again to coach me on pronunciation,
suggesting a different phrase, cutting the track in mid-yell when I went
flat or sharp.
Finally satisfied, he had me go back and double track all the lead
vocals, an unnerving trick that had me mirroring my prior track.
It created a third, otherworldly voice, like that of a time traveler from
the future bearing only terrible news.
He was looking for something beyond me, of course, but I stretched as
well as I could, hoping to please him for reasons I see now as the
obvious old search for paternal approval. *Papa-look at me!*

After we loaded the Blue & White, we sat with Robbie in the tiny outer
office, chatting easily about the future.
He seemed pleased with the quick session, and at the first lull in our
conversation he produced a stack of papers from his satchel.
"Ok, then," he said, "there's only the matter of the contract. Are we
ready to sign? Did you read through it?"

We each signed, of course, wedding our future to Robbie and his label for decades to come.

Posh collected the signed documents and tucked them back into his bag, then he talked to Kimm of details that held no interest to me, like cover art and first run numbers.

I only wanted to know when I could hear it. Those songs we just committed to tape as record, *a record.*

We were, for the first startling moment, to consider the songs as a commodity. Songs written on the edge of the bed, melodies daydreamed in class.

Lyrics scribbled in the back room of the Wild West store, a legal pad upon a box of Candies Rose Gold Pumps, size 9.5.

We were giving these things, *these songs*, name and weight.

It was another anarchy house in Ottawa, filled with crusties, feminists, and militant *vegans* before there were such things.

And discovering yet another American flag hung upside down in the cluttered living room I had a brief moment of patriotic indignation: *What? You can't hang the fuckin' maple leaf thing upside down, ya fuckin Canucks?*

Perhaps it was an attempt to make us feel more at home, or maybe just a bewildered statement regarding their obnoxious Yankee neighbors downstairs.

One wall was dominated by a worn bookcase, and above a full set of Encyclopedia Britannica was a collection of books befitting the earnest collective.

A Bible wedged between The Holy Qur'an and *Everyman's Talmud.*

Then: *Guerilla Warfare, Mein Kampf,* and, naturally, *The Anarchist Cookbook.*

The upper shelf leaned tastefully to the literary, Thoreau and Burroughs, Baldwin and *that dirty cat* Ginsberg.

A few inches of gem-like Black Sparrow paperbacks wedged against

my beloved *In Our Time*.
(Upon checking, Hemingway still claimed but a singular and
lonely "m," even up yonder, here in Canada.)
And at the end, its ballooned font unmistakable on its slim orange
spine, sat the punkiest volume of them all, that fable of persistence in
the face of denial, of the willingness to change for the better: Dr.
Seuss' *Green Eggs and Ham*.

The commune residents had thoughtfully whipped up a platter of cut
garden vegetables surrounding an earthen bowl of lumpy hummus,
which we grazed at politely while whispering plans to escape to a
McDonald's at our earliest chance.
But there was beer and unfamiliar cigarette brands, French accents
floating underneath the Clash's "Gates of the West."
It made me feel rather grownup and quite continental.

A mohawked punkette sidled up to me as I picked at the vegetable tray.
"Hey, good set. Short though, no?" she said.
She was wearing a homemade Crass tee over ripped leggings and
smelled alarmingly, yet somehow irresistibly, of body odor.
She gazed up at me and took my hand. *"Oh, la vache*, but you are so
tall, hmm?"
The French accent made me sure I was being seduced, and as she
motioned me down to whisper in my ear, I imagined all the naughty
things we would soon be performing, including unspeakable acts
involving her unshaven armpits.
"Listen," she whispered, her breath hot in my ear, "we ask for you to
be, hmm, *discreet*. Yes? The house is being bugged; you know?" And
here she looked around at the grimy walls with raised eyebrows.
"Under *surveillance*, hmm?"
"Get the fuck out of here," I said, laughing.
But she just nodded solemnly, looking once again around the room.

As she walked away, I felt the smartass child in me already formulating
a joke involving organic fertilizer and vegan blasting caps, but I pushed

it aside.

I could tell she was being serious.

And if they were indeed being "bugged" or just being paranoid, I had no doubt they had been hassled for their unwashed activism.

I wondered once again at the spectrum of this thing, *punk*.

Suburban knuckleheads, we who searched for no truth beyond cheap beer and women with terrible taste in men.

Here now, mingling with new radicals, CSIS listening to our gnawing upon both celery and carrot.

Mistaking the click and clack of mastication for ciphered Morse code, or perhaps the clatter of shell cartridges being chambered.

The sincere and the hopeful, the psychos and fiends, all of us sheltered under the same Tartan umbrella: *Punk*.

It was just the new music for some who bemusedly bought the records for the shock value.

For others, a wild phase to be outgrown, along with Barbie dolls or humping pillows to old issues of mom's *Cosmopolitan*.

But for some it became the lifestyle of a lifetime.

And they answered the frantic beat, those shouts of anger, as if turning toward Mecca at the clarion call.

Somehow, on the promise of those songs we recorded in a small room in North Hollywood, we were invited to join the rebellion.

And what I always found miraculous; they knew who we were.

We were *known* to them.

Later that night, as I lay in the Blue &White, I stared up at the lit windows of Anarchy House and imagined the passionate conversations inside.

Young people discussing the dim chances of a better world.

Resolved in their stubborn refusal to go along quietly with the known wrongs, the comprised life offered them in a trade for silence.

A block away, perhaps, bored men in short sleeves sat in an unmarked laundry truck, headphones on, pen in hand.

I took a bite of my Big Mac, but tasted a sudden bile that discolored my appetite, almost making me throw the corporate fast food into the wheel well.

Almost.

NINE

***W**e picked up Jill, our Toronto contact,* around 9 p.m. the
following evening.

We'd spent the day in Ottawa waiting around for the
promoter and his promised payment, and he finally met us with a
hundred and fifty Canadian dollars in Monopoly-colored bills.

He was apologetic about the delay, though, and treated us to a fine
lunch of prosciutto-blanketed pizza and potent Extra Old Stock beers in
nearby Hull.

As we left for Toronto, I discovered I was still a bit spooked by our
time at the Anarchy House and I kept an eye in the sideview for any
unmarked cars before reasoning that *all* the fucking cars were
unmarked.

Jill was the promoter and tireless den mother of Toronto punk, and she
had graciously invited us to stay at her house in Oakville.

We got to her quiet street where she sat waiting on the steps of her
house, looking all the world like a girl ready to go back in and turn off
the porch light, stood up by a lousy boyfriend once again.

She got in the Blue & White, and turning in her middle seat, said hello
to all in the van.

We slid shut the door and took off, Jill politely ignoring the odor
embedded in every fabric of the hold, of six sweating men braised there
for months.

She then fell into conversation with Kimm as they had been in phone
contact for months.

They chatted about other bands on the road that summer, set times for
the big show the following night.

We stopped for gas at an Esso station, and while we were filling up
another van pulled up to the pumps behind us.

California plates, the unmistakable roar of Ramones coming from their stereo, the music louder once they shut off the rattling motor.

The doors of the Dodge opened and a crew mirroring us (shaved heads, T-shirts grayed by careless sink washings, combat boots worn below shorts) piled out.

It took a moment to resolve the image with the realization that it was the *guys from fucking Youth Brigade.* In a chance meeting here at a Canadian gas station, a million miles from home.

It was a thrill to see faces from home, like viewing the same stars hanging overhead from a different country, the different perspective giving them a sudden new value and sparkle.

I tackled Shawn Stern and wrapped him in a bear hug, even deigning to lean down and plant a kiss upon his shaved scalp. "Go on," I growled into his ear, "Liberate yourself from my viselike grip!"

He pushed me away, swatting the spit from his head. "Get the fuck off me, Magrann," he said. "What're you, drunk again? *Drunk still?*"

We all emptied into the parking lot then, hugging it up and slapping backs.

I moved along, hugging Mark and Adam, checking in with their jolly road dudes Brian and Marc.

It seemed years ago when they had left me for dead atop that hearse in Austin, and we compared notes on the crisscrossed routes we had driven since then.

After the vans were gassed, we moved our happy reunion to a nearby party Jill directed us to.

Chris and Doug, still sober and grumpy, stayed out in the van.

The rest of us spent the night drinking and talking as if we were parked in front of the Cathay De Grande back home, just miles from our own comfortable beds.

Youth Brigade were on the bill the next night, Jill managing to stack a great bill with our bands plus Zeroption and the F.U.s from Boston.

We loaded in early and actually did a soundcheck, had time to hang out at Jill's for a few hours before returning to the club at dusk and finding the hall packed.

Jill had arranged seven gleaming cases of beer in the backstage room, iced piles of Brador and lethal Old Stock.

Doug and Chris could no longer abstain, especially when I reasoned with them (sweeping a hand at the stacks of icy beers) that a week of sobriety within this season of existence was insanity.

They fell upon the beer, upending bottles to their mouths and taking great gulping swallows, as if in a futile attempt to make up for lost time and to catch up to me.

The Stern dudes were from Toronto originally and could count on the goodwill of the locals: native sons *made good* down in Hollywood.

We, with our shaky pedigree, were looked upon by the stylish punkers warily, so we took no chances.

We played a fast set with almost no breaks between songs.

I kept the banter limited to a couple *Thanks ,Canada!* even daring once to utter *Merci* to the hooting crowd.

At Jay's urging, we played a set heavy with the newest songs, off our latest record, *After the Lights Go Out.*

By now we were familiar with the uneasy negotiation of the setlist, the temptation to load it up with known old songs against the artistic desire to showcase something new.

I knew the usual response when a new song is announced: that glazed look of disinterest falling over the shared gaze of the crowd.

People nudging friends with a nod, signaling time to go outside and have a smoke.

But we did play the new songs and the roiling pit continued, the crowd tuned into the beat and roar of guitars above lyric or melody.

As we so often did, we fell back upon that first EP to end the night, as if calling to our distracted grandchildren to come help us off the kitchen floor.

We played "Manzanar" right into "Waiting in the Wings," "Mannequin" before closing, as always, with "I Got a Gun."

And then, as an unrequested encore, I shed my guitar and jumped into the surging crowd for a manic rendition of "Wetspots."

As we left the stage, the wet planks a mess of tangled cords and broken beer bottles, I tossed the microphone to Shawn, who only shook his head and grinned.

We nodded in silent agreement, that we *got lucky* once again.

And then I went back to investigate that pile of beer backstage.

We had pestered Robbie after the recording session, like children asking yet again how many days until Christmas: *where was the record?*

He patiently explained the timeframes of pressing and packaging, using cryptic language like *masters and lacquers, plating and test pressings.* Terms that left Kimm speechless and nodding still, long after he'd hung up with Robbie, me listening at his shoulder.

Looking back, it all came about terribly quickly, but at the time the wait for the record was interminable.

We'd told everyone, of course, that we were making a record *-on Posh Boy!-* and were politely congratulated in the way a child might be for claiming to have actually *seen* Santa fly overhead in his sleigh.

There was no proof, and at times we doubted the existence of this record ourselves.

I'd make Kimm call Robbie yet again, only to be told of some new detour on the meandering road of record making, and Kimm would hang up once again, nodding.

We were finally summoned to Robbie's tiny office off Santa Monica, an alcove set in the old Alco record pressing plant.

Kimm and I walked in and discovered Robbie sitting at his desk in full ski wear, nylon bib overalls over a turtlenecked sweater, a tasseled beanie still covering his moppy hair.

Before we could question the outfit, he explained that he'd just come from Mountain High, where they allowed a couple hours of discount skiing on weekday mornings.

The office was decorated with the various album jackets produced at the plant, including a row of brilliantly rendered tropical birds on pastel

flats, covers of the *Train Your Bird to Talk!* series.
I wandered close to the wall to inspect the covers, discovering the track listings going something like, *1) Hello 2) How Are You 3) Hello, How Are You…* on and on, slight variations on the most mundane of bird-to-human greetings.
Naturally, there were albums in *Train Your Bird to Speak* in Spanish, French, and so on, though I could not find any editions that promised to train your bird to, say, cuss like a drunken longshoreman, or perhaps summon Satan with reverse incantation.

Robbie handed each of us a 12″ record in a plain white sleeve, which we each spun around in our hands, looking at the generic label for any clue of content.
The center label simply stated *Electrosound, Los Angeles,* beneath a series of stamped numbers.
"It's a test pressing," Robbie explained to our confused looks. "Before we go to production, hmmm?"
We walked out onto Santa Monica a bit dejected, having expected stacks of finished product: our faces smiling from glossy back covers, replicated by the thousands and shrink-wrapped for prosperity.
Robbie walked us out and waved as we pulled from the curb.

I watched as he went back into his office, bundled against the winter chill, back to those speaking birds of the tropics.
The hiss and stomp of records being pressed into existence beyond his snowy jungle.

When we got back to Cerritos we wordlessly ran up the stairs to Kimm's bedroom, his mom Lois calling up after us to see if we wanted some cookies, still warm from the oven.
Kimm took the album already resting on the turntable, Starz' *Attention Shoppers!* and replaced it with our own.
He placed the needle down with the slightest of scratch.
We backed away, as if from a lit fuse beneath a squat Mexican skyrocket, and waited for the sound.

Larry's "Manzanar" bass line came through the speakers, low and ominous, throbbing.
We looked at each other, then at the spinning record that conjured the strange rumble.
Then we realized that, like the T.S.O.L. EP, this one was recorded for 45 RPM.
Kimm lifted the needle, switched the speed on the turntable and started the record over.
We listened to side A, then B, then over to A again before we spoke.
Finally, Kimm spoke first: "Is that what it's supposed to sound like?"
It was harsh and fast, stripped of any depth or dynamic.
It was, for lack of anything better at hand, *hardcore.*

We invited Larry and Burton over, and we all listened to it together, standing in a circle in Kimm's bedroom, dropping cookie crumbs on the shag carpet.
Larry dug it, Burton shrugged and left to go lift weights at the gym.
Kimm and I reasoned with ourselves and each other.
We finally convinced ourselves that this music, this sound rushing past us out of the speaker, that this was now *us.*
That Saturday night Rodney played "Manzanar" on the radio, and if I could convey the feeling of hearing your song on the radio for the first time in any worthy way, I would do so now.
I will say that I remember standing motionless during the entire 125 seconds of play, as if I might break the spell by any sudden movement. And when Rodney reverse introduced the song, *(....and before Bowie we heard a new one from Posh Boy's latest group. That was Channel Three with Manzanar...)*, inevitably christening it as "amazing," I felt the threat of real tears forming in my widened eyes.

We left Jill's early, aiming for an early show back below the border in Cleveland.

We were all ditzy hungover, still buzzed and buzzing from the grand night.

We had all gathered backstage after the gig, the hall emptied out and the gear packed in the vans.

Doug and Chris got instantly and hilariously wasted, their spell of sobriety ended by those strong Canadian beers.

After the load-out they came roaring into the backroom with Brian and Marc from the Youth Brigade crew.

They kept pointing to their crotches, shouting, *"mange le fromage bébé!"* a term they learned from some of the local punks.

It apparently translated to *eat the cheese, baby!*

A bottle of whiskey inevitably appeared and was passed around, but I simply passed it on, sticking my tongue out at the jeering Sterns.

I stuck with the beers, my sister Barb's caution about our family's disastrous history with the hard stuff still fresh in memory.

I pictured gray Ireland, homeland of my drunken ancestors.

The thatch-roofed cottages vacated in the middle of the night, a family scurrying through the darkness just ahead of torch bearing creditors and the furious fathers of shamed daughters.

The *McGranns* sneak off the island, the family name altered by just one guilty letter on that vomitous steerage class journey across the Atlantic.

They landed as *Magranns,* upon a new land where they could once again gulp at the demon liquor and fuck things up anew.

I drove the Blue & White clearheaded, with the smug satisfaction of the drunk who had demonstrated the merest of self-control, while Chris and Doug groaned through their first hangovers in a week.

We got to the border by noon and took twenty minutes to watch the water rushing over Niagara Falls, gulping in the spray-flecked air to clear our heads.

My eyes naturally settled on the crashing climax below, to the foaming violence and roar, the awesome splash hidden by rainbowed mist.

On the walk back to the van I thought of the glorious death I might realize upon that rocky conclusion, after a fetal-positioned ride in a sealed barrel.

We got back into the Blue & White and skirted Lake Erie on the 90, everyone feeling comforted somehow that we were back in the States, singing along with Jay's mixtape.

Undertones came on, "Teenage Kicks," and we all sang along in goofy falsetto, serenading the passing cars.

Outside Buffalo we passed a wood paneled station wagon and as I looked over, I made momentary eye contact with the middle-aged man driving.

(I say "middle age," but now of course realize the guy was probably thirty, if that.)

He had on a wrinkled white shirt and loosened necktie, sleeves rolled up to the elbows.

I looked to the windows behind him where a tangle of kids -either three or four-were squirming and crying.

Their church clothes destroyed by the post-service jelly donuts they waved in their grubby little paws.

In the passenger seat the mother just sat, elbow on the arm rest and a hand shielding her eyes, defeated.

The man looked back through our windows as well; saw the fellas back there, everyone singing, Doug already swigging at a beer in attempt to right his hangover.

I could imagine the rest of his day: going home to take off his church clothes and sit in his darkened bedroom alone for five precious minutes.

Hearing his family down there: that *noise* that haunts his every moment of existence.

Yelling for more -*always more*- from down the stairs of his twice-mortgaged house.
He calculates the ammunition necessary to quiet them all, including the final round that will let him finally rest.
I hold up my beer then, salute him in cheers as he veers to exit the freeway while we drive on.

Kimm and I stood in Zed Records, a small strip mall shop just up the street from Long Beach State.
Zed's was the best record store in the area, stocked with rare import singles, T shirts, and a magazine rack holding Xeroxed fanzines along with glossy *Creems* and exotic *NME*'s.
There were punk buttons, Damned and Sex Pistols, stickers that could instantly transform a lowly Ford Pinto into a glorious punkmobile.

Kimm was a loyal customer, and by then his bedroom held a half meter's worth of shelf space filled with the records he'd gotten at Zed's.
To the left, the early singles that reflected the weird art bent of the early fringe: Suburban Lawns and Devo, Weasels and early B52s.
Moving starboard, the English anthems: Clash and Jam, Stiff Little Fingers, Damned and Pistols.
And then, filling the outer right edge, the new hardcore of SoCal.

Posh Boy was represented by the Rodney comp and *Beach Boulevard*; T.S.O.L.'s stark EP shelved next to their new full-length goth opera *Dance with Me.*
And there on the end, ready for easy and daily access, Adolescents' astonishing Blue Album.
I'd always thought T.S.O.L. and Adolescents were our own Stones and Beatles, respectively.
The former's inherent darkness and danger, the latter's mastery of harmony and songcraft.
And later, when we would share some of the same stages with those

bands, I was forced to consider our own English Invasion counterpart. And though I hopefully reasoned we might be considered the sly *Kinks*, I came to realize we'd probably be judged as a slighter footnote to the era, picturing only the goofy grins of Herman's Hermits or Freddie and the Dreamers.

But now, we casually stood in front of the racks in Zed's, pretending to be browsing along the records.
Flipping through the "A's" and "B's" before standing together facing the bands grouped under "C."
There, between Chelsea and The Clash, was a full separator holding the grainy image of my acoustic guitar cabinet, the same one handed down from my brother, Tim.
The cover of the album is a tight shot of the grill cloth, the texture rippling above a speaker cone.
And there, above it all, sloppily spray painted through a hardware store stencil: CH3.

We each grabbed a copy and twisted the shrink-wrapped records over and over.
On the back were shots of our four faces, in mugshot starkness, each of us in our own *Brady Bunch*-ed frame.
Robbie had asked for a group photo at the very last minute, and we rushed down to Cerritos Mall and stuffed two dollars' worth of quarters into a photobooth, pushed and pulled each other, laughing, into the booth between flashes of the strobe.
The result, which haunts us whenever the EP pops up online, (as ridiculously overpriced as an unwrapped *Star Wars* figurine) is jarring.
Upper left, Larry is somber and oversized in his frame, unsmiling as a Depression-era dock worker cheated out of a day's pay.
Below him, Kimm wears the startled look of a boy walking in on his cheating mother.
Bottom right Burton is wearing a bandana wrapped gangster style, one eye closed as if shut by violence and steel.
And then there's *me*, wearing a reasonable enough outfit of stripes

beneath black leather.
But below my crazed eyes I flash a leering grin, looking all the world
like the victim of either intestinal gurgle or untimely orgasm.
These - *these!* - were the images we okayed to show the world.

I stood on the sidewalk holding the EP.
I tore at the shrink-wrap, slipped the vinyl out of the sleeve 'til a
crescent of black vinyl peeked out.
I then reassembled it and held it at arm's length, as if in disbelief; a
record!
Tactile in my moist hands, a heft given something of the air.

PART IV

ay leaned between the seats, pointed at the dash.
"The journal. Pass it here."
We were heading up the 94W, having just left a huge cheese shop off the freeway. I passed Chris the tub of curds I'd been working on and pushed aside some things on the dash, searching for the notebook.

The dashboard of the Blue & White had filled with trinkets we had collected all summer, and by now it looked like a shrine to madness.
There was a full-sized set of bullhorns, taken from the back room of an El Paso VFW hall.
Upon one horn hung the sequined thong of a New Orleans stripper, while a pair of gag Groucho glasses (with a blunt penis for a nose, of course) sat atop the other.
Cassette tapes baked against the windshield, tapes given to us by other bands and tossed aside after a single listen.
A family of troll dolls appeared sometime after Florida, one of them in the perpetual agony of being half eaten by a rodent-sized T Rex figurine.
And the centerpiece, crowning the fuzzy span connecting the horns, was an upper set of dentures we were baffled to find in the back of the van after the gig in Oklahoma.

I found the Mead under some yellowed newspapers and pulled it out.
The notebook had filled these past weeks.
Pages stained and fattened by spilled beer, its coiled spine unraveling like a valve spring seeking escape from a tortured motor.
Before I passed the notebook back to Jay, I paged through the latest entries.

8/7 Sun

Left Jill's early for Cleveland-matinee- Got CLE by 5:30 but show was cancelled-Local bands were late? Promoter an ass……Stayed by ourselves in punkrock house, no tv. Read mags all night and crashed.

(Another cancelled gig, nothing. But at the bottom of the short entry, noted within a jagged caption bubble like a Batman fight onomatopoeia: *Highlight of the day-found a Taco Bell!*)

8/8 Mon

Sat around all day, changed Canadian money, lunch in gay bar. Promoter finally met, but still no money-left for Pittsb 5:30, stayed at Hell House, hot dogs, new wave bar-chicks! Slept on porch.

(That the margins remain clear on this page suggests none of our lads got lucky with the new wave chicks. I do not recall the gay bar lunch, but I applaud our younger selves for doing so without the expected homophobic commentary.)

8/9 Tues

Eggs for lunch, hamburgers for dinner. Did radio interview URCT and made funny I.D. Played Electric Banana w/ Real Enemy. J throws up on stage. 2 sets, promoter+gun! J stays w/L again, C&K at Girls' pad. HellHouse: Doug+me=porch. Jack got bed.

(Jay did indeed throw up and played most of the night perched upon a milkcrate, holding his pulsing intestines in check while we played both sets. The end notation does show, though, that Jay did in fact meet a sympathetic girl the night before and got to stay between her clean sheets once again.

Chris and Kimm also seemed to have gotten lucky.

Famously, the Electric Banana promoter was rumored to wield a pistol during payout. And though he paid us without comment, a gleaming .38 snub nosed revolver indeed sat just out of reach, holding down some papers on his cluttered desk.

8/10 Wed

Woke and took showers, wrangled the boys, made Jack drive to Cincinnati. Ate at chili joint, got 2 cases, Jay throws up all night. Played Jockey Club KY w/ Killing Children(?) Doug drinks massive amounts tequila, falls off barstool & cracks head. M & Jack stay w/ Teri/Amy/Diana downtown. BB

(So, apparently Jay was suffering from something beyond a hangover, and the poor guy had to play another barfy gig. Jack and I stayed downtown with some ladies, though the alliterative notation -BB, (as in blue balls!)- makes me think it was a platonic sleepover.

The rest of the guys ended up at St. Elizabeth emergency room, Doug having split his left eyebrow with a deep gash. The staff would not let Chris and Kimm carry him past the lobby, as his shorts were somehow now around his ankles and Doug threatened to beat any man who came near him).

8/11 Thur

Birthday day! Called Anele's (?) house to get Doug to pick us up. His head is jacked! Stayed @ Anele's, parents cool old Mods from UK. Fixed cords, watched MTV, spaghetti dinner. Went to Jr's Bar, smoked weed, crashed.

(We found out the happy coincidence that Jay and Doug shared the same birthday, August 11!

Shame that Doug was still concussed and worrying over his head wound, which still wept blood whenever he drank. Jay was still feeble with a pesky virus. We were staying in the clean suburban house of an angelic punkette, named *Anele* here but surely properly

spelled *Annalee*. She had kind young parents who bandaged Doug's skull and fixed us a huge platter of pasta.

I do remember doing laundry in the basement workshop while her father, a fine old Brit chap, regaled me with stories of pipe wrench fights with Teddy Boys back in his golden East London days.

Fixing cords, hah. We relied daily on soldering irons and gleaming pools of alloy to keep us going.)

8/12 Fri

Woke early& left Cinc, got to Chi around 5pm Waited for soundcheck w/ Mike Suckow, got McDonalds and OldE800 quarts with last of money. Doug head still bad…. Central American Social Club upstairs hall w/ Violent Apathy & The End–FOUND 1,000 LIQUORS! Slept on sidewalk in front of BigBlue (AOF house). 7, 8 if HJ count.

(Oh, they count.)

The Chicago promoter was Mike Suckow, and I find myself squinting at the memory of first meeting the guy, as he has remained a close friend since that summer.

We blew into town looking forward to a Friday show in a big city.

I remember a hot upstairs gig while the sun was still playing above the downtown skyline.

We were starting to get worried about Doug's gash, and I think I even called my father at one point to ask his advice- ("too late now, maybe just butterfly it and keep it clean," he'd said, before adding: "Chicago, huh? How're we doing with the ladies out there?").

Sensing correctly that he was in the company of fellow drinkers, Suckow took us by a store called 1,000 Liquors after the gig.

He ushered us into the store without a word, grinning like a proud parent.

We beheld the tall shelves and gleaming coolers for a silent moment, and then ran for the maze of booze like a shrieking pack of children upon an Easter egg hunt.

It was indeed a wonderland of alcohol; we searched the coolers for exotic beers, started counting the liquor bottles to prove the namesake.

It was only after we'd exhausted five minutes of stupid chatter that Kimm piped up a golden verse from a far corner of the store: "Hey, look at this-there's a fuckin' bar back here!"

For this kingdom had not just bottles destined for sloppy consumption at home, but there, behind swinging doors, an actual dive bar.
We'd never heard of such a thing, but Suckow assured us it was a Midwest taproom, and this being Chicago, it stayed open far later than we had any need to be drinking.
We left poor Jack to double park for 90 minutes while we drank as many of the potions as possible.
We ended up at the Articles of Faith house where people inside were having heartfelt conversations about punk rock.
I ended up out on the sidewalk drinking alone, a thousand liquors falling one by one.

8/13 Sat

No show-Woke up in an attic-Regroup, grocery for food to BBQ at lake. Made chicken thighs, swimming in the lake, weird fresh water! Doug's eye getting worse. ......went out to suburbs (Lon & his lizard!) got drunk in basement with gear, jam session back to Mike Suckow's house to crash.

When I look at the pages of the journal, I am amazed at how many weekend nights we wasted without a gig.
But this Saturday was a memorable day spent on the lake shore, hanging out and swimming in the fresh water of Lake Michigan.
We were used to the salted Pacific and missed that ocean's familiar buoyancy as we sunk into the lake's unknown depths.

Doug spent the day swimming, unconcerned about his open head wound (which we still had not really addressed).
It was a fine Midwestern day, chewing on brats and chicken breasts barbecued along the water's edge, drinking endless cans of Old Style that Suckow produced by the case.
By sundown we were drunk and unruly, cranky without a gig or a chance to meet and disappoint women.

Mike was tasked with entertaining us that evening and herded us into the van for a field trip to a small get-together in the suburbs inland. A couple of the AOF crew came along, and at one point a grinning hippy named Lon took the wheel of the Blue & White, a sleepy Iguana perched on his shoulder.

We finally stopped at a normal looking Midwestern house, all shrubs and picket fencing, no upside-down flags to be seen.
No girls.
But there was a basement set up with couches and a backline of gear, and the night dissolved into a sloppy jam session.
Everyone ended up with a different instrument than their usual.
At one point I was assaulting the drums, a double time version of "Baba O'Riley," all while smoking a cheap cigar.
Jack played bass and Jay sang lead until I'd inhaled enough blue stogie smoke to make me turn green and fall off the drum throne.
As I wheezed into the linoleum, I felt someone nudge me aside with a foot, take the sticks from my clutched fists, and continue the ragged song.

I was being impressed by these ruddy Chicago locals, their workmanlike approach to steady and serious drinking, their worship of summer sun after another long season of winter misery.
I somehow found Suckow had also just read Jim Harrison's *A Good Day to Die*, and we sat in the backyard and had a long wandering talk while we passed back and forth a bottle and watched the stars wheeling across the sky.
We settled on a pact to someday destroy some government-funded infrastructural monstrosity in an act of righteous futility.
That, or maybe learn to fly fish.

8/14 Sun
Woke at Mike's-and wife Sue! Took showers, did Jane Fonda workout video on TV. Leave around 4 for Battle Creek w/ Pat from AOF crew. Got butterfly bandages for Doug's

**noggin………Hank's Hideaway by 8pm, Pnut butter & Jelly
sammies for dinner in parking lot, played w/ Latin Dogs and
Violent Apathy. OK show
Monster girls! M+S, C+YV D=BJ ……*Rubi was here!***
(The last line, red inked and the "i" dotted with a heart, is evidence that
"Rubi" had flipped through the journal and then took up pen to
autograph it herself. She signed it thus, and underneath that, her
exhausted partner noted further: *SHE SURE WAS!!!)*

The notebook sits on my desk at this very moment as I write these
words, like an grimoire containing incantations for conjuring the
cranky ghosts of the past.
The pages yellowed by beer, bodily fluid… time.
I read, and I wonder at the pages covered, each representing a day of
our lives that summer in 1983.
And as for those candid confessions scratched down in code and
expletive, we were, after all, only children armed with adult genitalia;
unaware of its dangerous connection to those more tender organs, the
brain and the heart.

We spent our last morning in Chicago** at Mike Suckow's place, watching his wife Sue pad around the house in a baby doll nightie and fuzzy, cha-cha-heeled slippers. Mike worked for a local beer distributor, one of those choice jobs protected and dictated by a monolithic union.

Though just a year or two older, he was the first punker we knew with a wife and house.

We sat there in their tidy home smelling bacon being fried, Sue walking around with a coffee pot to top off cups, and I could feel a bittersweet tinge of envy for such a solid and regular life.

That perhaps a different vehicle could navigate life besides that stinking Chevy van sitting obediently at curbside.

Upon a stack of VHS tapes beside Mike's Barcalounger sat *Jane Fonda's Workout*, and we put it on as a lark, hoping only to see some lovely butts in prone presentation, the dancers' overshadowed eyes beckoning back to us over stretched spandex.

Suckow dared us to get off the couch and give it a try, to attempt those pelvic thrusts and spread-eagled poses.

Soon we were all splayed upon the shag, groaning to the aerobic hell, giving up one by one, panting, until only Doug, Chris, and Sue continued the prancing madness.

Before leaving, Sue urged us to tend to Doug's head gash.

Being "the son of a doctor" and my brief stint working in dad's wacky office, I was elected to do the job.

After fetching rubbing alcohol and butterfly bandages from a local Rexall, I stood over Doug in Mike's bathroom and inspected the cut.

It was an impressive laceration, deep enough to see whitish striation underneath, long as a generous line of blow.

I flushed out the cut with straight rubbing alcohol, Doug flinching enough to spill the anesthetic waterglass of Jim Beam Mike had poured for him.

I pinched the wound together, but when I released it, it splayed open once again and shed a single drop of oxygen-rich blood.

I cut the butterfly bandages down, halving the adhesive ends so they would fit vertically along the wound.

I applied these carefully, moving along as I pinched the gash shut, finally laying a larger stripe of cloth tape on top and swathing it in clean gauze.

"Good as new," Doug said, inspecting the clean white pad covering his brow. "Thanks Big," he said. "My own fucking cut man."

We had a record out now, but shockingly, the world remained unchanged.

The record just sat there for a month.

And as our twice-weekly reconnaissance visits to Zeds confirmed, the stock remained fat in the store, save the few copies we pestered our friends into buying.

Of course, we had not played any real gigs, and our name was still unknown beyond the jagged borders of Cerritos, Norwalk, and Artesia. We were back in school, Kimm and I both at Long Beach State now. I'd successfully lobbied mom into letting me move back home and go to the local state college. My dad, probably happy to save the astronomical tuition and board cost of USC, did not object.

I raced the arched hills that separated the classrooms on the new campus, which seemed laid out to purposely keep you tardy for every lecture and test.

We kept practicing in the garage, writing new songs (though there was no indication we'd ever see a recording studio again) and worked the shitty night and weekends shifts at the Wild West store.

Kimm and I would have a signal when any punks would enter the store. A quick double whistle when any shaved heads pushed through the entrance, punks wasting another Saturday by shoplifting their way through the mall.

We'd go hide out in the back stockroom, pretending to be doing inventory until the punkers left, lest our shameful identities as lowly clothes peddlers got out.

But even when approached by a spiked hair punk, we were never recognized as the goofs on the back of the EP.

As far as we could tell, no one bothered to even flip the record to inspect the back cover at Zeds.

I saw my stockinged love only one more time, and that was when she was rushing past my station, a screaming brat in her grasp.

The child, traumatized by the doomsday posters of BACK TO SCHOOL! plastered throughout the store, pulled back against his mother's hands as she aimed for Kimm's immaculate field of denim.

She glimpsed over at me quickly as she passed, and after I imagined a pained look of regret for the kinky future we would never realize, my eyes wandered downward to her retreating steps.

I was disappointed to see her in flat soled, sensible shoes. I'm talking Keds Women's Champions in ivory canvas.

The type of footwear that inspired nothing beyond a day of meaningless errands and a dinner of Tuna Helper across from her belching slob of a husband.

I went back to the stockroom and retrieved our shared Candies stilettos from their hiding place, then took one last look at the daring heels before replacing the worn box cover, by now grown soft at the edges from my dampened palms.

I tossed them into the unmatched return barrel, as if casting a stillborn lovechild into the sea.

"So, any plans of you guys playing a *show* so I might actually see the band I signed?" Robbie asked one day on a succinct phone call.

We booked our first show at The Cuckoo's Nest in Costa Mesa, a club we knew well from the vantage of dance floor but had never seen from up on the stage.

It was a sleepy Wednesday night gig, one of those affairs where you were issued a stack of colored tickets to shill to friends pressured into favor, like moving Girl Scout Cookies or ineffective weed for your lazy children.

They counted your crowd for the night, and you were moved later into the week if you pulled, until you might catch an opening gig on a sacred Friday or Saturday night.

Of course, we were doing all this backward: a record already on the shelf but without having played a real gig yet, still baffled by such language as "load-in" and "soundcheck."

We set up on that tall stage where we had seen so many local bands conduct the swirling cyclone of slammers.

I finally ran my hand along that oddly misplaced mural of dreamy white clouds that served as the stage backdrop.

We played our set to maybe thirty people, a crowd mostly made up of kids from Cerritos, carpooled down the 55 freeway at our pleaded request.

Chris stood side stage as our first roadie, Doug and his brothers were down on the floor instigating a tiny but ferocious pit.

Robbie showed up as well and seemed happy enough with the night, though that may have had more to do with the gal in the vinyl miniskirt who sat upon his lap and nibbled at his ear.

He waved me over after our set and gave me but one note on our debut performance:

"That shade of red you're wearing," he said from beneath the lobe nibbling ministrations of his perched punkette, "it's *all wrong.*"

Kimm came into the Wild West one afternoon and, after clocking in and pinning on his badge, came over to me clutching a rolled up copy of the *LA Weekly.*

Without a word, he flipped it open and pointed at the print.

And there, between yet another exposé involving LA's guilty water supply and the *La Dee Da* Hollywood gossip column, was the record review column by the music editor, Craig Lee.

It was a quarterly roundup of new releases, including a surprisingly lukewarm pass on X's *Wild Gift,* which Lee crabbily took to task for overly poetic language.

The final review introduced a *"new quartet of jerk rock geniuses from suburban Cerritos… without time nor ability to include any such lyrical flourish in these short blasts of hardcore purity."*

He went on to compare us to, of all things, *The Ramones*, and though he noted the serious fury in the song "Manzanar," we were redeemed as knuckleheads for the goofy prurience of the hidden closer, "Wetspots!" Craig ended up his glowing review with: *"Now, if only they didn't look so geeky!"* (Surely this was a comment on those photobooth grimaces plastered on the back cover).

Standing there among the columns of corduroy and denim, I read the review, once, then again, and could only nod in agreement to his final assessment.

If only!

THREE

We got to Milwaukee after midnight, woke the promoter with slaps on his door until the porch light came on.

He grumpily let us into his tiny apartment to crash.

The next day was heavy overhead, a gray blanket holding in the oppressive heat and moisture, everyone cranky with nothing to do until show time.

We spent the day staying away from each other, Jack napping in the van while Kimm took to a corner phone booth in a last-ditch effort to salvage a couple more shows before we crossed the Canadian border again.

Chris and Doug were back to skipping rope and doing pushups on the sidewalk as I sat on the porch drinking beers and occasionally shouting, "Hey, why don't you suck his cock while yer at it!" while they held each other's ankles for sit-ups.

They'd cast sideways glances in my direction, blaming me not only for shanghaiing them into this endless trip, but also for the food, the humidity, and probably the existence of *Milwaukee* itself.

A couple times I overheard them talking breathlessly between sets of pushups, and I could have sworn I heard the words "bus tickets" and "escape" among their grunted complaints.

But really, we were all considering blessed mutiny from these August doldrums.

Our momentum seemed stilled like a ship in a dead calm, its sails hanging impotently off the masts without flutter.

Only Jay was happy, spilled along the lumpy couch, playing an unplugged electric guitar mindlessly as if petting a sleeping cat on his lap.

An old Hope & Crosby movie was on the television, the guys mugging beneath pith helmets against some desert backdrop.

Jane Russell enters the scene wiggling up from a snake charmer's basket; her wondrous boobs served up as the scene's punchline.
I could tell Jay loved every moment of being here, if not on the road, then at least being *gone* for the summer.
His feline energy was suited for this life: the days of long naps and reading in a quiet spot of sun, stretched out on a couch and motionless for hours.
Then, with a nocturnal burst of energy, he'd hit the stage and the after party wild-eyed, well rested, and prepared to flirt and drink until dawn.

We pulled up to the show that night and were encouraged by the crowd of punkers milling around outside.
We said our hellos as we loaded in.
Got some back slaps, even had to put down the amps for a moment to autograph some vinyl with fragrant sharpies.
The local opening band was just finishing up to the empty room as we loaded in.
A few frat boy types at the bar sarcastically slow clapped as the band finished up, derisive yells of "woo, punk rock!" coming from their party.
We were puzzled that none of the crew out front seemed to be coming in, but I imagined they were just enjoying the cooling evening, the city finally surrendering its hold on the heat and noise of the day.

A couple of kindly punk girls, Jenny and Jordan, came up and introduced themselves, welcomed us to Milwaukee.
By the way they rolled their eyes and pronounced Milwaukee with an exaggerated Midwestern tang -*Mul WAH kee*- their greeting took on the chaste tone of apology.
They explained that the local punkers were boycotting the show, something about the cover charge being too high or some opening band getting screwed by the promoter.
One of those local dramas that we always seemed to be getting thrust into the middle of, like David Carradine or Bronson, those '70s TV

loners who only needed to kick the right asses and fuck the prettiest girl
to set the town back on track as they exited into the sunset.

The promoter was already making excuses as we set up to play,
wondering out loud *how in the world* he was supposed to pay us when
so few had coughed up the cover charge.
We decided to play the set loud with all the lights off in the bar,
somehow reasoning that way at least the kids outside could listen to us,
while none of the asshole frat guys would be able to see us.
Afterwards, the promoter hemmed and hawed a bit more, telling us
while we would *not* be getting paid, he *sure as hell hoped we were
hungry!* as he'd planned a feast of spaghetti noodles smothered in chili,
a local concoction he claimed was already simmering on stovetop.

Jenny and Jordan stepped in and rescued us, offering their pad to crash
after the party they were going to throw that night.
The girls were kind and brusquely hilarious, and after easily fending off
each of our separate and awkward advances, kept us housed and fed as
we waited for our journey to start again.

What we saw in these women we met all summer, aside from their
frank and victimless sexuality, was a fierce independence, living a life
claimed in those grimy inner cities.
Warriors beneath slashed haircuts and racoon-shadowed eyes, they
thrived within the context of Reagan Country America, being called
freaks, sluts, or worse.
They were making it on their own well enough to even care for *us*,
protecting us against their cities.
They watched over us, like little brothers or feral cats, strays bawling
for some appetite unsatisfied.

That it was quiet Jack that Jordan eventually allowed into her bedroom
shouldn't have surprised us, though perhaps she merely wanted to
cuddle this poor kid stuck out here with the savages.
And while we pestered him to the point of headlocks, gentleman Jack

never talked. Nor did he even scribble a single letter in the journal, cheating us of any coded secret he learned behind that locked bedroom door.

***We rode a startling rush after the* Weekly review**, Kimm coming into the garage each day with yet another piece of unbelievable news.
We got put onto choice support slots on Friday and Saturday nights at the Nest, as well as at the shows that started to pop up, for some strange reason, at dilapidated roller rinks throughout the Southland.

Without preparation or secret initiation, we were thrust onto shows with virtually every band that made up Kimm's record collection:
Adolescents to X.
We reported to these gigs in awe, sharing the cramped backstage with these bands.
Band that we'd seen only from the dance floors, a perspective that made the bands-*up there*-statuesque and untouchable.
I soon discovered I was taller than most of these people when we met at load in, and I soon developed a purposeful slouch to become supposedly invisible.
I also made it a habit to get grimly drunk in order to still my trembling hands enough to tune my guitar for the gig, shake hands with these musicians in passing.

Most of the bands we talked to were friendly, and we were relieved to find most of them just kids as well, just as lost backstage or lined up outside of locked doors after the show, yelling to get paid.
A lot of them were curious about our dealings with Posh Boy as Robbie had worked with so many bands on his compilation records.
We were told repeatedly how we got swindled out of our publishing, though I didn't understand why these bands (who had maybe *one* song on one of his compilation records) were getting so worked up over the very un-punk business side of the music business.
It was smiling Steve Soto of the Adolescents who pulled me aside at

some roller rink and put it in perspective: "Hell man, if it wasn't for
Robbie signing you guys, would you have a record? Would you be here
now?"
We touched beers together in cheers, agreeing that we surely would
not.

Robbie, in one of his mysterious deals, got a single of "I Got a
Gun" pressed with the UK label No Future, as well as placing the track
on the *Punk & Disorderly* compilation.
That record company wisely chose not to use our goofy band photos
but covered the record with a charming collage of gun tragedy,
including the iconic sidearm execution of Nguyễn Văn Lém, his face
forever torqued by the .38 slug entering his brain.
We were immediately taken for an ultra-violent British band in Europe
who lived a mysterious, twinned identity on the other side of the
Atlantic.
It was only decades later when we would finally tour there and dispel
any myths about being tough guys.

Kimm was starting to get calls daily, offers for shows, requests for
interviews.
He'd come into the garage late for practice, breathless with yet more
tremendous news:
Robbie wanted us back in the studio to record a full-length album.
John Peel of the BBC was said to be championing the No Future single
with serious airplay.
Guest columnist Wattie Buchan gave the EP a glowing review in the
latest *NME*, saying we had beaten *The Clash -for fuck sake!-* at their
own game.
I took all this news in as if from afar, as if witnessing something
crystalline and fragile being spun while I watched.
Afraid to breathe for fear of breaking the delicate magic that held the
moment together, fucking things up by naming the thing aloud.

But it was the day that Kimm came in with the news that we would be playing at the Whisky a Go Go (8910 Sunset Boulevard, Hollywood, California) when I allowed myself to believe such things could happen.

I'm sitting in the shadow of a huge Miller billboard, surrounded by a barricade of emptied plastic cups as the four-piece polka band finishes up their jaunty version of "Tennessee Waltz."
I brace myself for the next song, the big set opener of "Beer Barrel Polka."
And sure enough, with a Welkian *and uh one and uh two…* the accordion-driven nightmare begins its endless cycle once again.
We'd been sitting in the courtyard of the Miller Valley brewery tour for two solid hours, and I'd unwillingly memorized their repertoire, songs mentioning "beer" or "polka" set to the same chugging meter.
"Roll Out the Barrel" followed by a 3/4 version of the "Welcome to Miller Time," a setlist repeated with Teutonic precision.
The band, made up of three gray-headed gents plus an embarrassed teen bassist who continuously rolled his eyes in our direction, was probably used to tourists sitting for perhaps two songs.
Just long enough to toss back a 10-ounce cup of beer and move on.
Then they'd make their way out the gates, continuing their futile search for cheap entertainment, to see what Milwaukee offered to burn away another muggy weekday.
The plump girl at the keg stand disregarded the *Two Samples per Adult Only Please!* signage and kept us in full cups all afternoon, delighted by Chris's silly flirting and his wobbly-kneed dancing to the polka tunes.

That year Miller had been pushing their watery brand under the "Miller Time" campaign, promising that if we *had the time*, then they *had the beer*.
And oh, we had the time all right, brother.
We'd been stranded in Milwaukee for three days, a string of gigs canceled, and no payday on the horizon until a return to Canada the next weekend.

We spent three afternoons getting steadily drunk on free cups Miller High Life, self-tagged beneath their dated logo as the *Champagne of Beers*.

I knew what they were aiming for with the wordplay, some wag at McCann Erickson sitting the Miller team down and saying, *"Look, we all know this is the worst beer on the market. But what if we compared it to gasoline or urine… or-no wait, I got it-champagne…!"*

But after the tenth round of plastic cups were dispatched to yet another rendition of "Roll Out the Barrel," the words swam together and made as much sense as, say, the *Dog of Cats* or the *Hamburger of Hot Dogs*.

It was not lost on me that this was the second brewery tour of the summer, and I wondered if we might next year plan our tour around suds factories, the way some people travel the country to collect grinning photos in front of all the Major League baseball fields.

Kimm sat next to me on the picnic bench, on this day even drunker than I.

His tour planner tucked in his backpack, abandoned in frustration.

We were getting ready to start another leg of this tour, westward along the long Canadian highways until we'd finally meet the Pacific again in Vancouver. Then we'd start south, toward home.

I thought maybe Kimm had realized that his own summer vacation was rapidly running out, and that his memories of it would be mainly of sticky phone booths, a filthy handset held to his head for collected hours on end. That, and the daily herding and corralling of the rest of us, he fulfilling the most thankless task in all of music: Tour Manager.

"Whoo!" he shouted as "Roll out the Barrel" came to its *oom-pa-pa* crash landing.

"That was a good one boys! Again! Again!"

I *spent the night before the Whisky show in the drunk tank.*
We'd gathered at the Gold Brique after our last practice, confident that our set was tight, the guitar strings new, each of us sure but casually silent (this after hours of posing in front of the mirror) about which shirt and pant combo we'd wear upon that stage.
We aimed for the Whisky gig with humorless focus, so when mom flicked the lights on us at eight o'clock, we decided upon a few beers at the Brique to calm our preshow jitters.

The Gold Brique was a sweet little neighborhood bar in the bordering neighborhood of Artesia.
No hard booze but glass pitchers of Coors for four bucks, a sawdust-seasoned shuffleboard and a 45 jukebox.
A neighborhood joint that attracted a well-mixed crowd of local retirees, Cholos, bikers, and punks.
The owner was grouchy old Helen, who shook her head at our chopped hair and torn shirts as she passed over the sweating pitchers, warning us against starting any "crazy shit" in here.
But she never asked for ID, and it wasn't a surprise to see a couple of kids ride up on stingray bicycles and saddle up to the bar, barely tall enough to pour a glass from those heavy pitchers.
Everyone got along all right at the Brique, save the occasional flare up of drunken baseball arguments or the appearance of a furious wife, the bar suddenly lit by the high beams of a station wagon holding a trio of bawling kids.
The woman would rush in to capture her beer-drunk husband before the weekly paycheck was lost to cocaine or poker.

It just happened that this was one of the nights the cops swept through the place, on their monthly visit under the guise of weeding out the underage drinkers.

They checked some shady types for warrants, then nudged a few people to empty out their pockets.

The bar top was soon filled with pocketknives, glossy bindles of white powder, syringes, and surprisingly, some pointy 5.56x45mm military cartridges.

A mustached cop came up to us, waved his flashlight around and said, "Oh brother, you guys ain't of age. Out."

But then his beam of light found my studded wristband, the pyramid studs grabbing his attention.

He tugged at my arm then, "What's this, spikes?" He shined his flashlight to my eyes, then up to my shaved head.

He looked over at his partner, who was chatting and laughing with Helen, and said, "Hey Bob, we got some *punks* here. I'm scared, huh?" Then the other cop walked over, shaking his head.

"Totally," Bob said.

They cuffed me, calling my wristband a "deadly weapon," and took Chris as well, on the charge of not having any ID on his person.

We were kept all night in a freezing community cell, Chris and I huddled together, shivering under the glaring fluorescent light.

We were surrounded by a Saturday night's collection of snoring, farting drunks and one babbling madman who sat in the corner and talked through the night, urging us all to wake up and join the Communist Party before it was *all too late*.

We were released in the gray morning without charge: the cops merely taking our mugshots for their File of Known Punk Rockers, tagged like pesky campground bears before being released back into the wild.

It seems there was a real community concern about these new, wild-haired youths who could terrorize the mall food court with their very existence.

The local cops stayed abreast of the threat, as if we were some organized crew intent on burning the library or taking down a bank in Dead Kennedys T shirts.

They hauled us in, kept us without charge, recording our likeness
before releasing us.

Larry picked us up in the morning, laughing hysterically.
"How was jail, ya queers?" he asked. "Drop the soap?"

When I walked in the door, my mom only shook her head, furious to
the point of being silent.
Disappointed to have a child jailed, of course; but perhaps another
simmering rage was awakened.
The smell of diesel coming back to her, that freezing bus ride to camp.
When she was caged for the crime of looking different, of being
misunderstood.

We drove and drove toward Canada, Chris keeping a nervous eye on
the falling gas gauge, Kimm making peanut butter sandwiches and
passing them around.
At one point we stopped at a McDonald's and ordered six cups of water
and three Filet O' Fish with our last pooled money, adding the sheepish
request to *cut each one in half, please.*

But entering Minnesota on an eighth of a tank, Doug, as though finally
finding the perfect moment to display a learned magic trick, produced a
Sears credit card embossed with the name "Dan Everston."
I received it with two hands like a communion wafer, knowing not to
ask who Dan was.
At that moment we were *all* Dan.
The card worked at the gas pumps exactly twice, and got us, as if in
penance, into North Dakota.

As we drove along those oceanic plains, the skies before us grew slate,
then charcoal.
The rain dropped, and then gushed great sheets that washed across the
windshield sideways.
Eventually the wipers did nothing but clear a moment of terror, the
highway dividing lines vanished, the tilted horizon strobed in lightning.

Finally, the tires gave up all grasp of the road and we went sideways, hydroplaned on a quarter inch of water, the van veering into oncoming traffic as a big rig bore down, head on.

Time, that fucker, did its trick of slowing then, letting each of us utter a single syllable of shock.
We were held for the moment in the path of destruction, and I could see not only the inevitable crash but also the aftermath.
Red lights flashing above idling cruisers, county patrolmen smoking in the rain, shaking their heads at the carnage steaming on the asphalt.
Water drips off the brims of their plastic covered hats, mimicking the tears they shed at the loss of such fine young men.

Our front tires suddenly found purchase and the van shuddered on its turned wheels.
Chris spun the steering wheel back into our lane with his left palm, his right arm held out instinctively across the seats as if to keep a bus load of children from orbiting out through the windshield.
He overcorrected as we slid sideways, and just as the semi passed I heard the faintest *snick* of metal upon metal, a head on collision bargained down to a mere inch of contact to our rear bumper.
We pulled off to the side of the highway, the rain so loud on the roof that we could not talk over it, even if we could conjure up any words.
We sat quiet in the Blue & White, each of us dazed.
Cheated out of the death we'd just surrendered to wholly.

It was Doug who finally said, *"fuck it"* and slid open the door.
We watched as he ran into the open field, dark as night now, and he raised his hands to the skies, held back his head, yelling up to the pouring clouds.
I looked over at Chris, who shrugged, and opened my door.
One by one, we all got out of the van, all of us soaked through instantly, goofy to be alive.
We shouted up at the sky, whoops of relief, cursing the clouds, God, and anyone else who might listen.

"Hah! Why?" Kimm yelled, the words just audible above the howling storm.

Why? he repeated, and I knew he was questioning far more than just the terrific moment.

He lowered his hands and stood dripping, waiting for an answer.

If we were crying or laughing by then I could not tell, we stomped at the puddles and took off our shirts and shorts, danced like savages in our dirty boxers in the pouring rain.

We hooted in tongues, unintelligible sounds borne from deep in our guts, an instinct of survival awakened like sea monkeys rehydrated.

And then Jack came out of the van, stripped to his skivvies, holding a bar of soap.

I watched as he let the rain soak him, and then lathered his thin frame.

By the time he tossed the soap to me I dropped it into the mud, laughing so hard I had to brace my hands upon my knees.

We each took turns, lathering our armpits and crotches, giggling and dick punching as if in a locker room.

And I'd like to report that just then, with all of us survived and *cleansed*, that the storm passed and a single beam of moonlight fought its way through the parting clouds.

But nah.

It just kept on fucking pouring, and we moved on.

I plugged in my amp and moved aside, letting the Whisky stagehands set the microphones for soundcheck.

I walked to the edge of the stage and looked across the club.

Smaller now with all the houselights up, the entrance door was open to Sunset Boulevard, letting a trace of daylight thread through the room.

The smell of spilled booze and the cooking aroma of warming electronics perfumed the air, and beyond that; the earthy funk of sweat, borne of triumph and despair, hurried sex.

I looked down at the dance floor beyond the monitors, searching for the

vantage points where I usually stood, watching so many bands play.
We were told twice to turn down the amps during the quick
soundcheck, dismissed mid-song, and told to be back on stage at 9:30.

After soundcheck we hung out upstairs, somehow scoring the big
backstage room that overlooked the Strip.
We tried to calm our nerves with cautious sips of beer, nodding at the
conversations we were pulled into by well-wishing guests.
It seemed this was no backstage, that this upstairs room was just
another section of the club, and people crossed in and out at will.
I looked around the space, imagining the past doings here: the drugs
ingested and blowjobs traded, the careers launched and extinguished.
Deals made by drunken handshakes that would result in either gem-like
additions to *The Great American Songbook* or bitter lawsuits that
would last a decade.
The room was soon packed, filled with more strangers than familiar
faces. Robbie was there, holding court with Rodney in a corner, their
heads held close in conversation, probably already choosing the next
band to bless.

In a neat twist of destiny, the opening band was Unit 3 and Venus,
made up of Jack's brother, Henree, and his wife, Patty, with Jack's
seven-year-old niece Venus on vocals.
I watched them play a few songs from the balcony, and the crowd was
giving them a great response, shouting along to their big hit, "Beer."
"Beer, beer isn't good for you!" cried Venus, as the drunks held aloft
their foaming drinks in cheer.

I chanced a quick peek up at the house balcony across from me, where
my mom sat with Lois Gardener and Chris's mom, Carol.
They'd carpooled up, and I tried to imagine the conversation on that
ride. *(Terry, be a dear and lock your door, hmm? I believe that man is
defecating in the gutter!)*
My mother was not one to wander out of the house after dark, much

less visit the grimy streets of LA, but I knew she was here with a sense of pride, even after her youngest was now a jailbird.

Perhaps it was all those nights of hearing us practice in the garage, sitting just on the other side of an uninsulated wall and hearing us go from terrible to bad, finally to *pretty good*.
She would sit there as the house shook around her, struggling to lip-read Jerry Dunphy presenting the 7:30 news.
She had suffered along with us, overheard our dreamy plans as we sat at the kitchen table wolfing her Spaghetti Carbonara after practice.
And now she sat at a cramped table perched above the Whisky dance floor, sipping at an overpriced cola and waiting for us to get on stage and reveal what it had all been for.
Carol had probably been here in her own wild youth, and perhaps scanned the room for remembered go-go cages and cigarette machines.
Lois, laughing at the whole scene, shook her empty highball glass at the tattooed waitress, game to fulfill the two-drink minimum.

Jay was there, too.
He was Robbie's right-hand man by then, and we'd been working with him for a couple weeks on songs for *Fear of Life*.
He showed up at the garage one afternoon to hang out and do pre-production work, listened to our song arrangements before methodically breaking them all down and rearranging them with far better results.
He'd played at the Whisky plenty, most recently with his band The Stepmothers, and before our set he walked onto the stage with us and discreetly turned the guitar amps up two notches from soundcheck.

We stood on the stage in the darkness just before beginning.
The house sound still playing, Black Flag's "Jealous Again" pulsing out of the speakers, marinating the crowd with rage and fury.
I looked down at the packed house, strummed a quick chord on my guitar to the shouts and raised glasses of all that stood just below me.

I saw pockets of locals from Cerritos, here to share the night with us, along with faces I'd recognized from the clubs.
The nights standing shoulder to shoulder in the bouncing pits, watching a band from the floor.
Punk rockers, all of them, and in that moment, I had a weepy flush of love for my fellow man.
I had awoken that morning in a jail cell, arrested for nothing more than being a punk.
All these kids could share a similar story, the stares and jeers, the yells of *hey punk rock faggot!* shouted from the passing Camaros.
It only made us feel we were doing something *right* to so enrage the people we despised.

I took one last look up at mom, and she was holding tight to the balcony rail now, as if braced for an approaching storm.
I thought of her life, of the variations of *"Jap"* hurled her way, then at the other moms. Women who endured ass pinches and patronizing speeches daily.
Then we- who were gifted the better life-we, who were raised safely in the stamped suburbs, living the privileged life of the white middle class.
We had found a way to mutilate ourselves and become a minority.
If not just to break out of the mundane existence that lay before us, then to finally wake up, become alive, and exist in an uglier yet far truer world.

I was pulled out of my reverie when a cup of beer was thrown on stage, and the yell of *let's go ya dicks!* brought me back to the moment.
Standing upon a filthy stage before the rowdy crowd, frenzied like a pack of hyenas, ready to attack at the first sign of weakness.
The house sound cut off then, a delicious moment before the stage lights would come up and we would count off, and in the blackness the crowd roared.
I looked back at Burton, yelling "Ready? Ready?" Then to Larry, who only smiled and nodded me on.

And then Kimm and I nodded to each other, just as our fathers may have bobbed their heads to childhood friends in discrete farewell, a silent pact to find each other again after the war.
Burton clicked off four times and we launched into the staccato report of "I Got a Gun."
The stage lights came up and the place went off.

We got to the Pembina–Emerson border crossing** in the early morning, still dark.

We were prepared to sit in the van for hours as the Mounties dissected the Blue & White once again, searching for any crumb of indecency that would justify a shameful U turn back into the States.

We all held those SIN cards though, and the guys from Stretchmarks were heading our way to help.

Chris pulled into a turnout on the US side and turned off the motor.

We each fell asleep where we sat, our heads back and tongues out, gasping snores at the van roof, exhausted by the long drive.

It was a mere two-hour delay at the border this time, Mark from Stretchers and manager Matt showing up after dawn with some paperwork.

Documents were inspected, copied, stamped and handed back.

We were cleared, and then followed the green Stretchvan into Canada.

Once out of sight of the border we pulled the vans over and got out, hugged like reunited brothers, and all talked at once in hoarse shouts.

The boys brought out an iced box of Extra Old Stock, and we toasted the rising sun with those strong Canadian beers.

We followed them to the Stretchmarks pad, which we'd imagined as a Canuck-styled Monkees clubhouse, perhaps with a fire pole and wee backyard hockey rink, Molson dripping out of every faucet.

But it turned out to be another jolly punk mansion, a sagging farmhouse filled with farting punks, though I saw no evidence of the Stars and Stripes inverted in contempt.

It was warm and welcoming inside, Dik and Bill padding down the stairs to hug us as Kelly the drummer yelled out his greetings from the bathroom, where he was currently *dropping a wicked deuce* but would be out shortly.

One side of the kitchen was braced by stacks of beer boxes, each containing empties. We'd soon learn they took the recycling seriously, as the bottle deposit was an unheard of five cents apiece. A quick bit of math (and knowing the drinking habits of these sturdy lumberjacks), I realized they were probably draining enough suds to make the rent each month.

Upon tossing an empty into a trash bin later that night, Kimm was pinned to the kitchen wall for a five-minute lecture on bottle deposits and what wasteful shits we Americans were.

He retrieved the bottle and placed it back into its webbed case like a reproached poacher, replacing a Condor egg to its warm nest.

We spread out in the house, drank morning beers while watching weird TV, talking about our summer adventures since we split up in Texas.

I found a nice little patch of clean carpet in an alcove below the stairs and stretched out.

It was a luxury of flat space, and I reveled in nothing more than stillness; my body melting into the shag, finally free of forward momentum.

We slept then, and when we woke in the evening the Stretchmarks had already left for the club.

We showered quick and took off, as the Stretchers warned us to *not miss their goddamn set that night.*

We got to the Doghouse club and found a charming deli tray laid out for us backstage, a platter of cured meats and cheeses, hard rolls and pickles.

We fell upon the food like locusts and did not lift our heads until only parsley and a waxy slice of pimento loaf remained.

Mark showed us around the club, really an old warehouse that the guys had taken over and repurposed as a club.

I had a real respect for this zeal and gumption, though I, of course, did not mention that, but only asked where the goddamned drinks were.

As if waiting just for that question, Matt wordlessly opened a coffin-sized cooler packed with glistening beers on ice, and then he pointed a single finger at the sideboard behind us.

There, like a loaded weapon, sat an unopened 3-liter jug of Jack Daniels.

Speechless, I grabbed Matt around the neck.

And instead of daring him to break from my viselike grip, I simply kissed him squarely on the mouth.

It was a night we needed; the space packed with friendly punks who'd heard all about our tour hijinks from their local heroes.

A bald, raccoon-eyed gal came up and yelled in my ear, "So, which one is the slut, is it you?"

I simply pointed to Doug and Chris, who were both shirtless and drinking double handed, though I was unsure, really, which one of us was guilty or worthy of the crown.

We did finally see the Stretchmarks play, and they played their ferocious brand of hardcore so brilliantly that I felt a swelling of pride that I *knew* these guys.

Dik and Mark were held in mid-air most of the set, each making spread-legged leaps off the riser.

Bill slashing away on guitar, his brother Kelly holding it all together, his drumsticks a blur.

At one point they stopped their set and pointed us out to the crowd, their "drunken pals from Hollywood, California!"

Then Matt jumped onstage with them to play bass, Mark now wearing a second guitar and a red beret like Kimm had worn early in the summer.

And then they played one of our songs as *us*, a teasing but touching version of "Out of Control."

Dik wore a Japanese headband and stumbled the stage like a punk Dean Martin, chewing the words and oversinging the melody with an overwrought earnestness, a mimicry hilarious and unnerving.

I played the opening of a new song, "Catholic Boy" for Jay again, strumming each chord slowly while he studied my finger position on the frets. He shook his head, as if in wonder or disgust.
"Where the hell did you think that up?" he asked. "I mean, major to minor to 7th to… I don't know what to call the last one. Weird!"
"What, you don't like? How would you play it?" I asked.
"Oh no, it's great just like that. Just weird. I would have never thought of something like that."
We were in the garage, going through songs for the next record, Jay having called me from Lakewood Boulevard and Artesia where the Metro 266 bus had dumped him without ceremony.
"Where the fuck you guys live?" he asked from a payphone. "By a mall or something? *Where am I?*"
I told him I'd come pick him up, though he squinted at me over his sunglasses when I rode up on my brother's CB400 Honda.
I flipped down the passenger pegs and scooted forward, nodded for Jay to hop on.
As he slid onto the saddle behind me, he said, "Take it easy. I hate motorcycles."

Robbie thrilled us with the news that we'd be doing a full-length album, a quick follow up to the surprising success of the EP.
We imagined using the extra tracks afforded to us now to show off some of our more melodic songs, just as the Clash could smuggle in a piece of Mick Jones' pop perfection, like a gem hidden in the coal.
Posh assigned Jay to do the pre-production work, prepping the ten new songs that would make up the album *Fear of Life.*

The album would be rounded out to twelve tracks with the inclusion of "Manzanar" and the naughty "Wetspots." (A song that would haunt us forever, like the word *FUCK* tattooed across the knuckles of a petting zoo clown.)

Jay came into the garage and peered around at our gear, took in the band and motorcycle posters covering the studs.
We still had Aerosmith and KISS up there, bootleg posters bought on the stumbling walk out of the stadium gates.
Jim Pomeroy crossed up midair on an old Bultaco Pursang, sandwiched between a '77 Damned & Adverts tour poster and a faded poster of Simonon forever destroying his bass for *London Calling.*
I played the riff again at speed, choked downstrokes, and Jay nodded his head. "Yeah. guitar intro, we'll put a lead line over that before each verse."
"You know what that is, don't ya?" I asked then. "It's 'Green Manalishi,' dropped down to D."
And then I played the old Fleetwood Mac song (Judas Priest version) and Jay nodded in recognition.
"Ah, ripping off the greats. Good man."

It was the start of my long mentorship with Jay, he informing every aspect of my songwriting and stage work.
Always firm in his resolve, a confidence in his vision so resolute that it inspired in me a blind trust to hilarious and disastrous results (enough to, say, abandon the guitar for a bit and become a cock-loaded *lead singer*, cowboy-booted and cotton-candied haired. Another story…).
We'd first seen Jay with the Simpletones, the glorious ensemble group whose charming songs like "I Have a Date" and "California" seemed to destine them to be the West Coast Ramones.
It was a band with three lead singers, modeled after a teen pop band or perhaps a punk Sha Na Na.
But there was also a thrilling, sinister side to the band, and you just knew that after picking up that much-anticipated date, the lad was going to produce a Rorer 714 Quaalude in lieu of corsage and they'd end up fucking in the back seat.

We spent a few afternoons breaking down the songs to drum and bass, building them back up again. Always cutting them down: shorter, to the point.

Jay also discovered my mom's dinner table, always groaning with food and ready when we were cut off at eight pm.

He arranged to get to Cerritos for our evening practices then join us for a meal after.

We were comfortable with Jay immediately, though a bit star struck as we sat there eating, listening to his stories of his days in the Simpletones and stints with almost every other LA club band we could question him about.

Already beyond the slash and spike of punk rock style, Jay was now playing in The Stepmothers, a big sound rock band that ably shared the stage with bands like Motley Crue and Quiet Riot.

His hair was long and big, tinted a blowzy shade of red suited for aging Vegas showgirls and forty buck hookers.

We all met back at Brian Elliot's to record the basic tracks and captured the drums and bass in one quick, evening session.

I helped Burton load his red drum set into his lifted Toyota truck of the same exact color.

I shook his hand and told him it was good stuff, waved from the curb as he drove back to Cerritos.

His time with us is archived on those 2-inch reels, but within a couple months he was gone.

Jay guided us through the guitar tracks then, suggesting a half dozen licks that would fit into each song.

A few times picking up the guitar Kimm or I had laid down in frustration and quickly playing a compact and sparkling lead line with a shrugging ease that had me and Kimm cursing his skill under our grateful breath.

We returned a couple more times for overdubs and vocals, Robbie joining us for those sessions to see how things were shaping up.

He deemed the opener, "Out of Control" too short, and with razorblade and splicing tape, the second verse was magically duplicated and pasted in as a third, identical verse before the lead. We had recorded a quick song at the end of the session, the first song I had ever written, "You Make Me Feel Cheap."

It was a slight rip off of Aerosmith's "Mama Kin," played with a Stooges-like tempo and recklessness.

After I put on the lead vocals I watched Robbie in the control room, looking up to the ceiling as he listened, nodding to a thought that had just occurred.

I would get to recognize that mannerism, like the nostril-flared tell of a poker player across the table, holding a hand of cards that would sweep the pot.

"You know," he said when I came into the booth, "the empty tag at the end of each verse, it sounds like it's missing something, hmmm?"

And then he snapped his fingers, and started to sing: *Can't help it, the girl can't help it!*

He turned to Jay. "Am I right? The Little Richard song!"

Jay was nodding then. "Right. I can hear it."

I had no idea what the fuck they were talking about, and when we packed the gear and left the studio, the two of them were still hovering over the board like mad scientists, intent on creating life where there had been none.

A couple weeks later Robbie told us to be sure and tune in to Rodney, that he would be playing one of the new tracks.

We sat at Kimm's dining table, huddled over bottles of Lucky Lager, keeping an ear cocked toward the speaker for any familiar tone.

Finally, after following an interminable goth block of sludgy industrial moaners, we heard the rushed drum intro of Burton hammering the snare, my sloppy and slightly out of tune slashing at the E chord, Kimm's jarring overdub of syncopated response.

My voice comes in, somehow a pitch higher than normal.
The whole song seems sped up just lightly, like a record urged faster by a nudging finger upon turntable.
And then: a different voice, unmistakably female.
It appears out of nowhere, like the shadow of a restless spirit caught in the background of an old family photo.
The girl sings in duet with me, the whole song, and she seems to have a bratty answer to my every pleading verse.
As a kicker, at the very end, the gal seems to have a merciful moment of either desire or pity, and reconsiders giving this loser just one more chance.

We looked from the stereo speaker to each other.
In perfect unison, as if copied, cut, and spliced in the moment, we asked:
The fuck was that?

We didn't know that Rodney and his girlfriend Maria had dropped by the studio one night while Jay and Robbie mixed.
Maria was urged into the vocal booth and given the tag lines that Robbie had heard in his head.

I sputtered in rage after Rodney went to the commercial.

A chick singing? *A duet?*
I imagined a thousand hardcore punks hearing it as well and writing us off, discovered as the New Wave wimps we truly were.

It all worked out as a huge advantage, of course, as Rodney took to playing the song without fail each weekend.
We even garnered a few daytime spins on KROQ, the female voice making the song less threatening to the programmers, perhaps.
And all that rage at the song-*my song*-being transformed into something else entirely was forgotten.
Sometimes, I learned, *the grownups* are right.

We got up after the Stretchmarks and played our set.
It flowed and the crowd was into it, but it felt like just a preliminary warmup to the beer-soaked afterparty back at the Stretch house.
On the way there we stopped at the official beer vendor, apparently beer not trusted to be doled out through convenience stores or gas stations like back home.
The scene was hilarious, late-night Canadians rushing in for Saturday's last call, beer apparently not sold by package on Sundays in the province.

Pickup trucks and Camaros, their finishes equally blasted by the brutal winters and salted roads, all came flying into the parking lot and skidded sideways, sending up a spray of gravel.
Thirsty men hopped from the vehicles and dashed for the doors, their cars not quite yet coming to a full stop.
Walking through the store, Kimm held out some cash, fanning out the candy-colored bills the Stretchies had generously paid us for the gig.
We each grabbed a case of beer and got in line along with all the rest of the drunken Canucks, giddy to make it to the checkout line as they started to turn people away at the doors.
We piled back to the van, each of us proudly holding up cases of beer as if we'd managed to snag the last of an overhyped and worthless toy after a frantic Christmas Eve scramble.

The gigs were getting bigger now, shows at abandoned roller rinks and faded ballrooms drawing a thousand punks.
We played the glorious Olympic Auditorium, where Ralphie Valladares and his valiant T-Birds would infuriate their roller derby opponents, where Freddie Blassie and Gorgeous George would preen for the cameras.
My grandfather, Makoto, would watch grainy black and white feeds from the Olympic, probably mystified that such fake violence was necessary in an already brutal world.

The promoters were chased by police-instigated riots from one hall to another, and we would find ourselves upon stages of grand movie houses and shuttered theatres.
I would look up at the ceilings still scrolled with gorgeous piping, wander the art deco lobbies.
Investigate cloakrooms and silent phone booths.
Wondering if my mom had touched those same ornate banisters when she was a young girl in the city.
I would tell my mom about shows at the Palladium, getting drinks at the Biltmore, and she would gaze just over my shoulder, seeing the nights of her youth.
We'd soon see this in all the cities across the country: the abandoned downtowns of America repurposed as our playgrounds.
Only the punkers and gays saw beyond the filth and danger and moved into the ornate shells of the forgotten downtowns.

We returned to the strip, had our own headlining shows at the Whisky.
Played in every other storied club up and down that wonderful street.
One night we were backstage at the Florentine Gardens just after an opening set for The Professionals.
Sex Pistol Steve Jones popped his head into our dressing room and gave us the thumbs up.
"That was al'right lads, yeh?" he said, a girl -*a bird*- nestled beneath each of his tanned arms.
When he left us, Kimm and I looked at each other with raised eyebrows.
Kimm shook his head quickly, as if trying to wake from a long and crazily detailed dream.

I came to my senses at a Salisbury House in downtown Winnipeg, sitting across from a pierced-nosed girl who urged me to eat.

"Jeez, but we were a mess last night, eh?" she said, as a waitress set a plate of food on the table.

It was around 11a.m. the morning after the show, and I kept an eye on the front window.

Waiting for the appearance of the Blue & White at curbside to pick me up and hit the road.

I tried to focus my eyes on hers, but could only manage a blurry, distant image, as if looking though the wrong end of smudged binoculars.

She had wide blue eyes beneath umbrellas of purple makeup, a shock of red hair the color of dried blood.

I looked down at the Formica table between us and beheld a platter of potatoes, sausages, and a slab of ham, all covered with two goopy eggs.

I pushed the plate aside and reached for the steaming coffee mug.

"Oh, come on Pa, eat up." she said. "Edmonton? Jeez, but you fellas got a long ass drive today."

"Can't do it, Ma," I said over the coffee cup, "was never much of a breakfast eater. Evil stuff." I took a deep sip and burned the fuck out of my tongue.

I put the mug back down and swiveled in my seat. "Say, I don't suppose they serve Bloody Marys in this joint, hmm?"

She barked out a single laugh.

"Hah. You're a funny one," she said. She speared a sausage link off my plate and, placing it upon her extended pink tongue, took the thing down in one suggestive chomp.

I raised my eyebrows. "Impressive."

"Oh, you have *no idea*," she said, pushing the plate back toward me.

And truly, I did not have any idea.

Then, like a rescue craft bearing down on a sole survivor, the van pulled into sight.

We were given a choice of artwork for the new album and spent a night with photographer Edward Colver.
Larry, Kimm, and I crowded into his darkroom and watched Edward work.
Images appearing in the trays of developing solution like murdered corpses floating up from the depths.
We looked at group shots he had taken of us in alleys and train crossings, each of us slouched in unsmiling, tough-guy postures.
We looked at and rejected one photo after another, nothing quite capturing the *feel* we were going for, not that we could articulate that *feel*.

Finally, we saw the one photo that we all pointed at together, exclaiming *that's it* in unison.
We were thinking of naming the album after the track *Fear of Life*, and the photo claimed those words capably, if too literally.
"Ah, that one," Edward said, taking the print from my hands and inspecting it under a desk lamp. "Yeah, Black Flag was gonna use that for *Damaged*, but I think it's wide open if you want to use it."

It is a striking image: a pair of hands held together as if in prayer. But, instead of rosary beads, the hands clutch a nickel-plated Colt Python revolver turned, suicide style, back toward the shooter.
Chains form a handcuff-like bracelet around the shooter's left wrist, and his frayed sleeves are rolled down, perhaps to hide the scars or track marks that have brought him to this place of despair.
The gun seems not quite cocked and staring at the photo I always thought we were looking at the last moment of doubt.
The trigger just squeezed, just a fraction of a millimeter between hammer and cartridge.
And the ensuing mess left for the weeping relatives to scrub.

***After the beer run, we entered the Stretchpad with our treasures of
booze*** to the cheers of a packed house.
We took a spirited lap around the living room, cases of beer held high
on shoulder, as the Canadians jeered and sang incorrect (and filthy)
words to *The Star Spangled Banner*.
It seems like half the people at the gig had come over to the party, and
soon the old place was alive with smoke and laughter.
Cases of beer were torn open, bottles passed around like ammunition
before battle.

I was already staggering after the drinks at the club, but the few hours
we had left with the Stretchers gave the night an urgency that made us
all reach for another beer before the last was drained.
We hugged and laughed at our earlier adventures of the summer, like
gray men reliving the glory days of youthful battles.
Though it seemed that we, at least, were still engaged in the war.

Doug and Chris had disappeared upstairs with girls, hopeful of quick
sex and long sleep in a soft bed.
Kimm and Jack were passed out on the couch, their heads thrown back
in drunken exhaustion.
"These Cali boys, they're dropping like flies!" someone crowed.

"Lightweights!"

I mistakenly threw an empty bottle in the garbage and was cornered by
a fiery little dwarf of a girl who lectured me on the proper etiquette of
deposit and return. (And, for that matter, the general moral & hockey
superiority of *Le Canadien*).
That's when my flame-headed punkette stepped in to my rescue.
"C'mon, Shelia, leave him alone," she said, grabbing me by the elbow
and guiding me away.
"Don't worry about her," she said, a thumb jerked back toward the tiny
gal who was now digging through the trash barrel for further evidence

of American waste. "She just likes to hear herself talk, ya know?"
She pulled me into a dark hallway where people were lined up, waiting
for the head.
As one couple passed, she pushed against me to make room, then
stayed there. "Hey jeez, you're a tall one, right?" she said, looking up at
me.
And it wasn't until after we were pressed closer still, her tongue darting
around in my mouth like a hunted animal searching for shelter, that she
pulled back and said, "Corrine. And you are…?"

We got to her small cottage after a confusing drive through Winnipeg
in her Jeep, she talking the whole time over a blasting cassette of *Give
'em Enough Rope*.
I was reminded again of an earlier car ride through empty streets,
windows open to the summer night, shouting beloved punk rock while
a girl next to me shifted gears and drove us toward the unknown.
She drove with purpose, gunning the accelerator down each street, only
to brake hard just before each stop sign or light. I searched for seat belts
and found none.
When the tape got to "Stay Free" she turned the car stereo up even
louder, saying, "Ooh, it's my song–it's *our* song, sweetie," and
bellowed out every word.
And just like that, we had *a song.*

**Fear of Life *came out, and we held the shrink-wrapped album to the
light*,** flipping it over, marveling at the polished package.
CH3 in a startling clean boldface font hovers just above those suicidal
paws, and below the gleaming gun barrel, *Fear of Life* in careless,
paint-stroked response.
The back cover features a group photo, all of us crowded together
looking tough, closed-mouthed and weary.
But the photo is imposed on a funky portable television set, a motif that
would come to haunt us *(get it? Channel 3, like, on the TV!)* in a
hundred flyers and fanzine images.

It turned out to be a pretty good record.

Burton's drumming fits the songs perfectly; a hollow surf snare sound that somehow fits the songs' pushed meter.

Larry's single finger twiddling of the bass strings provides an oddly comforting bottom throb.

And then there are guitars -*guitars!*- all over the thing.

Jay's imprint of wiry lead lines snaking throughout the record, a celebration of riff and hook.

And while it is never mentioned in the same breath as those classic first LPs from Adolescents or T.S.O.L., it allowed us to claim a spot if not equal to, then at least *among* them.

The record got some good initial reviews, and the hardcore backlash to "Make Me Feel Cheap" never materialized.

The song became a crowd favorite, in fact, and allowed us to pull a different girl up onstage each gig to shout out the Maria parts.

It was only years later that we finally met Maria in person, and she was gracious to the point of *apologizing* for crashing our song.

We pulled her on stage that night, of course, and we were all startled to hear her crystalline voice in person.

Corrine's place was tiny and clean, the walls covered with black and white movie posters and framed European liquor advertisements.

There was a large glamour photo of Veronica Lake, one eye staring out longingly, the other one hidden beneath a ridiculously lush sheath of blonde. While I was studying the photo Corrine came up behind me and wrapped her arms around me, pinning my arms to my sides. "Don't you just *adore* that, hmmm?" she whispered.

I thought of her finding this photo in some thrift store and seeing herself: peering out at the world with one eye while the other beheld only darkness.

I sat on the couch and drank another beer while she busied herself in the bathroom after saying, swear to God, she was going to *slip into something more comfortable.*

I felt stuck in an old '40s movie with a swooning ingénue, but it was all endearingly kooky.

I was already forming the night into sentences, ready to tell the guys all about it on the long van ride tomorrow.

She came out holding a lit candle, wearing a silken kimono robe.

She walked to me, nudged my knees apart.

Then she stood looking down at me, finally silent.

Something was not quite right, and when I realized the problem I reached out for her body.

I slowly undid the sash holding her robe together, opened the robe to expose her shockingly white body, then closed the robe back up with the left side over the right.

"Bad luck wearing it right over left. To the Japanese, you know," I said. "Only dead people wear it like that."

She looked down at her robe puzzled, then laughed. "What? Oh you, you're a funny one."

I followed her into her bedroom, where she put the candle down on the nightstand.

She turned to me then, wearing the look of seduction that she'd probably perfected by a thousand minutes in front of her mirror.

And then her face changed with a notion.

"Say, you couldn't put this window shade back up for me, huh?" she said, pointing at a yellowed window blind propped in the corner.

"The thing fell off last week and the morning sun in here is *brutal.*"

A few minutes later I was standing unsteadily on her bed while trying to put the scroll back into the hooked slots.

I was experiencing some double vision and closed one eye as I navigated the brackets.

"You wouldn't happen to have a screwdriver, would ya," I shouted to the kitchen, where she was rattling around. "Phillips."

She came in with a paper sack split by tools, now wearing a flowered apron above her kimono.

"Here ya go, Pa, and don't call me Phillip," she said. "Hah."

I finally got the blind mounted and rolled it down over the window beside her bed.

I lay on the bed then, my head spinning, and she soon joined me with mugs of tea and some toast with jam and margarine.

And though it was not what I expected, I ate it and realized I needed it.

"Good toast, Ma," I said.

"Whatever you say, Pa," she replied, laying down beside me.

The domestic roleplay had somehow cooled our passions, and she rested her head on my shoulder then, and we both started to fall asleep.

"This is nice, hmm?" she whispered.

And it *was* nice.

It was all I desired, that lull after the act.

The murmurs and hugging, a finger tracing my chest as we told stories about our recent youth.

I knew the sex itself, handled quickly and drunkenly, was always tinged with guilt and sadness, shadowed by something that I would not be prepared to face for years.

I woke a few hours later to the muted splashing from her bathroom shower, and the sound of her singing "Stay Free" in a childlike voice. *"We met, when we were in school,"* she sang. *"Never took no shit from no one, we weren't fools…"*

The sun filtered yellow through the shade, and lifting my head a few inches off the pillow found I was still roaringly drunk.

I stretched out alone on her soft bed, resigned to never leave.

I imagined the life we would have here.

I would abandon both band and country in a single scandalous act, claiming sanctuary among my new beer-bottle-returning Canadian brethren.

I would remain north of the border, silent as a draft dodger, wearing nothing but flannel and Sorel boots, growing my hair long enough to ponytail.

Corrine and I, we'd sell hash.

Or perhaps we'd run a daycare center, yes.

We would adopt haunted indigenous orphans whose parents had frozen solid along the highway after huffing aerosol cans of Lysol.

I would grow old and bury Ma, then die in front of a fireplace, my dark daughter weeping over me, one eye glistening with tears while the other hid behind a curtain of thick black hair.

Corrine came out of the bathroom then, steaming and wrapped in towels. "Hey, let's go buddy," she said. "Mark already called. They're going to pick you up after I get some breakfast in ya'."

As a last-minute afterthought, Kimm had included a PO Box address on the insert, on the slim chance someone would take the trouble of writing.

We were shocked when we went by the Cerritos post office a few weeks later to find the slim box choked with a stack of correspondence. Most of them were requests for stickers and buttons, or requests for us to come out to their awful little town to play a gig.

We also received a handful of postcards reminding us that we suck, and that we had *sold out* in the short months between our hardcore EP and this limp-wristed "new wave" album.

These we pinned to a bulletin board in the garage, and would read aloud after each practice in Southern or British accents, toasting the letter writers with sloshing cans of beer.

And then we received thick envelopes, addressed carefully in chunky block or florid cursive, their stamps postmarked by unknown abbreviations.

A girl or boy would introduce themselves in a cheerful opening paragraph.

And then after a few compliments on the record, the letters would take

on a confessional tone, the writer letting us know that the lyrics somehow connected to them.
And how, incredibly, these songs had helped them through a tricky time in their young lives.
Often they would go on to let us know what tragedy they had endured.
Their bewilderment they saw mirrored in the songs, and the comfort they had somehow found in them.
As if they had received a coded message: *hang on.*
I was armed to roll my eyes at such flattery, of course, prepared to let my cynicism armor my heart once again with a snide remark.
But I could not.
I was touched by the thought of these people, taking the time to not only buy the record, but to *listen* to the songs and consider the lyrics.
To think that they would then take to pen and paper, find a fucking stamp, and address an envelope in long hand...

And, in these letters, it was their turn to write the lyrics.
Songs without music, their words in trade for mine.
More heartfelt and purer than anything I could ever hope to write.

I slid out of the booth at Salisbury House as the van honked at curbside.
I leaned down and gave Corrine a kiss on top of her head, and then she got up, wrapped her arms around me with a flourish and gave me a full-face smacker, probably lifting one leg to the swelling end credits orchestration she heard in her head.

She smiled, weepy, slipped me her address and said: "Write. "
I did write, and we nurtured an occasional correspondence for a decade.
She answered my four sentence postcards with three-page missives on perfumed lavender stationery.
She detailed her heartbreaks and romances through the years.
There was the marriage to a "swell bi guy" doomed to divorce, before finally moving in with an architect and "two great kids."

She confided in me so easily I wondered if she was mistaking me for another Mike from another band, perhaps a Mike who consummated the night and deserved such intimacy.

But in one letter she wrote, "I heard our song in the radio today darling..." and signed the letter, as she did ever after, with "Stay Free, Ma"

Later, that day, four hours into the quiet, hungover drive toward Calgary, I took the journal down from the dash and started another entry.

I wrote her name in the journal, and beside that jotted down "FWS." The boys later read that and conjured a dozen filthy interpretations of the abbreviation involving scenarios and positions that shocked even themselves.

But I stayed mum.

Smiling to the passing prairie, recalling the night: Fixed Window Shade.

*W*e drove all day, everyone cheerful after the wild night in Winnipeg, each of us taking a turn telling our version of the night.

In 200 miles the van was quiet again.

I looked in the rearview and saw everyone looking out the windows at the land rolling past.

We were finally turned to the West, and we each felt that migratory pull toward home.

Outside of Saskatoon the Blue & White coughed out a single *clunk* and then a billow of white steam escaped the hood, as if the van had finally allowed the watchful spirit it harbored to escape into the ether.

We piled out on the side of the highway and huddled around the open hood. The fan had spun off and lodged against the radiator, piercing it. The single gash in the cooling fins of the radiator was tiny yet dire as a hole in a life raft, the sharks circling closer as air escapes in a bouquet of bubbles.

We stood there, watching the green drips of coolant fall to the asphalt, the sky just turning to purple now, the bravest of the stars revealing themselves already.

I felt a stab of guilt seeing the Blue & White wounded and steaming. The six of us huddled around the vehicle that had been home and transport the whole summer.

It had gotten us safely, *so far*, galloping the continent through sun and storm.

Provided us with shelter, it became a prison cell of long drives, a fragrant boudoir for late night rendezvous.

We had denied the old gal a single oil change or even a wash besides the falling rain.

I rubbed the raised hood of the Blue & White, comforting it upon its faded muzzle.

We filled the radiator with melted water from the Coleman and limped into the next gas station, the fan and frayed belt sitting atop the cooler.

Luckily, a nice old guy was manning the pumps, and he looked under the hood, inspected the fan, then went into the garage.

He brought out a two-quart mason jar filled with assorted nuts and bolts, probably the flotsam washed up along the shores of the Saskatchewan Highway, collected like shells during his long boring shifts.

He was able to mount the fan again, and then emptied a bottle of Bar's Stop Leak into the weeping radiator.

"That'll hold ya'," the old guy said, closing the hood. "You boys are far from home, eh?"

I thanked him, and though he wouldn't accept any money for the help, we did leave him with four bottles of Extra Old Stock to see him through his Saturday night.

We drove on, Chris keeping an eye on the temperature gauge, which fluttered a bit above normal then settled down.

It was another Saturday night without a show, though we wouldn't have made it in time anyway.

We finally pulled into the Aurora Motel outside of Edmonton, shuffled into a room and, taking the mattresses off the boxes, made a single nest on the floor.

Everyone fell immediately asleep, filling the tiny room with a flophouse symphony of snores and farts, leaving me awake and staring at the stained ceiling.

When I finally slept, it was to dreams of the ocean, of being in a boat with my dad.

A tiny sabot that threatened to capsize with each foaming swell, my dad laughing at the thrill of it all.

The shoreline faded, then finally disappeared as we sailed further into the storm.

Of course the boat is leaking, a gash in the bow letting in the black sea.

Then I am in the water, clinging to the side of the sinking vessel, waiting on the unseen predators floating just beneath us.

"Remember, Michael," my father yells above the roaring ocean. "All tragedy starts off as an adventure!"

We were enjoying a strange momentum after Fear of Life came out, an exponential popularity we could not claim nor reproduce since.

The fact that we now had a proper album out on Posh Boy somehow meant we were now top billed in those drafty roller rinks and Sunset Strip clubs.

I could use my fingers to tick off the time between when we first recorded that demo tape to headlining the Whisky.

And it is measured like an infant's short and hopeful life, not in years but in months.

I kept waiting for someone to expose us as frauds, for some precocious child to finally stand and point out the King's shriveled foreskin as the parade passed.

But it was just accepted that this was our time, and we climbed ever higher on incredibly packed bills.

Headlining over other bands that would go on to break into the mainstream; the bands who sensibly capitalized on each new opportunity with focused ease.

They probably whiz along the Autobahn in a double decker tour bus as we speak, getting blown by a doe-eyed groupie as they check their stock portfolios on glowing tablets.

It was then that Burton left the band, flatly refusing to go out for longer than a weekend on tour.

We tried not to dwell on the loss of an original member, telling ourselves that his heart wasn't really into the band.

He worked sixty hours a week, piling up that overtime pay toward the next internal combustion toy on his wish list.

He saw no point in the long drives to play a short set, didn't see the

silly competition we were suddenly thrust into against the other bands.
Of trying to gain foothold atop those hand-drawn flyers, to sell a few
more records.
But we would forever miss his wild sense of the moment in the song,
the fills changing with each rendition to sometimes brilliant effect, the
cymbals crashing in on a *three* instead of the expected *four*.

***The next day the guys from the band SNFU came by to escort us to
the show***, an all-ages matinee in a rented hall.
We set up silently, by this time Chris and Doug plugging in the amps,
tuning the guitars, then taking a crouching point at either side of the
stage.
We all assumed our positions without words, even without looking at
each other, so ingrained was the routine and set list by now.
We played a hot, hour-long set, then two encores of songs we'd already
played.
The young audience wanted more, and we played until the hall finally
cut the power, leaving us shouting out the chorus of "I Got a Gun" over
Jack's drumming.
We'd ended up at a pizza parlor connected to a hotel in Edmonton, and
due to some Sunday loophole in the mysterious Canadian liquor laws,
were able to order pitchers of Labatt to go along with our pies: thick-
crusted, manhole cover-sized pizzas dripping with grease and slabs of
thin cut ham.
Doug loaded the jukebox with Motown, and we took over a long table
with some local girls and the guys from SNFU.
I sat next to Ken, the young singer, who quizzed me on my half-Asian
roots as he too was a Eurasian mutt.
He told me how much he liked how we jumped around when we
played, and the next time we played with them he was now "Chi Pig,"
transformed into a punk superhero.
He created his persona as if in a lab, informed by the touring bands that
passed through Edmonton.
Directing the rage of mixed race and confused sexual identity toward

his explosive performance, he spent most of their set airborne.
Taking huge leaps off the drum risers and monitors as he sang his
sardonic lyrics, fronting a band that eclipsed us easily and honorably.

Another round of heavy glass pitchers appeared at the table, and we
toasted each other all over again.
It was then that "Ain't Too Proud to Beg" came over the speakers, and
we all got up to dance. At one point, Chi and I falling to our knees, fake
microphones in hand, pleading with each other not to go away.

EIGHT

***T**hey kicked us out of the Aurora Motel at 1 p.m.*, long after the maid had given up rapping on our door with her exasperated calls of *housekeeping!*
The manager unlocked the door and looked into the darkened room of tangled bodies upon the deconstructed bedding, threatening the police if we weren't out in fifteen.

We drove to Calgary for a Monday night show at a long bar (or perhaps it was named Long Bar? The journal has both words capitalized), a show which I cannot recall at all.
The stained journal page notes only that it was a *Monday night show- ugh,* and we did an interview in the parking lot, then left for Vancouver at 2 a.m.
There are some asterisked footnotes following, noting that the radiator was holding steady, we scored some hash, and Doug's cut was healed and remarkably scar free.
And finally, at the bottom of the page: *Rasta Cat!*
The details escape me now, but we somehow left Calgary with a young cat in the van, a tuxedoed stray with huge green eyes.
He made himself instantly at home in the van, snacking on bits of food that had been ground into the rug, then sprawling out across the ice chest between Chris at the wheel and me in shotgun.

It was another long drive into the darkness, going through the cassettes we were by now sick of, even Poe's tales of darkness grown boring.
Soon everyone was asleep in the Blue & White save Chris and me, and the cat who sat wide eyed and purring through the night.
We turned the stereo down and talked, trying to keep each other awake as we raced through the dark void, saying names
like "Banff" and "Kamloops" aloud over and over, hilarious until the

hash high wore off.

We talked about the old motocross days, untouchable girls from high school who were now fat or discovered as idiots.

Each story started with "Remember that one time…" and ended up with a wheezing sigh, this after a crescendo of laughter.

Before we left on this tour, Chris had gotten a new race bike, a Suzuki RM 250 with seemingly invisible rear suspension.

We talked about bikes for a bit, how he couldn't wait to get home and start racing motocross again.

He nodded his head out at the dark highway before us. "I believe I've had enough of this stuff."

And I knew what he was talking about.

The endless driving, daily boozing, the hangovers chased away only by the next round of booze.

He and Doug were cheated even of that single golden hour onstage to justify this journey.

"What about you?" he said. "Ever gonna get another bike to race again?"

I thought for a moment, shook my head. "Nah, don't think there's any more motocross in my future." I picked up the cat and spoke into its furry little face.

"What? And quit show business?"

Chris suddenly stomped on the brakes, bringing us to a shuddering stop on the highway. "Whoa," he said. Then: "*Whoa, Nellie!*"

The headlights shone upon a lanky bull moose who posed defiantly on the centerline, lit up and magnificent as if on stage.

From our seats the moose appeared impossibly tall and moved its mouth nonchalantly.

He turned to face us, displaying a great rack of fuzzy horns.

"Whoa, shit, what do we do?" I said. "Wait?"

I slapped at Jay's legs, and when he woke, I pointed out the windshield.

We were all awake, staring at the massive mammal blocking the highway, forbidding us passage.

The cat jumped up the dashboard and stared out along with us, purring contentedly, his tail twitching its secret code to the creature outside.

Jack was 17 when we grabbed him, plucking him from Retaliation, his high school garage band.
There was already a new generation of young bands playing parties around Cerritos, bands inspired not by the AM pop of the '70s and our beloved Brit punks of '77, but by the current hardcore.
They *started* with Black Flag and Circle Jerks and only aimed to surpass that sheer speed and intensity.

Jack knew enough to come to the first practice knowing all the songs, and he kept his mouth shut, just nodded when asked if he was willing to go on tour.
And when I questioned him, he assured me he had no desire to be a *singer.*

He did prove a solid, if silent partner in the band, though his silent reserve could eventually become haunting.
Like a girlfriend's cat who sits upon the sill and witnesses vile acts of passion in mute judgment.
It's only commentary a single leg lifted impossibly high, allowing his spiky tongue access to those furry balls.

The shows got more violent, started to end in a riot half of the time.
The cops seemed to enjoy it while the punks resigned themselves to it.
It became a cartoonish relationship: the cops armed by Acme; the punks slippery as roadrunners.
Both sides thrilling at the chance to hit a uniformed man or underage child in the face.
No lawsuits were posted, no cell phone video ever sparked online outrage.
The violence was simply accepted on both sides as part of a regular Saturday night in LA, some shows stopped before a note was played.

We would show up, make a U-turn as the battles spilled into the streets, go back to Cerritos to unload the gear back into the garage, cross another date off the calendar.

I realize now that perhaps this was why we were the headliners at so many shows.

As I squint at those old flyers online, incredible lineups for 5 or 6 dollars, I realize that the show never came off.

The flyers exist as mere fan fiction, and on some we are the gleaming headliners atop a bill of SoCal legends.

A gig that never happened, but slipped into history by scan and upload, and therefore now the truth.

W*e reached Vancouver at 2 p.m.*, having completed another overnight drive. By now we simply and stoically endured those long stretches, like committing to a series of root canals, say, or having one's entire back covered with a tattoo of the Last Supper.

We could sense, if not actually smell, our beloved Pacific Ocean, just beyond the pines that lined the street of faded old houses.

We got out of the Blue & White and stretched.

Sniffing at the air like stray dogs released from kennel cages: grateful, though unsure if the next destination be adoption or slaughter.

The cat huddled further beneath the second bench, looking wildly about at the suddenly still world outside the sliding door.

Rasta seemed to enjoy the long drive, finding maternal comfort in the van's shuddering chassis, the white noise hum of the tires.

He'd claimed the Blue & White as home, to the point of spraying his new territory (as well as Jack's Vans slip-ons, alas).

He also left a discrete poo in the back recesses of the gear, discovered as a fossilized trio of marbles a month later.

He spent the long drive sitting atop each of us in turn, languidly pulsing his sharp little claws into each lap until he was pushed onto the next.

I looked back at one point and Doug, reading through *Catcher in the Rye* once again, held the cat and was stroking it absently in his lap.

I took out the Instamatic, said, "say cheese." Doug held it up by the scruff of the neck, its tiny lion face next to his.

We pulled up at yet another big, Victorian-styled house, the type of sprawling compound that had probably housed a prominent family back in the day.

I looked up to its maze of windows and faded eaves.

Moldings with ornate carvings rotted beneath chipped layers of paint,

each exposed shade revealing a past decade of its former glory.
I imagined the original occupants, now long dead, in sepia-tinted
portrait:
The tow-headed twins in sailor suits, the unsmiling mother in stiff,
high-necked collar, her bosom guarded by a galaxy of tiny cruel
buttons.
They stand behind the seated, mustachioed patron, his fortune built on
some ruthless endeavor involving bloodshed or environmental rape.
Not pictured, the Chinese nanny kept in a tiny upstairs alcove, silent to
the nocturnal visits of the master: guided nightly by lamplight and
engorged, uncircumcised lust up those rickety stairs.

But it was neither a cuckolded society matron nor a shamed immigrant
slave who opened the front door.

It was Ken, DOA's tireless manager.

He bid us into The Plaza, now DOA's headquarters, the old house big
enough to house a rotating crew of musicians and local artists.
The place was busy as a hotel lobby, so many people passing through
that Ken gave up on individual introductions, just waved a hand over us
and presented us as "the Channel Three boys."
He told us that Joey and the DOA guys were down at the club setting
up gear, and we had a few hours to relax before soundcheck.

We uncapped beers and spread out, letting Rasta Cat wander the dark
corners.
Off the front parlor was a great room, vast enough to house some
pieces of experimental art.
Jay and I wandered through the tiny exhibit, stood before a female
mannequin, its head replaced by a ball of barb wire, her arms toilet
plungers.
From each breast protruded an emerald cord of dynamite fuse.
Jay and I looked at each other and cried, "yes, yes, but what does
it *mean*?"

The Stalag 13 club was set in another disused warehouse, and just as
we'd found the abandoned mansions of America's past now repurposed
as punk refuge, so too had the stilled warehouses become its nightclubs.
Factories and shops downsized; craftsmen pink-slipped as the
warehouses made room for the latest numeric controlled mills that
could be operated by a low paid moron.
This, decades before the notion of *gentrification* dawned upon a
generation of cowards.
Punks discovered the dead remnants of a prosperous past and gave it
new life, a new purpose, armed only with futon bedding and a
borrowed PA system.

We loaded the gear into the dark industrial hall, found Joey Shithead
and Dave from DOA rigging up speakers.
Joey shook my hand firmly, and as always, I was amazed to find myself
embraced by a punk hero.

It was their astounding work ethic that partly inspired Kimm to start
doodling on the map of the American continent.
We sat before showtime and drank beers, telling Joe of the cities and
shows this past summer, the good nights and bad.
But inevitably, whenever we mentioned a place or a person, Joe would
just listen politely to our breathless yelping before calmly replying, "Oh
yeah, sure. We know them. *We've been there.*"

It was a fun show, and though DOA was not on the bill the guys were
there, Dave and Wimpy playing before us in their side project named
Judas Goat.
We were gifted *two* encores by the weeknight crowd, though I suspect
that had much to do with the sight of Joey Shithead crouching by the
side of the stage and shouting *"Yes! Ok!"* after each song.

We adjourned back to The Plaza for an all-night party among the
weaponized mannequins and the pierced denizens who wandered down
from the labyrinth of upstairs rooms.

The air was thick with smoke and reggae music, shouted conversations and laughter.

Once or twice I glimpsed a darting movement in the periphery: Rasta Cat racing along the walls, hunting wide eyed along the scrolled baseboards.

Joey came around with a coffee can, taking up a collection for the defense of the Vancouver Five, an activist group captured earlier that year.

Joe told us of their daring raids, their Harrison-esque attack on a hydroelectrical power station and a pornographic video chain.

I pushed a couple tens from the night's pay into the shaken coffee can, but I knew that was the extent of our activist altruism.

We were mere cowards in comparison to, not only the Van Five, but also to the bands like DOA who used those punk rock stages to better the world.

In later years, I would quit apologizing for our lack of activism as a band, explaining that we were indeed political, though concerned mainly with the politics of the heart, and for that matter, the groin.

As the party quieted down we started making our way up the stairs to vacant mattresses or into the arms of sympathetic Vancouverites. Strong Canadian beers in hand, Joe calling up the ornate banister, bidding us *sweet dreams* like the benevolent master of the manor he was.

Toward dawn, as I lay tangled in the sheets of a floored mattress, I turned to a streak of gray across the open doorway.

A feline bolt of speed rushing across the hall, Rasta once again feral in the wilds of that creaking old house.

And when we left Vancouver the next day the cat was not in the Blue & White, for he had found a home now.

We left him at The Plaza to join those other noble yet wild animals.

Beneath those latticed gables and spires: though rusted, still pointing upwards.

The year turned to 1983, nothing between us and summer but a few easy classes at Long Beach and those boring shifts at the Wild West store.

That is, until I was finally dismissed from my post at Wild West due to too many shifts missed due to "Unexplained Absence" (code for hungover).

I did not protest, though I imagined Kimm would join me, throw down his badge and march out of the store in solidarity.

But he merely shook his head at me and returned to those sunset canyons of denim and corduroy in Trouser Gulch.

When I went to pick up the last meager paycheck and hand in my badge, I looked one last time at Boot Hill, the shoe department where a silent romance had existed for an achingly perfect season.

Mom was getting fed up with my lazy college workload and daily hangovers, not even a three-hour shift to get me out of bed.

I overheard her on the phone with my dad one afternoon when I was coming down the stairs.

"1p.m. and he's just rolling out of bed, your son the *rockstar*. Will you talk to him, please?"

I knew mom was concerned if she involved my dad.

They'd both settled into life without each other; my mom satisfied with a quiet, nun-like existence without the wild Irishman to deal with.

Dad, he'd usually summon me to lunch or dinner to fulfill some unseen calendar interval of fatherly duty.

He would be staying a week at a grand resort off Laguna or La Jolla.

A bedroom door of the suite closed off, his latest disco date sleeping off the night while we'd look over the room service menus.

But always, the room would face the sea, his beloved Pacific, and between our stumbling sentences I would catch him just staring out at the ocean.

That blue expanse that bordered his journey west, yet somehow bid him further.

But later that evening, when I answered on the third ring, it was not my dad on the line but Robbie.

He said hello, then asked when we would be ready to get back into the studio.

"You know, for the next record you owe me," he said. "The contract?" he added.

The pause in the connection that followed was finally broken by a breath of sigh, either Robbie's or mine, as I looked at the acoustic guitar sitting on my bedroom floor.

The one I used to write songs, which had sat untouched for months.

TEN

I'*ve heard a story, I'm sure of it,* of some little elf or goblin that makes shoes for a failed shopkeeper at night.
Can't recall the details, but the old guy finally gets greedy and tries to make the elf blow him or fill out a W9 or something.
Ruins the magic, the deal is off.

Those first two records came so easily, the songs appearing as if conjured overnight by a wee benevolent cobbler.
But once we had to sit down and write specifically for a new album, try to put a leash around the thing we could not describe, we found ourselves dry.
Abandoned by both inspiration and nocturnal fairies.

Kimm and I tried to write songs together, gathering in the garage to just *jam* (by God I hate that word, which brings back memories of melting into the Anaheim Stadium turf on a blazing summer day while Santana tortured us *–jamming–* for twenty-minute stretches of fretboard wanking).
But we soon found out we were terrible at collaborating on the spot.
Kimm or I would start with a few chords, and then Jack and Larry would kick in.
Then, lacking any new trailheads to venture off, the noodling would veer back onto familiar territory.
We could only find the direction where someone had gone before; we'd all meet at the same bridge and realize we were playing the song we'd tried to rip off in the first place.
Our inspiration revealed as nothing more than petty theft.
We'd inevitably just end up playing "Sheena is a Punk Rocker" or "White Riot" for the next half hour, and then unplug the guitars, defeated, and tear into the next twelve pack.

I found it better to sit alone in my bedroom and write, playing simple chords on the Suzuki acoustic while singing nonsensical sounds into a portable tape recorder.

If I came up with a pleasing enough melody, I would take the wordless melody of the big chorus (*Bah da-dum dah*!) and walk around for a day singing those syllables like a Tourette's safe word.

I would look to the corners of my bedroom ceiling for inspiration, page through paperbacks, scan the comics, all the while mouthing the sounds that only needed *words*.

Bachan would look up from her ironing as I passed, saying, "*Nani Wa*? What you say, 'bada um,? hmm?'"

I'd bring in two or three ideas each practice.

I would try to sell them on each idea, trying to avoid name dropping the song I was badly ripping off.

"This one, we'll play with kind of a Bo Diddley thing, see?" I'd say, trying to convey the song I was hearing in my head.

We would stumble along a few times, the guys never quite coaxed in the direction I wanted, until I'd finally confess, "You know, like "Hateful!" off *London Calling*?"

And then, with the original inspiration forever shadowing the *new* song, we would assemble it in its image.

Our crossing back into the states was uneventful, a bored border guard merely waving us through.

We were almost disappointed by our anticlimactic return to the United States, as we had hidden two cases of Extra Old Stock beer inside the amp cabinets, hoping some bottles would make it home.

As we crossed into northern Washington, the sun suddenly peeked from between the towering pines.

It was a brief welcome home as the sun retreated once again behind a Pacific Northwest shroud of cloud.

We got into Seattle and hit a music store, piling the countertop with guitar strings and drumsticks, a couple new cords to replace the frayed lines that we'd finally surrendered to the trash after weeks of patchwork.

We were resupplying; not just for the last couple road dates in Seattle and San Francisco, but for the final show at Perkin's Palace in Pasadena.

Kimm had booked a big gig at the end of the week featuring the Circle Jerks, MDC, the Dicks, and D.R.I., with us grabbing the choice main support slot just before the Jerks.

And though it meant shortening the original route by a few dates, it seemed a great homecoming show, if indeed that would be the end of the tour.

The Seattle show was held in a small storefront record store, and we played fast and loose for a small crowd.

There was the usual bullshitting and flirting with girls after the gig, but it seemed as though no one's heart was really in it.

There was a damp coolness in the air, though it was still late August. The "back to school sale" signs would be hanging in the Wild West now, and we were just days away from Jerry Lewis' goddamn swan song, killing another summer with his weepy telethon croaking of "You'll Never Walk Alone."

We were left alone in the parking lot as the shop shut off its lights, and for the first time it occurred to me that I hadn't even packed a sweatshirt as my arms dotted with chill.

We sat for a while in the van drinking beer, and after calculating the drive time to San Francisco, decided to leave in the middle of the night once again and head down the coast for our last overnight drive.

Chris took the wheel again, by now not trusting anyone else to drive through the darkness.

He was unable, anyway, to sleep when anyone else was driving.

When someone else did take a night shift he would stay awake, hovering between the front seats the whole time, muttering things like "God bless me!" and "sweet fucking Jumpin' Jehoshaphat, that was close!" to the startled driver, before the steering wheel would be surrendered back to him.

We all stayed awake that last overnight drive, though. Even Jack, who had by now mastered the art of immediately falling asleep as soon as he hit the back bench (either real slumber or feigned, I still don't know; I suspected him of employing a possum-like defense to escape our rambling and filthy van conversations).

We were buzzing, all of us, for our descent back into Southern California.

Kimm and Jay talked about the last show, about the size of the Perkins Place stage, Jay already suggesting the extra guitar cables we should get to extend our reach.

Kimm mentioned that though we were getting back into LA on Friday, there was still the possibility of continuing on and picking up shows in Las Vegas and Salt Lake City, a suggestion that was met with utter silence.

I just looked out the window at the night landscape racing past, the distant lights of yet another city floating upon the black.

My heart tugged with the bittersweet dread of going home, this summer ended, life resuming its normal programming.

I allowed myself a brief fantasy of being back in the blue car with the girl who drove stick, of a romance unsullied by meaningless sex and regret.

Doug sat in the back with Jack.

I watched the two of them talking easily, Jack probably still wary of a sudden headlock or fart attack.

Doug had simply satisfied himself with the idea that Jack had survived the summer. Another little brother still standing after his drill sergeant abuse, all the tougher for it.

Doug was probably thinking of the reality that faced him when he got home, a return to the back-breaking work that paid so well but took so much.

He would be back to rising at 5a.m. to swing that sledge hammer in a week's time.

But he'd taken this summer off and spent it as one whirling chaotic motion. Perhaps the routine of a job, food, and bed would all be infused with a treasured value from now on.

Doug would finally make his own separate peace, retreating to the Sierra Nevada mountains to patrol ski lodges, eventually gaining the awesome responsibility of firing Howitzer shells into the snowpack in the name of avalanche control.

And when we loaded out for the last time, he just walked away, not bothering to take any of his clothes or any souvenirs of the tour, keeping only the crimson-covered copy of *Catcher in the Rye.*

ELEVEN

e had collected just enough songs in six weeks to let Robbie set a recording date.

"Jay says you've got some good songs, hmm?" Robbie said on the phone. "Fast songs, is that what we're doing?"

I assured Robbie that we had a few different things to try, asked about the recording schedules and studio.

"Brian Elliott's again?" I asked, assuming we'd meet once again in the familiar room.

I heard a slight chuckle over the line, could picture Robbie shaking his head, preparing to correct me once again.

"Well, Mike," he said, "You have heard of Gold Star Studio, now, haven't you?"

And though the name spurred a certain image of old Hollywood, of golden convertibles and flaming desserts prepared tableside, I confessed that I was unfamiliar.

That chuckle once again, then he said, "Well, look it up. You're booked there, starting Wednesday at noon."

Toward dawn everyone in the back had fallen quiet, only Chris and I still chatting up front. We talked idly about anything that popped into our heads, anchored in our usual spots, keeping each other awake through another long night.

Chris had planned on getting into construction when we got home, though he eventually found his calling as a facility manager for large corporations, his maddening attention to detail finally finding a righteous cause.

He would build an impressive career out of correcting shoddy subcontractors, pointing out flaws in the drywall and weeping plumbing joints as easily as shaming a careless driver from the backseat.

Chris would continue racing motorcycles before switching to the new sport of downhill bicycles, finding his long frame and manic focus ideally suited for the silent sport.

That he stayed far away from our band adventures after that summer yet remained the closest of friends I attribute to some sort of shared survivors' guilt.

Perhaps he was the wise one for never picking up a drumstick or bass (even after we urged him to), knowing that the unrelenting neediness of being in a band was enough to strain the strongest of brotherhoods.

The sun rose as we passed Medford, and just after 7 a.m. we pulled into a California gas station.

As I filled the tank, Chris went into the convenience store and came out grinning, a six pack of Coors Banquet in each raised hand. It was the first Coors we'd seen since leaving Texas.

We parked behind the gas station in a gravel lot that looked into the dark green shadows of pine, got out with beers in hand then toasted toward the morning sun.

"Good job, man; all the goddamn driving," I said.

Chris nodded back, "Oh, yeah. Well," he said.

The sliding door opened and Doug came out to join us.

I drank in deeply of the thin, pale pilsner, recalled its origin from that factory nestled in the mountains of Colorado.

I squinted at the faded yellow can, our beloved home team beer.

It seemed the only constant of these past whirlwind years, the beer tied always to our Cerritos youth, the river running through the garage, subtle and awesome in its power of erosion.

Jay, Jack, and Kimm got out then.

We were all out there, holding the beers inherited from our fathers, stolen from our mothers.

I think it was then, back on California soil and clutching those familiar cans, that we may have all huddled for the last time.

We all knew that there would be no grand farewells after the last show in LA, that we would be scattered once again in all directions, finally freed of the Blue & White.

Cut from our tether to that dear old rusting hulk, a connection tenuous as the corded strand that keeps a floating astronaut from drifting off into solitary fate.

Perhaps we all had a moment of reflection, or perhaps it was just another day on the road.

Another day to navigate meager meals and stolen showers, claim a single moment of quiet to shit while the opening band played.

We stood together and touched cans, none of us saying a word.

Unwilling to jinx it with language, half of us hoping to make it home safely, the other half hoping to *never* go home.

And then, not bothering to turn away, we took out our wieners and pissed, baptizing our home soil in weary salute.

***It was indeed* that *legendary Gold Star Studios that Robbie had directed us to*,** and when I relayed the message to Kimm he asked me to repeat it twice before going wordlessly to his record shelf.

We were up in his bedroom with acoustic guitars, going over the songs one last time before the basic sessions.

Lynn and Lois were downstairs with the evening highballs, and as I was going up the stairs to Kimm's room, Lynn yelled after me, "Don't go shaking his right hand for God's sake, Mike. That's the one he holds the damn thing with!"

Now Kimm traced his finger along the spines of his collection before selecting and tossing half a dozen records upon his bed. "*These,*" he said, pointing at each in turn with a determined finger. "All recorded at Gold Star."

Upon his quilt lay *Eddie Cochran Greatest Hits*, Ike and Tina's *River Deep–Mountain High,* Iron Butterfly's *In-A-Gadda-Da-Vida.*

The Beach Boys' *Pet Sounds*, and a Herb Alpert record that I suspect Kimm bought solely for the album cover: a naked young lady wearing

only a gown of whipped cream.
And finally, like a precocious yet ultimately doomed child created by generations of inbreeding and despair, that collaboration between Phil Spector and The Ramones: *End of the Century.*

We were quiet for a moment, feeling once again out of our league and placed ahead of our time.
Back in the familiar dream of being called to the front of the class to deliver a book report on *Moby Dick,* wearing only yellowed jockey briefs and a raging hard on.
Robbie had, through one of his backroom dealings (probably featuring shadowy favors traded like wartime schematics of a bomb or windmill), landed us recording time within those hallowed halls.

Gold Star was located at 6252 Santa Monica boulevard.
And though it was just a mile and a half from Oki Dog, I'd never noticed the austere stucco entrance.

It was a building as faceless as a janitor supply warehouse or an S&M dungeon. No windows to the streets, no views of the sullen hustlers and leering chicken hawks who favored Santa Monica Boulevard over its boring older brothers, Sunset and Hollywood.

We met on the appointed day, and loaded into a vast, high-ceilinged room, a space big enough to house a full eighteen-piece orchestra.
I pictured them there, tuned up and prepared to be bullied by a hungover Frank Sinatra: just in from a Vegas all-nighter, still reeking of Jack Daniels and Angie Dickinson's intimate musk.
We never confirmed that this was the room used by Phil Spector (indeed, when we asked the young receptionist Johnette to show us just where the actual *Wall of Sound* was, we were answered with only a smirk), but I was testing the room's natural depth, clapping and singing "Be My Baby" into the rafters when an older gentleman walked in and introduced himself.

"Hello boys, hello," he said.

He had a fine helmet of gray hair, gold rimmed glasses of slight gradient tint, a cardigan sweater atop the salmon splash of a polyester golf shirt.

He looked like one of those stock characters out of a 1970s Quinn Martin TV production: the police chief who favored thin brown cigars, or maybe the all-knowing confidante of the show's namesake, a private investigator who is constantly being knocked out after trusting the wrong woman.

He looked down at a clipboard. "Is it C-H, is that a three? Like chapter three?"

Then he shook our hands, repeating "Stan" to each of us in turn as we introduced ourselves.

It was Stan Ross, *that* legendary founder of Gold Star who sat at the helm on most of those classic songs, and who would be, apparently, engineering our second album.

We got on with Stan immediately; he was just the comforting presence we needed.

We were over that initial giddiness of tracking in a studio, but our anxiety was amplified now by the historic room.

We stood in a tight circle, finally ready to lay one down.

Despite the vast space we still huddled close, like rescued strays that will forever favor the safe confines of the kennel cage to the open backyard.

I now think of poor Jack: not just his first session in a real recording studio, but thrown into *this* storied shed.

Where Brian Wilson once sat tortured by the sounds within his ringing head, where Spector held the Ramones at gunpoint, demanding yet another opening chord.

Where Stan Ross now sat beyond the glass of the control room, asking for the song title.

Robbie had left a note at the studio, telling us to record the Rolling Stones' "Stupid Girl," his request written out as casually as a reminder to water the plants or take out the garbage.

We resigned ourselves to Robbie's vision, hoping the ill-prepared version we came up with on the spot would be so bad it couldn't possibly be included in the final product.

Jack had a hard time nailing the double time beat, so Stan rigged a simple drum loop and had Jack double it.

We recorded the song quickly, letting us move on to our *own* sexist songs.

Stan seemed like a kindly old uncle.

Horrified by the thought of early retirement, he returned to those halls and rooms that once bustled with hit makers and hustlers.

I think he was willing to take on our project just to be surrounded by a new generation, kids eager to hear stories of the glorious past.

He got a kick out of our loud and fast songs, sometimes catching him off guard by just how short the tracks were.

"Is that it?" he would say into the talkback, laughing. "Jeez, the tape wasn't even up to speed yet."

When I got done with a vocal take, sometimes I'd ask Stan what he thought about it.

"Oh yeah, I heard every *fuck* and *suck* in there, baby," he'd say with a chuckle.

He'd shake his head, probably wondering how he'd come from tracking Sonny and Cher to *this.*

Then he'd hit the talkback once again: "And the hits keep coming!"

And though Gold Star would shut its doors not long after that (and suffer the inevitable suspicious fire that seems to finalize the history of every Hollywood landmark), I always think back to those few short weeks we gathered in that hall.

To hear the stories of the songs we'd loved, to add our own meager notes to its golden history.

We are driving over the Bay Bridge just as the sun touches the top of the Transamerica building.

I imagine the star pierced by the tip of the pyramid, a torrent of molten ectoplasm and poisonous gases raining down upon the financial district.

As the world settles into darkness, all credit and debt have vanished. Only the packs of wolves descending from the hills are left in charge of accounting.

Everyone in the van rouses at the sight of the familiar city; the grime and wonderful sleaze of those streets as we make our way to the North Beach neighborhood.

And although San Francisco had always felt like slightly enemy territory (the locals seem to eye our sloppy, poppy hardcore with suspicion and indifference), we were finally back to familiar territory.

After loading into the On Broadway and blowing off soundcheck, we all wandered over to Vesuvio's tavern and grabbed an upstairs booth. We sat there and the table was soon crowded with pitchers of beer and glasses.

We told ourselves stories of the last few months, as if we had not all been there, not heard these tales repeated in the van already a dozen times.

It was as if we were rehearsing them one last time before telling the folks back home, *finally* a new audience that would hear only the payoffs and punchlines.

We'd spare them the hours of boredom and endless driving, the arguments and frustration.

On the way back to the club we passed the glowing windows of City Lights bookstore, the room illuminated by Fante and Ferlinghetti.

I pulled Doug inside and pointed out a wryly titled companion to his
Salinger, a first edition *Ham on Rye*, which he immediately took off the
shelf and tucked down his shorts.

Robbie sat in the control booth listening to the rough mixes, his head
cocked to one side and eyes closed.
Stan sat to his left, constantly adjusting the mix.
Pushing a fader here, twisting a wee, candy-colored EQ knob there.
His hands dancing over the board, divining out the sweet spots of tone
like a man finding precious water with a wishboned twig.

Kimm and I sat on the couch behind them as Jay paced back and forth
behind the console, his head nodding to the accents and riffs that we
had piled on over the last couple weeks.
We had layered track upon track, Jay sometimes grabbing a guitar out
of our hands, exasperated, and tracking his own take in an instant.
We went through a box of shakers and tambourines, laughing at the
thought of sneaking pre-school instruments onto a hardcore record.
And when Kimm wondered aloud if a *saxophone* might work for the
song "All My Dreams," we came back to the studio the next day to find
Robbie had arranged a humorless session guy to meet us there.
We watched him lay down the tootling riff in a flat fifteen minutes.

Jack and Larry had packed up and left the overdubs to me and Kimm.
Larry heading back to work on his father's used car lot, Jack back to
finish the twelfth grade.
And though we speculated on the amount of *pussy* the lucky kid must
be navigating, coming back into social studies with his tardy excuse
scribbled on *Gold Star Studio* stationery, Jack was too good to act on
such a petty windfall.

As for Larry, he was starting to realize we weren't kidding about a
summer-long tour.

And after he finished his bass parts, he finally admitted that he could not possibly go.

He was the only son to a hustling entrepreneur, good old Bob Kelley, who was involved in half a dozen ventures at any given time.

Besides a car lot, his pop had an interest in a commercial meat delivery business in East LA and a bustling Mercado complex in downtown Santa Ana.

Old Bob used to wander in whenever we gathered at Larry's house and (Old Fashioned in hand) tell us about a *hot little four piece* he used to manage.

"Used to *rake* it in," he'd say, rubbing his thumb against middle and index finger, as Larry rolled his eyes toward the ceiling.

"Weddings, bar mitzvah, boat shows… *the works*." And then, before turning to mix the third cocktail of the evening, he'd say, "You know what you boys need? Vests. *Matching* vests."

And here he'd hold a spread hand at arm's length, as if to shield his eyes from a glittering vision of the past.

"Sharp, I'm telling you. *Sharp*."

Larry inherited his dad's business savvy and knew that his future lay in far more profitable ventures than sitting in the van for a season, the miles counted by the hundreds.

He quit the band reluctantly, staying throughout the writing and recording of the record and playing the last few shows we had booked before summer.

But I thought he never left the band, really.

He was just not on stage with us anymore.

His finger-flicking bass sound stayed the constant on those early songs, and he remained a close pal, taking me out for lunch in ever smaller and more expensive Ferraris throughout the years.

He went as far as *literally* handing the bass over to Jay, on stage and mid-set, that hot June evening at the Cathay De Grande.

THIRTEEN

I **watched Robbie listening to the rough mixes**, but I could see no clue of approval or distaste.

He had his mirrored sunglasses on, an eccentric gesture that seemed to fit the *Spector* specter that haunted the room.

The song "Can't Afford It" ended, and then he turned from the board.
He nodded. "Some good things going on. Fast though, hmm?"
He conferred with Stan then and looked down at the track sheets.
"We're only at twenty minutes of music here."
It was then that Jay tugged his elbow as Stan cued up the final track, telling him to pay attention to this one.
It was the track "I Didn't Know."

I could see the wheels spinning atop the Studer 24 track (as well as within Robbie's inspired head!) as we listened to the song.
It was an audacious 4 minute 50 second track, easily three times longer than anything we'd ever recorded.
The track was simple: intro, verse and chorus built over the same four chords.
Bridge nonexistent, as if washed out by an unseasonable flash flood.
From the spare intro the song crested at the end, into double time beat with dynamic washes of guitar.

It was, finally, a song that mirrored the sound I'd heard in my head all my life: the pop melodies of an AM radio played beneath a tented bedspread, the syrupy '70s rock of our feather-headed teenage years.
The crash of guitar and cymbal, the rage of our Brit Punk heroes, the flourish of our stadium gods.

Robbie turned to me again, and I could only see my eager reflection in

his Aviators, yearning paternal approval, awaiting his next words:
"Why Mike, this is a *pop song*, really!"
Then he turned back to the board and whispered the fateful words to no one in particular:
"*I hear abstract background vocals on this one!*"

And that's how we ended up sitting in the studio the very next day, watching three short, bald men sing along to the track.

Again, thanks to the mysterious deal making machine that *was* Posh Boy, these professional jingle singers appeared at Gold Star, ready to work.
We watched in amazement as they lay down the sweetest of background vocals, without thought or practice.
Then, calling for another pass with a finger circling the air, added another tight harmony on top of that.

But the sweetening made me instantly nauseous.
I immediately had panicked visions of losing all the hardcore credibility we had ever somehow gained.
Would there be record burnings outside gigs, boycotts of our shows?
Would the strict hardcore community (based on "individuality," hah) reject us?
Would we, I realized as my true fear, be somehow *revealed*?

We listened to the track again, now enhanced throughout by soaring background harmonies, every spare space of it filled by chirping *onomatopoeia*.
I stood, tapped Stan on the shoulder, and when he turned his head to me, slid my index finger across my throat
He stopped the track mid-*doo doo bop*.
I stood over Robbie now, reflected as petulant twins in his sunglasses.
"It's too much," I said, sweeping my arm out toward the empty studio, where just an hour before three old pros did their weary magic and were probably across town in another studio already, singing the

praises of cat food or laxative in three-part harmony.

Robbie looked at me silently, then lowered his shades down the bridge of his nose until his pupils were connected to mine.
"You don't like?" he asked.
I shook my head. "No, I don't like."
And then Stan got up and left to grab a coffee.

He knew from his decades of working with pouting *artistes* and exasperated producers when it was time to step out.
Kimm and Jay followed him, leaving me and Robbie alone.

Robbie at first tried to reason with me, letting me know that we might have stumbled onto something here, something that would take us beyond the roller rinks and riotous shows.
And after all, Robbie asked, *isn't that what we really always wanted?*

I wanted all the background vocals, and the heavy effect on my own vocals, gone.
But there was something else, though I couldn't articulate just what it was.

Maybe I was really talking, *too much,* about the storied recording studio and the packed shows, the overwhelming opportunity offered us while our hands were already full.
And, as any good coward knows, when offered what you *really* want, you run from it.

We came to an uneasy truce just as the others came back into the control room, having heard our shouting quiet down to hushed tones.
Robbie agreed to cut the background vocals from the start of the song, and we allowed the abstracts to kick in at the very end.

"Wow Mike, I'm impressed," Robbie said, finally taking off his sunglasses. "I don't think I've seen you so… *passionate* about your music."

And though he may have been teasing me for my red-faced tantrum, he seemed to respect my stance.

"But you know," he added, "when they open the doors for you, they only hold them open for so long."

It was the last time in the studio with Posh Boy, having apparently fulfilled the contract we'd signed just 26 months before.

But our career would be forever tied to Robbie, to that cast of characters who did his bidding upon favor and time.

With each new bit of technological repackaging, those songs would be revisited and renegotiated, first as CDs, then reissued albums.

Finally, and fatally, the songs were rendered to MP3 and lost to the internet. Like unleashing a feisty rescue dog for the first time, in the futile hope that given a taste of freedom it will eventually return.

People, when they think of us, they think of those first songs.

That same catalog of 27 tracks, written by children, barely an hour's worth of music.

Robbie would soon abandon LA, and live a proper ex-patriate life, checking in from Phuket or Johannesburg on rare, scratchy phone calls. I would listen to the static on the line, imagining him sitting upon rattan, a sweating gin and tonic at his elbow.

Perhaps in the middle of exotic and dangerous dealings:

Waiting on a visit from a mute courier who would deliver either a blood diamond or a manila envelope containing photos that could destroy an ambassador's career.

I didn't see Robbie again until years later, at Kimm's wedding, where I was the best man.

I stood and gave a rambling drunken toast to the new groom and bride, ignoring Kimm's gestures to wrap it up, his eyes pleading for me not to bring up the specifics of *that one time in 1983 when we embarked on a long tour…*

Afterward, Robbie found me at the bar.
We hugged and smiled at each other, each of us remembering a time in our lives that glowed like a wildfire retreating toward the horizon.

Had there been arguments over the catalog in the past years?
Did we sometimes descend into petty bickering over these shared creations, like divorced parents using their bewildered children to inflict pain upon each other?
Sure.
But then it wouldn't, after all, be much of a show business story without a *little* heartache.

I remember the words of Steve Soto, who asked me to consider where we would be if not for Robbie.
Would we have *ever* gotten out of the garage ourselves?
We stood at the rail watching Kimm and his new wife dance their first dance. We toasted them, then turned to each other and touched glasses.
"To the Professor," I said to him.
"To the Poet," he replied.

FOURTEEN

*T**he gig in San Francisco was with the bands** Hose, Scream, and Fang.

There is no notation of the actual show in the journal, but the very grouping of bands is startling.

If only for their destined fortunes and tragedies too fantastic to mention here.

Before our set I was the last to leave the dressing room, reluctant to leave the bottle of Jack and iced beers there.

I thought of that first party we played, then the first club gig, the ever-larger stages under more brilliant lighting.

Each step as terrifying and awkward as a high school dance.

It was booze I relied on to help me through.

But now, as I get ready for another darkened stage, it is not nerves I feel.

If I am honest, I barely feel anything, really.

I am drunk with numbness.

I fill a shot glass and debate whether to down it or save it for after the set.

I detect a stabbing tinge of truth, like a ghostly vision that appears only in the periphery, but I refuse to investigate my gut any further.

I take the shot, and as I head to the stage I promise myself that I will address this someday soon.

An appointment that I will postpone for decades.

We got the albums just a week before leaving on tour, and the spare black cover was a fitting match for the cold dark album inside.

Holding those black-on-black covers up to the light that first time, we must have enacted the entirety of the *Spinal Tap* album scene, this a year before the movie was released.

It was a frenzied and thin record, filled with anthems of confusion and dread. Indeed, we titled it *After the Lights Go Out*, an ode to darkness, fitting for the times.

Shows were canceled in riot or police harassment, the punk community splintered by incestuous violence; the happy boozing replaced by hard drug use.

Not content to get drunk and sniff at powders, close friends decided to now inject drugs into their veins.

People were committing real crimes, suffering real tragedy, and every week the phone seemed to chime in doom.

Calls starting with a breathless, *"Did you hear about…"* as the recipient of the latest overdose, stab wound, or gunshot was revealed.

Unfortunately, lyrically, the album was a humorless reflection of the times as well, and it reads like an insincere suicide note.

In an attempt to pad my credits toward graduation I had enrolled in both PHIL039-Existentialism in Philosophy and Literature- and ENG569 -The Southern Gothic.

Their twinned syllabi had me highlighting passages of Camus and Dostoevsky Monday and Wednesdays, then spending Tuesdays and Thursdays with those party gals, Carson McCullers and Flannery O'Connor.

Sometimes after class I'd sit on the breakwater in Seal Beach, smoking unfiltered cigarettes and drinking brown bagged Olde English.

Wishing only that the unrelenting California sun would retreat behind the clouds and give me a proper gray day to match my weepy mood.

I had learned the cheap trick that it is far easier to make people cry than to smile and filled the lyrics with bleak, sophomoric whining.

Daring to insert the phrase "cold dark world" into at least three of the tracks, hoping that some Gauloises-smoking critic might discover the theme and declare me a lyrical genius.

I read those lyrics now and cringe a bit, but smile.
Like seeing photos of unfortunate high school haircuts and pastel prom tuxedos, yellowed with age, burnished to a certain wistful charm.

FIFTEEN

I took a copy of the record to show my father.

I sat in his office while he had his usual lunch of dry roasted peanuts and two cans of Coors.

Out in the waiting room a dozen patients waited into a second hour as we drank beer together. He took his time reading the lyric sheet, tracing the words with a finger, at times smiling or shaking his head slightly.

Finally, he put the insert down and he looked at me.

"Your songs… they're so angry," he said. "Angry and sad."

And here I could only shrug, though I knew what he really meant: *what the fuck do you have to be angry about?*

I was, after all, raised in luxury.

Gifted with parents who knew real hatred and trial, who only wanted to give their children a better life.

And what indeed did I have to be angry about, what sorrow had I known beyond their divorce, which had only spurred them to treat me nicer?

I played upon their guilt to put a new motorcycle in the garage or stay out late getting fucked up in Hollywood.

I could always rely on my dad's boozing and womanizing as balm to my guilt.

Of course, it would not be long before I woke, two thousand miles from home beneath an inverted American flag.

Hungover and heartsick, unable to recall the name of the woman curled to my chest.

I left him still holding that black record in front of him, and then passed a roomful of people who wanted only a moment with this man: to be cured.

He went on to practice medicine until they wouldn't let him, his generous hand with the prescription pad finally noticed.

But he kept up his raging crusade against the politicians and insurance companies, the ever-present "crooks" that justified his own angry lyrics.

He was silenced only, finally, by Alzheimer's.

And then he returned to the grey slush of Philadelphia, playing football in the corner lot with the other twelve-year-old kids.

My mother was furious that the matron in "Separate Peace" was a drunk, no matter how much I tried to convince her the song was not about our own family.

But I knew she was also proud of me, of the band, of *us.*

Her boys of the garage, who shook the popcorn off the ceiling while she tried to watch the six o'clock news.

Who took cases of beer from her ever-replenished stock.

She bought every copy of the record she could carry from Best Records, then sent them out to all our bewildered Japanese relatives.

A week later she stood at the curb with *Bachan* in front of the Cerritos house, the Blue & White loaded, everyone excited at the adventure to come.

She hugged me goodbye, then said, "Hey. No funny business."

She took care of my grandmom until *Bachan* finally passed at 108 years, her January,1900 birthday cheating her out of living within three separate centuries by only a couple weeks.

And then, in the way Japanese women seem to do, mom turned overnight into a gray-haired grandmom herself.

Bachan to the next generation of grandchildren.

SIXTEEN

We played through all our remaining mixtapes on the last drive.

Some of the tapes were stretched thin and garbled by the constant play, sticky from baths of dashboard beer, warped from the heat and humidity of the season.

We listened to Jay's mixtape one last time, all of us singing along loudly to Hall and Oates' "She's Gone" until that tape accordioned into the Blaupunkt.

Jettisoned out the window at eighty-five mph, the cassette bounced along the asphalt, the tape unfurling along the highway like the brown entrails of a roadkill rodent.

We played Kiss and the Clash, our beloved underrated heroes 999 and Starz.

We listened to the first side of 2112, then the Monkees.

Playing "Daydream Believer" three times in a row, crying at the image of Doug fucking along to Davy Jones' hopeful vocals.

After our final piss stop just before climbing the Grapevine, I took over the driving.

Kimm got in shotgun, and we cracked a Coors Banquet for the final leg of the trip.

Kimm had finally let his calendar rest in his backpack, and now his hands held nothing but a cold can of beer and the calluses born of gripping pen and phone for a season.

The final phone calling card number had been cut off somewhere above Portland, though we would all answer calls from MCI and PacBell for months to come, a weary operator trying to trace calls from a Pittsburgh phone booth to Cerritos.

I held my beer can across to him, and he touched it with his in toast.

Nothing remained to be said, though I believe we both shared the dread and relief of coming home.

I looked into the rearview and saw Chris and Doug napping in the first bench, their heads slowly tilting forward with exhaustion only to be jerked back in a losing battle against sleep.
Chris had finally relinquished the steering wheel.
He and Doug could only think of the Blue & White stopping, finally, or at least slowed enough for them to jump out and escape.
Jack sat awake in the back, staring out the window.
He probably suspected that this tour would be his last with the band.
And Jay, well, he was back there, sipping a beer with the acoustic guitar on his lap.
If he was planning on his full integration into the band or was just happy to be home, I could not say.
He just smiled at the passing scenery and strummed that guitar.

We would never be together again, this group, this close, but the constant of Kimm and I up front remained.
And though the band had tested our childhood friendship with the nasty introduction of *business,* it also galvanized us against all outside threats.
We both knew the band would change again soon and came to the unspoken realization that we would simply carry on.
To just keep playing, regardless of who would join us in hope, or quit us in disgust.
I imagined we might turn into old men with guitars, be allowed to revisit these places and people of this summer.

Perhaps like old bluesmen, who can somehow still manage to play without penalties for waistline or hairline, punk rockers could carry on until death.
We would continue, riding the small victories and countless heartbreaks in kind, as if adrift upon the pulsing tide of our beloved Pacific.

SEVENTEEN

We got to Pasadena around five, after just hitting the start of rush hour
traffic as we descended into the Valley.
Into the pit of Los Angeles, the air warm but dry, the smog hanging
over a galaxy of brake lights. The shimmering waves of carbon
monoxide cast the summer sky with a golden halo.
Even rush hour on the 5 seemed charming somehow, a forgotten sting
of Southern California life.

We pulled into the Perkins Palace lot with the Misfits once again
blasting out of the speakers, all of us yelling along with the *ohs* and the
whoas, sliding open the side door to the clatter of empties, an avalanche
of aluminum announcing our homecoming.
We piled out and walked away from the Blue & White then, a final
escape.
I turned and looked back at the trusty old gal, half expecting the wheels
to finally fall off or perhaps the van would vanish altogether, its
existence fulfilled for a dreamt season.
But the Chevy Beauville sat silent, ready to roll on.

Doug's brothers, Duane and Darren, were there to meet us, and the
three brothers locked in hug for a moment before their embrace
dissolved into wrestling and chest punches, the brothers showing their
love for one another through the shared language of violence.
We loaded onto the huge stage from the freight ramps, a line of kids
already camped out along the front and sides of the building.
I looked at the waiting crowd, already in the hundreds.
After the months of half-filled bars, the shacks and warehouses
connecting the coasts like an underground railroad, I appreciated anew
the huge crowds back home.
A couple thousand kids assembled for just another Friday night.

The Circle Jerks were just getting done with their soundcheck and we set our amps in front of theirs.
Keith and Greg came up as we loaded in, and we talked a bit about the summer. The cities where we'd just missed each other, the people who became mutual friends, the discreet keepers of secrets and kinks.

Jack set up quietly for soundcheck on the tall drum riser, separate from us.
The end of his tour finally here, though he looked nervous as a prisoner on the eve of release: prepared for the inevitable shank between the ribs, the Governor's last-minute reprieve intercepted.

After the gig Jack would simply load up his drums in a friend's car and leave.
Jack joined the Air Force, of all things, becoming the only man in the band's long roster to ever have the notion of enlisting.
Serving, if not his country, then at least something beyond the needy whims of a touring punk rock band.

Jay taped extra guitar cords to the stage, extending our guitar cables to fifty feet, correctly anticipating the chaos of the slam dancers and stage divers who would invade our space all night.
Jay's mother, Sharon, came to greet us at soundcheck, their family house in Arcadia just down the way.
She would become our favorite stage mom, offering to tell us on any given night if we played well or truly sucked.

Jay would stay on with the band as a full member, holding tight to the bass guitar relinquished by Larry until we would eventually expand to a five piece.

Jay became my song writing partner for the next few years, as Kimm concentrated on the business deals that would lead us far away from the hardcore riots of 1983.

We spent long afternoons in Cerritos watching *The Last Waltz* and Elvis' *'68 Comeback Special*, as if we were immigrants trying to learn the language of a new country.
And then we would write new songs, songs that would alienate even the most loyal of our hardcore fans.

Jay eventually moved to Germany, after discovering the laid-back cadence of European life a perfect fit.
We chat still, talk like the old men we have become.
The conversations tend toward aches and pains, girls we used to know, worries for our grown daughters.
But Jay only has to pick up that guitar next to the couch, and without thought, without breaking conversation, begin to play.
Then I am reminded once again of his ridiculous skill, and of the cruelty of the music business.
Of gifts doled out at random, as if from powers above.
By cruel gods content to laugh at our folly, for equating talent with success.

EIGHTEEN

I wake in a bed, and it's quiet.

I instinctively sweep my arm around before opening my eyes, checking if there is a breathing body beside me.

Expecting one of the guys to be next to me, also claiming some of this flat soft space.

Or perhaps there is a girl who, in a drunken lapse of judgment, had taken mercy on me.

Brought me home and is now lying wide-eyed, wondering how to get rid of me.

But I feel nothing there, I am alone.

When I open my eyes, it is not to an upside-down American flag pinned upon the wall of a weed-reeking commune.

And it is not to the sticker-covered ceiling of the Blue & White, where I have been designated the blackout drunk watchdog yet again.

It is a boy's room, the walls covered with posters of motocross bikes and rock and roll bands, and at the foot of the bed Paul Stanley and Gene Simmons pose on either side of a crouching Ace Frehly.

Ace's head tilted back and eyes closed, his guitar literally smoking.

It's my bedroom, and I am home.

I get up to piss, and when I open the door, I find all my clothes from the tour have been washed, ironed and folded neatly on the floor next to my room.

Bachan having already gone through my bag at dawn, probably thrilled at the treasure of filthy laundry.

My mom, at the foot of the stairs, calls up to me.

"Are you awake, finally? Going to the store, be back later. Making *tonkatsu* tonight!"

The front door closes behind her and I know that she will cook enough to feed eight, even though it will just be the three of us at the table. Save the missing first cutlet, served to my dead grandfather at his shrine in *Bachan's* bedroom.

I sit down on my bed, look about my small bedroom.

It is odd, the sensation of sudden stillness.
Above all it is quiet, the noises of the summer all the more evident in their absence.
No hum of the radial tires upon highway, no conversations continued long into the night in guard against sleep and highway death.

No out of tune guitars, no screech of an opening band.
No yelling over the forgotten annoyances of another day past.

Just the tick of the thermostat as the central air kicks in, and *Bachan* down in the kitchen: the soft swishing of the evening rice being cleaned, soothing as receding surf foaming against warm sand.

The houselights went down at Perkins, and we kicked off with "I Wanna Know Why."

We were locked in, the songs familiar as memorized prayers after so many nights in a row.
I knew when Jack would hit the crash (whose crack had now completed its journey, rendering the cymbal split from bell to edge), when Kimm was going to pick slide into a lead, when Jay was about to leap, spread legged, on a downbeat.

Bands often describe it as being tight, but truly it is being loose.
If not loose, then *free.*
The moment of letting the machine fly beneath you, guided by the track.
A sloppy precision borne out of all those nights together, the good gigs and the bad.

Those sweat-corroded guitar strings, dulled just enough to make us strum harder.

The music starts, the threat of explosive violence in the air again, familiar as the electric smell before a summer storm.
And then it starts, the churning pit, the scattered fights, the pockets of people scowling at us, the drunks cheering us on, slutty girls wagging their tongues.

On the stage it is as crowded as a dance floor, enough people crawling up onstage with us that we can barely see each other.
They dance and shout into our microphones, take flying jumps out into the darkness, a literal leap of faith that hands will be there to catch them.

Someone kicks my guitar cord out of the jack, a punch lands on the back of my head.
As a stage diver rushes past me, he pushes off my shoulder and I fall to my knees upon the stage.

I stand and catch Kimm's eye across the stage.

We shake our heads at each other once again, still astonished to be on this side of the hall, up on the stage.
I think of all the years together, of the nights spent listening to records in his room, of the shows we saw together, covetous of the stage lights.
The days in the garage, nurturing the tinnitus that would eventually haunt our every waking moment.

I lose sight of Kimm's spiked blonde hair as another group of punkers crowd around his microphone to sing along to the songs we wrote together.
And then, just as I'm about to escape into the multiplication tables, to think of anything *but* this moment, it occurs to me that I *want* to be here.

In the present, up on this stage.

In front of a thousand kids, a few who will perhaps be inspired to pick up the guitar tomorrow and start their own band.

I think, for the first time, that we *deserve* this.

The show has dissolved into lovely chaos, and I feel it would carry on of its own momentum even if we walked off the stage.

A group of Pasadena rocker girls yell for Jay, and I see his mom, Sharon, watching from the side with a grin.

I see breasts exposed; Nazi salutes raised by cowardly packs of boys flanking the pit.

Arms waving from the center of the pit like the last gestures of drowning men just before they surrender to the black depths.

A beer can is launched high into the air, its contents foaming into the spotlights, and it narrowly misses my head as it crashes to the floor behind me.

Someone yells out, "fags! Play 'Wetspots' and get the fuck off!"

I almost cry.

I am home.

NINETEEN

I *noticed a girl in the front of the stage*, blonde and tall. She stood steadily at the center, watching me, fending off the slam dancers with good natured swats and kicks.
At one point I saw a mohawked goon try to grab her by her waist and pull her into the swirling pit, but she quickly elbowed him in the face, sending him reeling back, both hands holding his blood-spouting nose.

I recalled the night before we left on tour, those stockinged legs working both pedals of the blue Rabbit, the Damned tape blasting, the ride through the South Bay on a cool night in June.
She was a girl I had seen on campus, noting the black streaks beneath her blonde, bobbed hair.
The black funeral gowns she wore to class even on blinding hot Indian Summer days, dressed like a mourning widow among our preppy classmates.

When the pit grew more violent, just as we finished the song "Mannequin" and rolled right into "Wetspots," I reached down and grabbed her hand, helped her up on stage.
She shouted: *"Welcome home!"* into my ear as the drums kicked in and the stage filled with divers.
I waved off the bouncer who ran toward us and motioned her to go sit side stage with Doug and Chris.

As she drove me home in the Rabbit, I watched the lights of Downtown LA pass, then the dark industrial alleys of East LA, until we hit the Southbound 605 toward the sleeping suburbs.

She drove and I talked nonsense, as if recalling a vivid dream that begins to fade a moment after waking.

A rambling monologue about the awful and wonderful America I had seen, the heroes and villains I had met.
And the ocean of alcohol I had to consume to save them all.

I reached and put my hand on her fishnetted knee, but when I moved it higher on her thigh, she swatted me away.
"Listen buddy," she said, smiling. "No funny business."
I shut up then and knew that we would not devalue this night with the mindless friction of meaningless sex.
She worked both her long legs on the pedals, the practiced dance of clutch and gear.
She slipped in the Damned tape again, *their* Black Album, and we sang along to "Wait for the Blackout" at the top of our lungs.

I imagined the life we might have, moving in together and living that romantic struggle of young, broke couples.
A time that is somehow always looked back upon as the very best days of a relationship.

I would start my own business, cutting wood or metal, something far removed from music and stage.
And I would again be down on the floor with the other fans, unnoticed.

We would marry by the ocean, honeymoon on a beach, move from modest homes inland until we were once again by the sea.

Punk rock would inform every aspect of our life, from the jarring colors of our bedroom walls to the kind of cars we would drive, hers always adorned with a Damned sticker as soon as it came off the showroom floor.

Our first and only child would be fair haired, yet almond eyed, a stubborn strain of Japanese determination and Irish loyalty shining through her infant gaze.
We would teach our daughter to make her own T-shirts, and to fight the bullies who teased her fashion,

Mom showing her a quick way to bloody a nose with an elbow.

And I would be a father.
I would discover the faults and triumphs of my own father then, and forgive him all too late.

I would become addled, of course, and bore my grandchildren with my tales of a time in my life so long ago.
I would page through the dashboard journal yet again, though the pages had long ago turned to dust.

Yet I would read it aloud to them still, from memory, a story of one shining season when I dared to rise from the dance floor and stand on the stage.

I would die old, in the sun, the journal of that summer finally slipped from my hands.

Photo by Arthur Siegel

Please visit the Miles Per Gallon companion page for rare photos and extra content. Scan QR code or visit facebook.com/CH3band.

Contact Mike Magrann at mpg.magrann@gmail.com.

A C K N O W L E D G E M E N T S

My sincere thanks to Kimm Gardener for the decades of friendship and support, and to Robbie Fields who took a chance and got us out of the garage.
To Jay, Chris, Jack, and Doug for allowing me to share a bit of our adventures.

Steven DiLodovico, my editor and guide through this new world, and to Amy Yates Wuelfing for getting these words to print.

Ben Schafer and Lisa Glatt for their early guidance, Eileen Magrann-Wells for the family history lessons.
To the writers that generously lent their advice: Keith Morris, Nancy Barile, Jack Grisham, Dave Scott, Brad Logan, Jerry A. Lang, David Ensminger.

Cheers to all the bands that inspired us and share the stage with us still.

Contact:

Mpg.magrann@gmail.com
www.facebook.com/mpgmagrann

Back photo rendered by John Magrann & Karen Ide